Vocabulary Expansion II

Dorothy Rubin

Trenton State College

MACMILLAN PUBLISHING CO., INC.
New York
COLLIER MACMILLAN PUBLISHERS
London

With love to my understanding and supportive husband, Artie,
my delightful daughters, Carol and Sharon,
my precious granddaughter, Jennifer, my dear brothers Herb and Jack,
and in memory of my dear mother, Clara.

Printed in the United States of America

The bulk of this book
is reprinted from *Gaining Word Power,*
copyright © 1978
by Dorothy Rubin

Macmillan Publishing Co., Inc.
866 Third Avenue, New York, New York 10022

Collier Macmillan Canada, Ltd.

Printing: 5 6 7 8 Year: 5 6 7 8 9 0

ISBN 0-02-404240-4

PREFACE

Vocabulary development is an essential factor in reading comprehension. It is an important element in the successful completion of any academic curriculum and forms a standard component of academic achievement and aptitude tests. *Vocabulary Expansion I* and *Vocabulary Expansion II* provide a systematic, participatory approach to building and retaining a functional college-level vocabulary.

The two texts apply a number of sound psychological learning principles to vocabulary building. Words are presented in graduated levels of difficulty. The learning process in each lesson is stimulated by exercises and puzzles and reinforced by access to the solutions for self-evaluation of progress. Students' individual differences are accommodated not only in the self-contained chapters that permit each reader to work at his or her own pace, but also in the extra practice for those who need it and in the extension into more difficult words for those who are ready to absorb them.

Overlearning, the repetition of experience in different circumstances, shapes the instruction because it is essential to the retention of information. A word once introduced will usually recur in many subsequent exercises, for the later exercises build on what has been presented in earlier ones.

Although each book has a pedagogical structure, the structure is diffused among a variety of practices and drills, as well as in the crossword puzzles, word scrambles and squares, analogy activities, and cartoons. To heighten interest, more difficult words are presented in a more challenging approach. Extra practices appear in each chapter as a separate section labeled "Additional Practice Sets," in which a variety of alternative exercises cover words introduced in the chapter. Tests and scoring scales permit users of the book to determine their rate of achievement.

Vocabulary Expansion I emphasizes combining forms and words derived from them. (Combining forms are defined in both texts as word parts that join with a word or another word part to form a word or a new word.) A knowledge of combining forms is fundamental to the accurate use and construction of words as well as to the understanding of their meanings.

Vocabulary Expansion II presents words derived less obviously from combining forms. Although both books present words in context, Vocabulary Expansion II stresses the use and interpretation of context clues to learn word meanings.

The two volumes are derived in large part from a single precursor, *Gaining Word Power,* Macmillan, 1978. Because each is an expanded part of one whole, the two may be used consecutively in a comprehensive vocabulary building program; each, however, constitutes a self-contained unit that can be used independently in a conventional class or in a tutorial or self-instructional program.

ACKNOWLEDGMENTS

I would like to thank Anthony English for being the personification of a perfect editor. His valuable suggestions, creative editing, intelligent insights, and uncanny wit have made working with him an extreme pleasure and privilege. I would also like to thank John Travis for being such a patient, kind, considerate, and helpful production editor. In addition, I would like to express my appreciation to the administration of Trenton State College and particularly to Dean Philip Ollio and Dr. Barbara Harned for their continued support.

CONTENTS

Chapter One 1

The Importance of Vocabulary Growth 1
The Organization of This Book 2
How Exercises Are Presented 2
How Words Are Presented 3
Special Notes 4
Extra Word Power 4
Additional Words 4
Understanding Analogies 4
Combining Forms 5
Pronunciation Key 5
Understanding the Term *Overlearning* 6
Suggestions on How to Study Vocabulary 7
Introduction to Context Clues 7

Chapter Two 11

Exercise 1 11
Exercise 2 16
Exercise 3 22
Crossword Puzzle 1 30
Word Scramble 1 32
Analogies 1 32
Multiple-Choice Vocabulary Test 1 33
True/False Test 1 35
Scoring of Tests 36
Additional Practice Sets 37
Answers 40

Chapter Three 45

Exercise 4 45
Exercise 5 51
Exercise 6 59
Crossword Puzzle 2 66
Word Scramble 2 68
Analogies 2 69

Multiple-Choice Vocabulary Test 2 70
True/False Test 2 72
Scoring of Tests 73
Additional Practice Sets 74
Answers 77

Chapter Four 83

Exercise 7 83
Exercise 8 89
Exercise 9 96
Crossword Puzzle 3 102
Word Scramble 3 105
Analogies 3 106
Multiple-Choice Vocabulary Test 3 107
True/False Test 3 110
Scoring of Tests 111
Additional Practice Sets 111
Answers 114

Chapter Five 121

Exercise 10 121
Exercise 11 128
Exercise 12 135
Crossword Puzzle 4 141
Word Scramble 4 142
Analogies 4 143
Multiple-Choice Vocabulary Test 4 144
True/False Test 4 147
Scoring of Tests 148
Additional Practice Sets 148
Answers 152

Chapter Six 157

Exercise 13 157
Exercise 14 164
Exercise 15 170
Crossword Puzzle 5 176
Word Scramble 5 177
Analogies 5 178
Multiple-Choice Vocabulary Test 5 179
True/False Test 5 181
Scoring of Tests 182

Additional Practice Sets 183
Answers 186

Chapter Seven 191

Exercise 16 191
Exercise 17 197
Exercise 18 203
Crossword Puzzle 6 210
Word Scramble 6 212
Analogies 6 213
Multiple-Choice Vocabulary Test 6 214
True/False Test 6 216
Scoring of Tests 217
Additional Practice Sets 218
Answers 220

Appendixes 227

Appendix A: The Dictionary 227
Appendix B: Glossary 234

CHAPTER ONE[1]

The Importance of Vocabulary Growth

The Organization of This Book

How Exercises are Presented

How Words are Presented

Special Notes

Extra Word Power

Additional Words

Understanding Analogies

Combining Forms

Pronunciation Key

Understanding the Term *Overlearning*

Suggestions on How to Study Vocabulary

Introduction to Context Clues

This chapter discusses the organization of this book and how one can best go about improving one's vocabulary. Let us begin by considering the importance of vocabulary growth.

THE IMPORTANCE OF VOCABULARY GROWTH

A good vocabulary and good reading go hand in hand. Unless you know the meaning of words, you will have difficulty in understanding what is read. And the more you read, the more words you will add to your vocabulary. Read the following statement:

> In the ravaged village there was a great amount of morbidity.

Do you understand it? Unless you know the meanings of *ravaged* and *mor-*

---

[1] It is very important that you read Chapter One. This chapter introduces you to *Vocabulary Expansion II.* It gives you the information you will need to use this book successfully.

bidity, you are not able to read the statement. In order to *read*, you must know the *meanings* of words and the way words are used in sentences.

Acquiring word meanings is an important reading skill. Because of its importance, this skill is being presented in a text by itself.

THE ORGANIZATION OF THIS BOOK

Vocabulary Expansion II consists of words that are not easily made up from combining forms. (The meaning of combining forms is explained to you later on in this chapter. See also *Vocabulary Expansion I.*) These words, like the words in *Vocabulary Expansion I*, are those that are used very often in lectures, textbooks, and newspapers, and the emphasis in this book is also on the *overlearning* of the words. (The term *overlearning* is explained later on.)

Answers for the exercises are provided at the end of each chapter.

HOW EXERCISES ARE PRESENTED

The exercises are presented in three steps. The steps are the same for all exercises:

Step I. *Presentation of words in sentences with context clues for each word.*
You are challenged to figure out the meaning of the underlined word from the clues in the sentence. Sometimes the clue to help you figure out the word is in the next sentence or sentences.

Step II. *Presentation of vocabulary.*
Learn words with their meanings and other information as you see the words used in sentences.

Step III. *Practice.*
Use the words in several different practices to ensure overlearning. After every three exercises, crossword puzzles, word scrambles, and analogies are provided for the given words. A multiple-choice vocabulary test and a true/false vocabulary test are supplied for Step II words. Scoring scales are given so that you will know where you stand. If you score below a certain level, you are provided with additional practice sets. In these *additional practice sets*, you are directed to restudy only the words you have missed. You are provided with different practice exercises to help you learn the words you have missed.

HOW WORDS ARE PRESENTED

The words presented are a base from which you can increase your vocabulary quickly and easily. The words have been selected on the basis of how often they appear in novels, stories, poems, textbooks, and other nonfiction books, newspapers, and magazines. Words that are commonly used in college lectures are also included.

Words are presented with the following information to help your understanding of the word:

1. Correct spelling and plural (abbreviated *pl.*). Only irregular plurals are shown.
2. Division into syllables. For example: can • did.
3. Pronunciation. The phonetic (pronunciation) spelling of the word may differ from the regular spelling to describe the pronunciation of the word. For example: **candid** (kan′ did). The syllabication and pronunciation aids are combined in one entry if the phonetic spelling of the word is similar to the regular spelling of the word. Otherwise, an extra entry is given following the syllabication entry. If a word is a one-syllable word, there is obviously no syllabication entry for the word.
4. Kind of word it is: *v.* for verb, *n.* for noun, *adj.* for adjective, *adv.* for adverb, and *prep.* for preposition.
5. Meaning of the word.[2]
6. Use of the word in a sentence. Only one sentence is given for each word even though the word may have more than one meaning.

Here is an example of the presentation of a word with an extra entry:

correct spelling — division into syllables — pronunciation

candid (can • did) (kan′ did) *adj.* Honest, outspoken, frank.

sentence — kind of word — meaning of word

It is refreshing to have a candid politician who is not afraid to speak out and give his views.

---

[2] The meanings of the words are based on *Webster's Third New International Dictionary,* Unabridged; Funk & Wagnalls *Standard College Dictionary*; *Random House Dictionary of the English Language*; *The American Heritage Dictionary of the English Language*; *The World Book Dictionary*, and *Webster's New Twentieth Century Dictionary,* 2nd ed.

SPECIAL NOTES

A "Special Notes" section includes special information about words that might cause you unusual difficulty.

EXTRA WORD POWER

The combining forms presented in the "Extra Word Power" section are those often used with thousands of words. For this reason they are presented in a special boxed section. The "Extra Word Power" section will give additional help to your vocabulary growth. (An explanation of *combining forms* is given in this chapter.)

ADDITIONAL WORDS

The "Additional Words" section presents some more difficult words. You can unlock their meanings by using context clues and combining form clues when applicable. To help you still more, practice activities are provided for these words.

UNDERSTANDING ANALOGIES

Analogy practice is presented after every three exercises. Analogies have to do with relationships. They are relationships between words or ideas. In order to make the best use of analogies or to supply the missing term in an analogy proportion, you must know not only the *meanings* of the words, but also the relationship of the words or ideas to one another. For example, "*doctor* is to *hospital* as *minister* is to _____." Yes, the answer is *church.* The relationship has to do with specialized persons and the places with which they are associated. Let's try another one: "*beautiful* is to *pretty* as _____ is to *decimate.*" Although you know the meanings of *beautiful* and *pretty* and you can figure out that beautiful is more than pretty, you will not be able to arrive at the correct word to complete the analogy if you do not know the meaning of *decimate. Decimate* means "to reduce by one tenth" or "to destroy a considerable part of." Because the word that completes the analogy must express the relationship of more or greater than, the answer could be *eradicate* or *annihilate,* because these words mean "to destroy completely."

Some of the relationships that words may have to one another are similar meanings, opposite meanings, classification, going from particular to general, going from general to particular, degree of intensity, specialized labels, characteristics, cause-effect, effect-cause, function, whole-part, ratio, and many more. The preceding relationships do not have to be memorized. You will gain clues to these from the pairs making up the analogies; that is, the words express the relationship. For example: "*pretty* is to *beautiful*"—the relationship is degree of intensity; "*hot* is to *cold*"—the relationship is one of opposites; "*car* is to *vehicle*"—the relationship is classification.

COMBINING FORMS

As a means of helping you to use combining forms to increase your vocabulary, some terms should be defined. There are a great number of words that combine with other words to form new words, for example, *grandfather* (*grand* + *father*) and *policeman* (*police* + *man*)—both compound words. Many words are combined with a letter or a group of letters—either at the beginning (prefix) or at the end (suffix) of the word—to form a new, related word, for example, *replay* (*re* + *play*) and *played* (*play* + *ed*).

In the words *replay* and *played, play* is a root, *re* is a prefix, and *ed* is a suffix. A *root* is the smallest unit of a word that can exist and retain its basic meaning. It cannot be divided further. *Replay* is not a root word because it can be divided into *re* and *play. Play* is a root word because it cannot be divided further and still keep a meaning related to the root word.

Combining forms are usually defined as roots borrowed from another language that join together or that join with a prefix, a suffix, or both a prefix and a suffix to form a word. Often the English combining forms are derived from Greek and Latin roots. Because the emphasis in this book is on the building of vocabulary meanings rather than on the naming of word parts, prefixes, suffixes, English roots, and combining forms will *all* be referred to as combining forms. *A combining form in this book is defined as any word part that can join with another word or word part to form a word or a new word.* Examples: *aqua* + *naut* = *aquanaut* (a word); *re* + *turn* = *return* (a new word); *aqua* + *duct* = *aqueduct* (a new word). *Vocabulary Expansion I* is completely based on the building of vocabulary using combining forms, as well as context clues.

PRONUNCIATION KEY

The pronunciation (the way a word sounds) of the words in this book is a simplified one based on the key presented on the next page. In order to simplify pronunciation further, the author has given only long vowel markings and included only the primary accent mark (').

The accent mark (') is used to show which syllable in a word is stressed. This mark comes right after and slightly above the accented syllable. For example:

pilot (pī′ lot) **biology** (bī · ol′ o · jē)

In the preceding two words, the syllables *pi′* and *ol′* are sounded with more stress and are called the accented syllables. The dot (•) is used to separate syllables. Note that no dot is used between syllables when the syllable is accented. Also note that the *y* in *biology* has been changed to an *ē* and the *g* has been changed to a *j* to aid you in pronunciation.

The long vowel mark (¯) also helps to indicate pronunciation. A vowel that has a long vowel mark sounds like its letter name.

A slash through a letter means that the sound it stands for is silent. Examples:

bāke̸ nōte̸ āte̸ bōa̸t

As an aid in pronunciation, the following key may be used:

Words ending in *tion, sion,* sound like *shun,* as in *nation.*

Words ending in *cian, tian,* and *sian* sound like *shin,* as in *Martian.*

Words ending in *cious* sound like *shus,* as in *delicious.*

Words having *ph* sound like *f* in *fat, foot,* as in *phone.*

Words ending in *ique* sound like *ēk* in *lēa̸k,* as in *critique, unique.*

Words ending in *le* preceded by a consonant sound like *ul* in *bull,* as in *bubble, candle.*

Words ending in *cial* sound like *shul,* as in *special.*

Words ending in *ce* sound like *s* in *safe, so,* as in *notice, sentence.*

Words beginning in *ce* or *ci* sound like *s* in *safe, so,* as in *cent, cease, citizen.*

Words ending in *c* sound like *k* in *like,* as in *picnic, traffic.*

Words beginning in *ca, cu,* or *co* sound like *k* in *kite,* as in *cat, cut, cot.*

Words beginning in *qu* sound like *kw* as in *queen, quick.*

Words ending in *ture* sound like *chur* as in *adventure.*

UNDERSTANDING THE TERM *OVERLEARNING*

Although you may have at one time or another met many of the vocabulary words presented in this book, you may not be able to read or use the words because you have not *overlearned* them. Throughout this book, the emphasis is on the overlearning of vocabulary. *Overlearning* is not bad like *overcooking* the roast. Overlearning will help you to hold on to information over a long period of time. To overlearn the material, concentrate on the words to be learned, memorize them, and do all the exercises. Overlearning will take place only if practice is continued even after you think you have learned the information. The additional practice you engage in after you think you have mastered the material is called *overlearning.* As practice is the key to overlearning, you will continue to meet in the practice sets of later exercises many words that you have learned earlier.

SUGGESTIONS ON HOW TO STUDY VOCABULARY

1. You should choose a time best for you so that you do not feel pressured.
2. You should try to find a place free of things that may disturb your studying.
3. You shouldn't try to do all the exercises in one sitting. Studies have shown that you will remember your material better if you space your studying over a period of time. The thing to do is to find and work at a pace that is good for you.
4. *Recall,* which refers to how much you remember, is very important in learning. Recall is used as part of the teaching method in this book. After the presentation of the word and its meaning(s), you should cover the meaning(s) to see if you can recall it (or them).
5. When the entire exercise is completed, go over the words you have learned. In addition, take a few minutes before a new exercise to *review* the previous exercise.
6. To make sure you remember the vocabulary words, try to use them daily in your written work or speech. In addition, see how many times you meet these words in your classroom lectures and readings.

INTRODUCTION TO CONTEXT CLUES

The words in this book are used often, and you will meet them in your subject matter courses, in newspapers, in magazines, and so on. The majority of the words in *Vocabulary Expansion II* are not derived as easily from a knowledge of combining forms as are the words found in *Vocabulary Expansion I.* Because you will not have as much help from combining forms to unlock word meanings, you should be especially aware of other helpful clues. A most important clue is context (the words surrounding a word that can throw light on its meaning).

If the writer wants to make sure that you get the meaning of a word, he or she will define, explain, or describe the word in the sentence. In the following examples, the writer actually defines the word in the sentence. (Sentences such as these are generally found in textbooks or technical journals.)

Examples:

1. A parallelogram all of whose angles are right angles is called a *rectangle.*
2. A *diameter* is the length of a straight line passing through the center of an object.

In the next two examples notice how the writer gives you the definition of a word by using a synonym (a word that has the same or nearly the same meaning as another). Notice also how this makes the writing more expressive and clear and avoids repetition.

Examples:

1. Although my friend John is *rational* on most topics, there are a few on which he is not too *reasonable.*
2. In the movie, the men on the desert kept seeing one *mirage* after another, and each time they thought that the *delusion* was real.

In the next examples notice how the writer *describes* the words that he wants you to know. See if you can figure out the meaning of *hippodrome* and *diligent.*

Examples:

1. In ancient times the Greek people would assemble in their seats to observe the chariot races being held in the *hippodrome.* (From the context of the sentence, you should realize that *hippodrome* refers to some arena or place in which races were held in ancient Greece.)
2. Sharon and Carol are *diligent* persons who never complain about working hard. (From the context of the sentence, you should realize that *diligent* means *hardworking.*)

Sometimes you can actually gain the definition of the word from the sentence or following sentences.

Example:

The house had a cheerful atmosphere. At any moment I expected *blithe* spirits to make their entrance and dance with joy throughout the house.

(From the sentences, you can determine that *blithe* refers to something joyful, gay, or merry.)

Another technique that a writer may use to help you gain the meaning of a word is to give you examples illustrating the word. See if you can figure out the meaning of *perilous* and *perjured.*

Examples:

1. Many of the men feared for their lives on the *perilous* journey because the mission that they were on had never before been accomplished. (From the context of the sentence you should realize that perilous means *dangerous.*)
2. Everyone knew that he had *perjured* himself when he said that he did not know anything about the crime and didn't know the victim, because there was a picture of him and the victim that had been taken during the robbery. (From the context of the sentence, you should be able to figure out that *perjured* refers to someone who has *sworn falsely* about something.)

Alert readers can also use contrasts or comparisons to gain clues to meanings of words. What do you think is the meaning of *ethereal* in the following sentence?

Example:

He was impressed by the *ethereal* grace of Jane's walk rather than Ellen's heavy-footed one. (If you guessed *light, airy* for the meaning of *ethereal,* you were correct. You know that *ethereal* is somehow the opposite of *heavy.* This is an example of contrasts.)

In the next example, see how comparisons can help you.

Maria was as *fickle* as a politician's promises before election. (In this sentence *fickle* means "not firm in opinion" or "wavering." Because politicians try to court all their constituents (voters) before an election, they often are not firm in their opinions, make many promises, and are wavering. By understanding the comparison you can get an idea of the meaning of *fickle.*)

Special Notes

1. The word *or* may be used by a writer when he or she uses another word or words that are similar in meaning. Example: Jim told the grocer that the butter he had bought the day before was rancid *or* spoiled.
2. The words *that is* and their abbreviation, *i.e.*, usually signal that an explanation will follow. Example: The elephant, rhinoceros, and hippopotamus are pachyderms; *that is,* they are animals with thick skin. or: The elephant,

rhinoceros, and hippopotamus are pachyderms; *i.e.*, they are animals with thick skin.

Context clues are especially important in determining meaning for words that have more than one meaning (homographs). For example, note the many uses of *capital* in the following sentences.

1. That is a *capital* idea.
2. Remember to begin each sentence with a *capital* letter.
3. The killing of a policeman is a *capital* offense in some states.
4. Albany is the *capital* of New York State.
5. In order to start a business, you need *capital.*

Each of the preceding sentences illustrates one meaning for *capital.*

In sentence 1 *capital* means "excellent."
In sentence 2 *capital* means "referring to a letter in writing that is an uppercase letter."
In sentence 3 *capital* means "punishable by death."
In sentence 4 *capital* means "the seat of government."
In sentence 5 *capital* means "money or wealth."

Some words with more than one meaning (homographs) are spelled the same but do not sound the same. For example, *refuse* means "trash"; *refuse* means "to decline to accept." In sentence *a* in the examples, *refuse* (ref′ use) meaning "trash" is pronounced differently from the term *refuse* (re fuse′) meaning "to decline to accept" in sentence *b.* In reading, you can determine the meaning of *refuse* from the way it is used in the sentence (context clues). Examples:

a. During the garbage strike there were tons of uncollected *refuse* on the streets of the city.
b. I *refuse* to go along with you.

Good readers use all these clues to help them to determine word meanings.

CHAPTER TWO

Exercises 1–3

Crossword Puzzle 1

Word Scramble 1

Analogies 1

Multiple-Choice Vocabulary Test 1

True/False Test 1

Scoring of Tests

Additional Practice Sets

Answers

EXERCISE 1

Step I. Vocabulary Words in Sentences

Directions: Sentences using the ten vocabulary words from Exercise 1 follow. See whether you can figure out the meanings of the underlined words from the clues in the sentences. Blanks are provided for your estimates of the definitions. Check your meanings with those in Step II.

1. My associates say that I must be unsophisticated or childish because I am so naive as to believe that the board of directors will vote for such an innovative proposal as mine. ____________________
2. They feel that there is a tacit agreement among board members to vote down anything new, especially a plan to integrate the different research departments into one. Because none of the board members will come right out and say that he or she is against uniting the research departments, we never know for sure where the board members stand. __________________; ____________________
3. Because I am a very candid person, people usually know exactly where I stand. ____________________

4. My associates told me that when I present my proposal to the board at our next conference, I'd better be terse and not verbose. The board members can't stand persons who are too wordy. ________________ ;

____

5. Although there are some members who might be against segregating the different research departments, they would probably not be too vocal about their views. ________________

6. My associates told me not to be frustrated when my plan is defeated.

____

7. Because the board members do not like to answer too many questions, they dislike inquisitive people. They feel that they are prying.

____

8. It is difficult to believe that the stockholders would sustain the board's policies. But many stockholders seem to support the board's views.

____

Step II. Vocabulary Words

1. **candid** (can · did) (kan′ did) *adj.* Honest; outspoken; frank. *You know that Frank is* ***candid*** *about his political views because he is so outspoken and open about everything.*

2. **frustrate** (frus′ trāte̸) *v.* To defeat; to bring to nothing. *adj.* frustrated: Filled with a sense of discouragement and dissatisfaction as a result of defeated efforts, inner conflicts, or unresolved problems. *After a great amount of effort, they were able to* ***frustrate*** *the politicians' plan, so that it was defeated.*

3. **inquisitive** (in · quis · i · tive) (in · kwiz′ i · tive̸) *adj.* Curious; given to asking many questions; unnecessarily or improperly curious; prying. *The* ***inquisitive*** *neighbor asked too many prying questions.*

4. **integrate** (in · te · grāte̸′) *v.* To unite; to make whole or complete by adding together parts. *When we* ***integrated*** *all the separate parts and saw the whole plan, we realized how good it was.*

5. **naive** (na · ive) (nī · ēve̸′) *adj.* Foolishly simple; childlike; unsophisticated. *He is so* ***naive*** *that, like a child, he will believe anything you tell him.*

6. **segregate** (seg′ re · gāte̸) *v.* To set apart from others; to separate. *In school some students tend to* ***segregate*** *themselves from others by forming special clubs that are not open for membership to everyone.*

7. **sustain** (sus · tāi̸n′) *v.* To maintain; to keep in existence; to keep going; to uphold; to support. *Because the judge* ***sustained*** *the defense lawyer's*

objections, the prosecuting attorney had to resort to a different line of questioning.

8. **tacit** (tac • it) (tas′ it) *adj.* Unspoken; not expressed openly but implied. *There seemed to be a **tacit** agreement because everybody knew how to behave even though no one said anything.*

9. **terse** (terse̸) *adj.* Brief; concise. *Remember to be **terse** because the audience doesn't like long answers.*

10. **verbose** (ver • bōse̸′) *adj.* Wordy. *Her speech is so **verbose** that the audience is becoming restless from listening to her.*

Special Note

The combining form *ten, tent, tain* means "hold." *Sustain* is derived from the combining form *ten, tent, tain.*

Step III. Practice

A. Directions: Each sentence has a nonsense word. Choose the word that *best* replaces the nonsense word.

Word List

verbose, terse, frustrate, tacit, candid, integrate, segregate, naive, inquisitive, sustain.

1. Jim tends to elois himself from others because he is a loner. ____________
2. My boible friend Jane went to this guy's apartment to see his etchings, but he had other things on his mind. ____________
3. It pays to be lopple most of the time; however, there are times when being outspoken can cause you a lot of grief. ____________
4. The proint reporters continued to pry into the affairs of the government officials until they came up with the truth. ____________
5. Many persons tried to drepe the reporters' attempts at discovering the truth. ____________
6. I prefer persons who use as few words as possible rather than croible ones.

   ____

7. In the film the students had a malon agreement to bang their desks every time the teacher turned her back to write on the chalkboard.

   ____

8. Jennifer's answers are never zelle because she likes to elaborate on everything. ____________

9. In times of galloping inflation, it's difficult to breable a decent standard of living. ____________

10. When the two towns merge, they will craim their administrative staffs.

____

STOP. Check answers at the end of Chapter Two (p. 40).

B. Directions: Ten sentences containing the meanings of vocabulary words presented in this exercise follow. Choose a word from this exercise that *best* fits the meaning.

1. Jim found out the hard way that it's difficult to maintain oneself on a meager diet while working and going to school. ____________

2. The unsophisticated candidate appeared childlike next to the worldly diplomat. ____________

3. I do not like to attend one of my classes because the instructor seems to do everything in his power to defeat my desire to learn. ____________

4. The police said that the reporter had been murdered by the mobsters because the prying reporter had uncovered some information that the mobsters wanted concealed. ____________

5. One of the outspoken students in the class told the instructor that her lectures were over most of the students' heads. ____________

6. There seems to be an unspoken agreement among students not to ask questions at the end of the class period. ____________

7. One of my instructors is so wordy that it takes him about five minutes to say "Good day." ____________

8. We were told that there is a plan to unite the two school systems.

____

9. The judge told the lawyer to be brief because it was close to noon.

____

10. On the plane nonsmokers separate themselves from smokers.

____

STOP. Check answers at the end of Chapter Two (p. 40).

C. Directions: The words from Exercise 1 follow. Match the words with their meanings.

________	1. candid	a. curious
________	2. tacit	b. wordy
________	3. verbose	c. to unite

________	4. terse	d. honest; outspoken
________	5. integrate	e. to maintain; uphold
________	6. segregate	f. to defeat
________	7. inquisitive	g. unspoken; not expressed but implied
________	8. sustain	h. unsophisticated; childlike
________	9. frustrate	i. brief; concise
________	10. naive	j. to separate

STOP. Check answers at the end of Chapter Two (p. 40).

EXTRA WORD POWER

> **dom.** State or condition of being; rank; total area of. *Dom* is added to the end of many words. For example: *Christendom*—the Christian world; *dukedom*—the rank or title of a duke; the area governed by a duke; *freedom*—condition of being free; *kingdom*—area controlled by a king; *stardom*—the status of being a star; *wisdom*—the state of having knowledge. How many more words that end in *dom* can you supply?

Additional Words

From your ability to use context clues, can you figure out the meanings of the following words?

1. **listless** (list′ less) *adj. Mrs. James was upset when her usually playful and energetic child behaved in such a* ***listless*** *and apathetic manner.*

   ____

2. **ecstasy** (ec • sta • sy) (ek′ sta • sē) *n. He was in a state of* ***ecstasy*** *when the homecoming queen said that she would go to the dance with him.*

   ____

3. **peruse** (pe • ruse) (pe • rūze̸′) *v. I will* ***peruse*** *the material at my leisure because I need time to go over it carefully.*

   ____

4. **terminate** (ter′ mi • nāte̸) *v. We decided to* ***terminate*** *our contract with that firm because it was always late in delivering our goods.*

   ____

5. **tentative** (ten′ ta • tivɇ) *adj. The arrangements we have made are only **tentative** ones because we want to see how well they work before we commit ourselves to something more permanent.*

____

STOP. Check answers at the end of Chapter Two (p. 40).

Practice for Additional Words

A. Directions: Match each word with the *best* definition.

________	1. listless	a. done on trial
________	2. peruse	b. great joy
________	3. terminate	c. spiritless
________	4. tentative	d. to read carefully
________	5. ecstasy	e. to end

STOP. Check answers at the end of Chapter Two (p. 40).

B. Directions: Here are five sentences that contain the meanings of the additional words presented in this exercise. Choose the word that *best* fits the underlined word or phrase in the sentence.

Word List

listless, ecstasy, tentative, terminate, peruse.

1. Some people find it very difficult to <u>end</u> any kind of relationship.
   ____
2. Although Susan was only hired on a <u>trial</u> basis, she expected to keep the job. ________________
3. When a young man from our town won a gold medal in the Olympics, the whole town was in a state of <u>great joy</u>. ________________
4. After having the flu for two weeks, George felt <u>spiritless</u>. ________________
5. You should <u>read carefully</u> any contract that you sign. ________________

STOP. Check answers at the end of Chapter Two (p. 40).

EXERCISE 2

Step I. Vocabulary Words in Sentences

Directions: Sentences using the ten vocabulary words from Exercise 2 follow. See whether you can figure out the meanings of the underlined words from the clues in the sentences. Blanks are provided for your estimates of the definitions. Check your meanings with those in Step II.

1. Hostile nations that are on unfriendly terms usually maintain very sophisticated spy systems. ____________________
2. Persons who read about spying operations feel that they are all fictitious. On the contrary, they are real. ____________________
3. The training that spies go through is as intense as that of astronauts because the consequences of an error could be fatal. Because their lives depend on making no mistakes, spies must be very careful. ____________________
4. One of the first things spies learn is to keep their spying activities covert and tell no one about them, not even their spouses. Some spies have kept their spying activities a secret for decades. No one except certain government officials knows who these spies are. ____________________
5. They could be affluent persons or persons without money. ____________________
6. They could be people with whom we deal all the time and who seem to do everything in an open or overt manner. ____________________
7. One thing that's sure is that when a spy is asked to do something, he or she must curtail everything else that he or she is involved in and carry out orders. ____________________
8. Many times what spies are asked to do may not seem relevant to them because it doesn't seem to relate or apply to anything else. However, they do not choose their assignments. ____________________
9. Did you know that spies carry a lethal dose of poison so that they can kill themselves if they are captured? ____________________
10. If a government discovers a spy in its midst, the chances for a pardon or amnesty are not very high. ____________________

Step II. Vocabulary Words

1. **affluent** (af′ flū · ent) *adj.* Having an abundance of goods or riches; wealthly; flowing freely. *Although Jane is very* ***affluent****, you would never know she has money from the way she acts.*
2. **amnesty** (am · nes · ty) (am′ nes · tē) *n.* (*pl.* **ties**) A pardon from the government; act of letting someone off. *The government changed its policy on the granting of* ***amnesties*** *so that more persons would be able to receive pardons.*
3. **curtail** (cur · tail) (kur · tāl′) *v.* To shorten; to lessen; to cut off the end

or a part. *In order to **curtail** expenses, we are buying fewer clothes and not eating out as much as we did before.*

4. **covert** (co • vert) (kō′ vert) *adj.* Secret; concealed; covered over; sheltered. *They behaved in such a **covert** manner that everyone knew that they were trying to hide something.*

5. **fatal** (fa • tal) (fā′ tul) *adj.* Resulting in or capable of causing death; deadly; bringing ruin or disaster; having decisive importance. *When someone has a **fatal** accident, his insurance company pays money to the members of his family who survive him.*

6. **fictitious** (fic • ti • tious) (fik • ti′ shus) *adj.* Imaginary; not real; made up; fabricated. *Janet's story was completely **fictitious** with no basis in fact.*

7. **hostile** (hos′ tile) *adj.* Unfriendly; referring to an enemy. *The **hostile** audience did not applaud the speaker and behaved in a very unfriendly manner.*

8. **lethal** (le • thal) (lē′ thul) *adj.* Causing death; deadly. *The **lethal** blow caused his death.*

9. **overt** (ō′ vert) *adj.* Open to view; public; apparent; able to be seen. *Because his actions were **overt**, nobody could accuse him of trying to hide anything.*

10. **relevant** (rel′ e • vant) *adj.* Applying to the matter in question; suitable; relating to. *Is what you are saying **relevant** to the issue, or does it apply to something else?*

Step III. Practice

A. Directions: Each sentence has a missing word. Choose the word that *best* completes the sentence.

Word List

affluent, amnesty, curtail, covert, fatal, fictitious, hostile, lethal, overt, relevant.

1. A karate expert's hands and feet are considered to be ________ weapons.
2. We had to ________ the discussion because time was running out.
3. In a film flashback, we learned why the main character treated his brother so badly and was ________ to him.
4. Many persons were disappointed when they learned that the government had again changed its ________ policy and that they would not be granted a pardon.
5. Everything that you have said so far is not ________ to the case at hand.

6. Although Bill comes from a very ________ family, he refuses to ask them for any financial support.
7. It's difficult for me to believe that my friend and I will not be sharing good times anymore because he was in a(n) ________ accident.
8. Mr. Brown is aboveboard and ________ in all his business dealings.
9. Although the author claims that all the characters in her book are ________ ones, I think that she has based them on real people.
10. We became suspicious about Mr. Roulf because he behaved in such a(n) ________ manner.

STOP. Check answers at the end of Chapter Two (p. 40).

B. Directions: Here is a list of definitions. Choose the word that *best* fits the definition. There are more words in the list than you need. Some of the words are from Exercise 1.*

Word List

affluent, amnesty, curtail, covert, fictitious, hostile, lethal, overt, relevant, candid, tacit, terse, sustain, verbose, naive.

1. Wordy ________________
2. Secret ________________
3. Deadly ________________
4. A pardon from the government ________________
5. Open to view ________________
6. To shorten ________________
7. Unfriendly ________________
8. Unsophisticated ________________
9. Frank ________________
10. Suitable ________________
11. Imaginary ________________
12. Wealthy ________________
13. Unspoken ________________

STOP. Check answers at the end of Chapter Two (p. 40).

*To emphasize overlearning (see Chapter One), you will continue to meet in the practice sets of later exercises many words that you have learned earlier.

C. Directions: Define the underlined word in each of the following sentences.

1. From the way that Jane dresses, you would think that she comes from a very poor home rather than from an affluent one. ______________

2. The boxer was grief-stricken when he learned that the blow that he had given to the other fighter had been lethal. ______________

3. When Mike was little, he used to invent people to play with, and he would give each one of his fictitious persons a special name. ______________

4. After Jack's dog, Alfie, met with a fatal accident, Jack said that he would never own a dog again. ______________

5. When the workers found out that Jim was a company spy, they became very hostile toward him. ______________

6. After Mary's heart attack, she had to curtail a lot of her former activities.

____

7. The operation was such a covert one that no one in the organization except the head of security and the head of the company knew about it.

____

8. The government said that it would not grant amnesty to any of the persons who had attacked the visiting ambassador and kidnapped his wife.

____

9. Our instructor told us to make sure that all of our statements were relevant to the questions asked on the exam. ______________

10. There were many overt signs to warn us that George was suicidal, but we ignored all of them. ______________

STOP. Check answers at the end of Chapter Two (p. 40).

EXTRA WORD POWER

y. Having; full of; tending to; like; somewhat. When *y* is added to the end of a word, it changes the word to an adjective. For example: *dirt, dirty*—full of dirt; *health, healthy*—full of health; *stick, sticky*—tending to stick; *wave, wavy*—like a wave; *horse, horsy*—like a horse; *salt, salty*—full of salt. How many more words with *y* can you supply?

Additional Words

From your ability to use context clues, can you figure out the meanings of the following words?

1. **crafty** (craf • ty) (kraf′ tē) *adj.* *I like truthworthy people who are above-board in everything they do rather than* ***crafty*** *ones.*

____

2. **versatile** (ver′ sa • til~~e~~) *adj.* *The* ***versatile*** *actor was able to play many different types of roles with ease.*

____

3. **tenure** (ten • ure) (ten′ yur~~e~~) *n.* *After persons receive job* ***tenure,*** *it is very difficult to dismiss them.*

____

4. **temerity** (te • mer • i • ty) (te • mer′ i • tē) *n.* *What* ***temerity*** *the driver had to pass four cars on a curve on a two-way road that had only one lane for each way.*

____

5. **tenet** (ten′ et) *n.* *One of my basic* ***tenets*** *is that hard work pays off.*

____

STOP. Check answers at the end of Chapter Two (p. 41).

Practice for Additional Words

A. Directions: Match each word with the *best* definition.

________	1. tenure	a. turning with ease from one thing to another
________	2. tenet	b. the right to possess something
________	3. temerity	c. sly
________	4. versatile	d. belief
________	5. crafty	e. rash boldness

STOP. Check answers at the end of Chapter Two (p. 41).

B. Directions: Each sentence has a missing word. Choose the word that *best* completes the sentence. There are more words in the list than you need.

Word List

tenure, tenet, crafty, listless, ecstasy, tentative, peruse, versatile, terminate, temerity.

1. The school board decided not to give ________ to one of the teachers.

2. What ________ she has to go right up to the president of the company, shake his hand, and then proceed to tell him what she thinks is wrong with the company.

3. Carol, who is usually so full of energy, is behaving in such a(n) ____________________ manner.

4. The ____________________ salesman had everyone convinced that his product was a steal at the price even though the product was overpriced.

5. "Everyone should have an equal opportunity to an education" is a ____________________ that most American educators strongly believe in.

6. Tony is such a(n) ____________________ person that he can easily switch from playing one role to playing another.

7. We were all distressed to hear that our jobs would ____________________ in a month.

STOP. Check answers at the end of Chapter Two (p. 41).

EXERCISE 3

Step I. Vocabulary Words in Sentences

Directions: Sentences using the ten vocabulary words from Exercise 3 follow. See whether you can figure out the meanings of the underlined words from the clues in the sentences. Blanks are provided for your estimates of the definitions. Check your meanings with those in Step II.

1. Many times in life we do not have alternatives or choices. There are tasks that have to be done, and we must do them. ____________________

2. Sometimes these tasks may be such formidable ones that we are frightened by them. However, most of us usually persist and overcome our fears and accomplish our tasks. ____________________

3. Many times tasks seem more difficult to us because we are either fatigued or famished. Obviously, if we are overtired or starved, we will have difficulty in doing anything. ____________________; ____________________

4. Sometimes persons have difficulty in accomplishing some tasks because they are such pessimists. They are gloomy about the task before they begin. ____________________

5. I concede that it's difficult to be cheery about a difficult task, but I am an optimist. ____________________

6. Have you ever found that you can become nostalgic about some mundane or ordinary task you accomplished almost a decade ago? Looking at some pictures reminded me of some everyday job my mother had me do. The pictures made me feel very homesick. ____________________; ____________________

7. Actually, the pictures also made me feel so sentimental that I was overcome with emotion. ____________________

8. As a result, I wrote my parents a long letter rather than my usual concise one. ____________________

Step II. Vocabulary Words

1. **alternative** (al · ter′ na · tive̸) *n.* One or more things offered for choice; a choice between two or more things; a remaining choice; a choice. *adj.* Offering or providing a choice between two or more things. *As the* ***alternative*** *to paying a fine was to go to jail, I chose the first penalty.*

2. **concise** (con · cise) (kon · sīse̸′) *adj.* Brief; terse. *The* ***concise*** *statement was brief and to the point.*

3. **famish** (fam′ ish) *v.* To make or be very hungry; starve. *adj.* **(famished)** Very hungry. *I am so* ***famished*** *that I could eat almost anything.*

4. **fatigue** (fa · tigue) (fa · tēgu̸e̸′) *n.* Physical or mental tiredness; weariness. *v.* To tire out; to weary; to weaken from continued use. *I was so tired from working today that I was completely* ***fatigued.***

5. **formidable** (for · mi · da · ble) (for′ mi · da · bul) *adj.* Dreaded; causing awe or fear; hard to handle; of discouraging or awesome strength, size, difficulty, and so on. *That is such a* ***formidable*** *task that it may be too hard to handle.*

6. **mundane** (mun′ dāne̸) *adj.* Referring to everyday things; referring to that which is routine or ordinary; referring to worldly things rather than more high-minded or spiritual things. *After listening to a lecture about the kinds of activities that the archaeologists engage in, my tasks sounded* ***mundane*** *and ordinary.*

7. **nostalgic** (nos · tal · gic) (nos · tal′ jik) *adj.* Homesick; longing to go back to one's home, hometown, and so on; longing for something far away or long ago. *When I saw some of my childhood things, I became very* ***nostalgic.***

8. **optimist** (op′ ti · mist) *n.* One who is hopeful; a cheerful person; one who tends to take the most hopeful view or expects the best outcome. *Carol always looks at the bright side of things because she is such an* ***optimist.***

9. **pessimist** (pes′ s̸i · mist) *n.* One who expects the worst to happen in any

situation; one who looks on the dark side of things; a gloomy person. *George is such a* ***pessimist*** *that he seems to expect only bad things to happen.*

10. **sentimental** (sen · ti · men · tal) (sen · ti · men′ tul) *adj.* Marked by tenderness, emotion, feeling, and so on; influenced more by feeling or emotion than by reason; acting from feeling rather than from practical motives. *At my parents' fiftieth wedding anniversary I behaved like a* ***sentimental*** *fool because I was so overcome with emotion.*

Special Note

1. The word *sentimental* may also mean "having or showing exaggerated or superficial emotion." This meaning is often used in literature.

Step III. Practice

A. Directions: Ten sentences follow. Define the underlined word.

1. Everytime Sharon attends a wedding, she becomes very <u>sentimental</u>.
   ____

2. After having the flu and not being able to eat for a number of days, I was <u>famished</u>. ______________________

3. Everything I do must seem so <u>mundane</u> to Jim, who is a noted ski instructor and a skydiver. ______________________

4. No one likes to work on a project with Susan because she is a <u>pessimist</u>.
   ____

5. My autograph album always makes me feel <u>nostalgic</u>. ______________________

6. Because John is so verbose, his instructor expected his report to be quite wordy; however, it was a clear and <u>concise</u> one. ______________________

7. Management said that it had no <u>alternative</u> but to close the plant because the company was losing too much money. ______________________

8. The company of an <u>optimist</u> is preferable to that of one who is always expecting something horrible to happen. ______________________

9. The players were in a state of <u>fatigue</u> after exercising for five hours.
   ____

10. The employees at the plant try to avoid meeting with their boss as much as possible because he is such a <u>formidable</u> person. ______________________

STOP. Check answers at the end of Chapter Two (p. 41).

B. Directions: In the Word Rectangle there are thirteen words from Exercises 1, 2, and 3. Find the words and match them with their correct meanings. Note that there are *more* meanings than words. If there is no word in the rectangle for a meaning, write *none,* and give the word.

WORD RECTANGLE

N	O	S	T	A	L	G	I	C
O	P	T	I	M	I	S	T	O
F	E	D	P	U	L	M	A	V
A	S	C	O	N	C	I	S	E
M	S	I	F	D	A	N	T	R
I	I	T	A	A	N	A	E	T
S	M	A	T	N	D	I	R	A
H	I	X	A	E	I	V	S	I
E	S	I	L	R	D	E	E	T
R	T	F	A	T	I	G	U	E

Meanings *Words*

1. Wealthy ____________
2. Brief ____________
3. Starve ____________
4. Homesick ____________
5. Marked by tenderness ____________
6. One who expects the worst to happen ____________
7. Referring to everyday things ____________
8. Deadly ____________
9. Unfriendly ____________
10. One who is hopeful ____________
11. Hard to handle ____________
12. Physical or mental tiredness ____________
13. A choice ____________
14. Frank ____________

15. Secretive ____________________

16. Open to view ____________________

17. Unsophisticated ____________________

STOP. Check answers at the end of Chapter Two (p. 41).

C. Directions: Ten sentences that contain the meanings of vocabulary presented in Exercise 3 follow. Choose the word that *best* fits the word or phrase underlined in the sentence.

Word List

alternative, concise, famished, fatigued, formidable, mundane, nostalgic, pessimist, optimist, sentimental.

1. I become overwhelmed with emotion when I see things that relate to my early childhood. ____________________
2. After working all night on a paper, I was so mentally and physically tired that I collapsed. ____________________
3. Writing three themes in one week is hard to handle. ____________________
4. When I don't eat breakfast or lunch, I feel starved by dinner time.

   ____
5. Sharon is a person who always looks on the bright side of things.

   ____
6. Jack is a person who always looks on the gloomy side of things.

   ____
7. What is routine or ordinary to one person may not be for another.

   ____
8. We had no choice in the matter, so we let him go. ____________________
9. Answer the questions in a brief manner. ____________________
10. After being away from home, I started to have homesick feelings.

    ____

STOP. Check answers at the end of Chapter Two (p. 42).

EXTRA WORD POWER

ful. Full of. When *ful* is added to the end of a word, it means "full of" and is spelled with only one *l.* In words ending in *y* after a consonant, the *y* changes to an *i* when *ful* is added. For example: *beauty, beautiful*—full of beauty; *pity, pitiful*—

full of pity; *tearful*—full of tears; *shameful*—full of shame. How many more words with *ful* can you supply?

Additional Words

From your ability to use context clues, can you figure out the meanings of the following words?

1. **tactful** (tact • ful) (takt′ ful) *adj. Because Mary does not like to hurt anyone's feelings, she is trying to think of a* **tactful** *way to tell Mrs. Brown that her son has been arrested.*

   ____

2. **expedite** (ex • pe • dite) (ek′ spe • dīte) *v. The buyer said that because he needs the order now, he wants the salesman to* **expedite** *the delivery of the goods.*

   ____

3. **obfuscate** (ob • fus • cate) (ob • fus′ kāte) *v. Everytime he spoke, instead of clarifying the issue, he* **obfuscated** *it even more.*

   ____

4. **constraint** (con • straint) (kon • strāint′) *n. One of the* **constraints** *of the job was that I could not leave whenever I desired.*

   ____

5. **variable** (var • i • a • ble) (var′ ē • a • bul) *adj. n. Because the weather has been so* **variable***, it's difficult to know what to wear.*

   ____

STOP. Check answers at the end of Chapter Two (p. 42).

Practice for Additional Words

A. Directions: Match each word with the *best* definition.

________	1. tactful	a. to hasten
________	2. obfuscate	b. changeable
________	3. constraint	c. to confuse
________	4. variable	d. skillful in dealing with people
________	5. expedite	e. restriction

STOP. Check answers at the end of Chapter Two (p. 42).

B. Directions: Each sentence has a missing word. Choose the word that *best* completes the sentence.

Word List

tactful, obfuscate, constraint, variable, expedite, crafty, peruse, temerity, ecstasy, tentative.

1. Although Mary had been told that the arrangement was a(n) ____________________ one, she had hoped that it would be permanent.
2. No one knows what she is going to say or do from one moment to the next because she is so ____________________ .
3. Mary tried to think of a(n) ____________________ way to tell her boyfriend that she was unhappy with their relationship.
4. We were all in a state of ____________________ when we learned that we had been chosen as representatives of our school to tour Europe.
5. Mr. Brown asked if the manufacturing department could ____________________ the delivery of the needed parts because his department had promised delivery to its customer a week ago.
6. Make sure that you ____________________ the contract before you sign it.

7. The rigid time schedule is a(n) ____________________ that will probably prevent me from taking this job.

8. The man showed such ____________________ when he leaped from one building to the next to avoid being captured.

9. At the juvenile center we met a ten-year-old child who is so ____________ that he can outwit the staff members.

10. Please don't invite Bob to explain the issue because he will do more to ____________________ it than anyone I know.

STOP. Check answers at the end of Chapter Two (p. 42).

CROSSWORD PUZZLE 1

Directions: The meanings of a number of words from Exercises 1–3 follow. Your knowledge of these words will help you to solve this crossword puzzle. Note that *combining form* is abbreviated as *comb. f.*

Across

1. Way of saying *mother*
3. Opposite of *stop*
5. Female pronoun
6. Brief
9. Third letter of the alphabet
10. Opposite of *happy*
11. Comb. f. for *one who*
12. Comb. f. for *not*
14. Same as #12 Across
15. Wordy
18. Abbreviation for Civil Defense
19. Past tense of *to send*
20. A dog and car are household __s
21. Unspoken
22. Indefinite article
23. A long-tailed rodent
25. A girl's name

Down

1. Pronoun referring to *self*
2. Comb. f. for *one who*
3. A supreme being
4. Opposite of *off*
5. A plant used for seasoning in cooking
6. Outspoken; honest
7. Hidden; concealed
8. Arrange
9. Cut off
10. To accomplish what you wanted to accomplish
12. Employ
13. Meshed fabric used to catch fish
16. A verb ending
17. A person who always looks on the bright side of things

27. Ending for the past tense of regular verbs
28. Homonym of *two*
29. Meaning of *fatigued*
32. Slang for *to catch*
33. Unsophisticated
35. Imitated someone
36. Meaning of *alternative*
38. You walk on these
41. A cover
42. Abbreviation for *pint*
44. To turn around
45. Betsy __ made the first American flag.
46. In school you go through the __s
47. Comb f. for *back*
48. Opposite of *go*
50. Imaginary
51. Marked by mental strain
54. Same as #47 Across
56. Same as #22 Across
57. Separate
62. Two thousand pounds
63. Same as #55 Down
64. On earth there are plants and __s
65. When a female conceives, an __ unites with sperm
67. Without this part, a plant would die
70. Abbreviation for civil law
71. When you stop breathing you __
72. Girl's name
73. When you're famished, you __
74. Abbreviation of *Common Era*
75. Spelling of the letter *T*
76. Fifth letter of the alphabet

19. A plural ending of some nouns
22. Abbreviation for advertisement
23. Dried grape
24. First three letters of the alphabet
25. Unite
26. Infant makes this sound and parents think it means "father"
29. You leave this for the waiter
30. A tenant __s an apartment
31. Same as #27 Across
32. Homesick
34. __ and vigor
35. Title used for both married and unmarried women
36. Fresh and firm: __ vegetables
37. Latin for *this*
38. To defeat
39. Doing something with __ is the opposite of doing something with difficulty
40. Same as #27 Across
42. He is a __ -med student
43. You sleep in this on a camping trip
46 Same as #3 Across
49. Same as #42 Down
50. Sixth letter of the alphabet
51. To make known
52. Homonym of *sew*
53. Same as #16 Down
55. Comb. f. for *one who*
58. Same as #16 Down
59. Opposite of *take*
60. Rhymes with *ham*
61. A skill in dealing with people
65. Same as #27 Across
66. An interjection used to express surprise or enthusiasm
68. Being a single unit
69. Same as #68 Down

STOP. Check answers at the end of Chapter Two (p. 42).

WORD SCRAMBLE 1

Directions: Word Scramble 1 is based on words from Exercises 1–3. The meanings are your clues to arranging the letters in correct order.

		Meanings
1. nidadc	________________	honest
2. treatsurf	________________	to defeat
3. rintatgee	________________	to unite
4. resgteega	________________	to set apart
5. catti	________________	unspoken
6. reets	________________	brief
7. snatsui	________________	to maintain
8. ulfantef	________________	wealthy
9. tocrev	________________	secret
10. yestman	________________	a pardon
11. claiurt	________________	to shorten
12. ehsolit	________________	unfriendly
13. nervealt	________________	relating to
14. nativealter	________________	a choice
15. maihfsde	________________	starved
16. moreifbald	________________	of discouraging difficulty
17. numenad	________________	ordinary
18. glonstica	________________	homesick
19. spessiimt	________________	one who expects the worst
20. stimiopt	________________	one who expects the best

STOP. Check answers at the end of Chapter Two (p. 43).

ANALOGIES 1

Directions: Find the word from the following list that *best* completes each analogy. There are more words in the list than you need.

Word List

naive, defeat, temerity, curtail, mundane, posterior, concise, tacit, sustain, obfuscate, ecstasy, amnesty, optimist, tactful, verbose, vociferous, voiced, tenet, prying, covert, happiness, bad, good, pathetic, spiritless, tentative, clear, lucid, candid, terminate, commence, tenacious, changeable, termite, expedite, constraint, incredible, term, steady, famished, integrate.

1. Fictitious: real :: sophisticated : ________________.
2. Covert : overt :: segregate : ________________.
3. Concede : surrender :: starved : ________________.
4. Affluent : wealthy :: frustrate : ________________.
5. Hostile : friendly :: clarify : ________________.
6. Relevant : irrelevant :: unusual : ________________.
7. Permanent : tentative :: variable : ________________.
8. Lethal : deadly :: terse : ________________.
9. Crafty : sly :: listless : ________________.
10. Sentimental : unfeeling :: pessimist : ________________:
11. Pat : strike :: joy : ________________.
12. Dreaded : formidable :: foolhardiness : ________________.
13. Positive : definite :: rear : ________________.
14. Contemporary : ancient :: begin : ________________.
15. Post : position :: pardon : ________________.
16. Pacify : calm :: belief : ________________.
17. Species : kind :: inquisitive : ________________.
18. Archetype : model :: clamorous : ________________.
19. Dormant : active :: lengthen : ________________.
20. Animate : deaden :: spoken : ________________.

STOP. Check answers at the end of Chapter Two (p. 43).

MULTIPLE-CHOICE VOCABULARY TEST 1

Directions: This is a test on words in Exercises 1–3. Words are presented according to exercises. *Do all exercises before checking answers.* Underline the meaning that *best* fits the word.

Exercise 1

1. candid	a. happy b. frank	c. cheerful d. to the point
2. frustrate	a. to defeat b. anxious	c. to separate d. foolish
3. integrate	a. to separate b. to unite	c. force d. race
4. inquisitive	a. prying b. a quiz	c. wise d. going before
5. naive	a. happy b. sophisticated	c. childlike d. apathetic
6. segregate	a. to unite b. regulate	c. foolish d. to separate
7. sustain	a. to help b. to maintain	c. unnecessary d. to go
8. tacit	a. to the point b. open	c. unspoken d. friendly
9. terse	a. unspoken b. brief	c. frank d. a pardon
10. verbose	a. quiet b. brief	c. wordy d. friendly

Exercise 2

11. affluent	a. result b. wealthy	c. cause d. secret
12. amnesty	a. short b. wordy	c. a pardon d. honest
13. curtail	a. curious b. cheerful	c. to shorten d. inactive
14. covert	a. open b. concealed	c. prying d. spy
15. fatal	a. poison b. secret	c. open d. causing death
16. fictitious	a. story b. real	c. imaginary d. unsophisticated
17. hostile	a. friendly b. unfriendly	c. kill d. hurt

18. lethal
a. poison
b. hurt
c. dangerous
d. deadly

19. overt
a. open
b. closed
c. secret
d. relating to

20. relevant
a. friendly
b. open
c. secret
d. relating to

Exercise 3

21. alternative
a. relating to
b. choice
c. imaginary
d. unfriendly

22. concise
a. wordy
b. long
c. to cut off
d. brief

23. famished
a. tired
b. long
c. starved
d. food

24. fatigued
a. hungry
b. starved
c. tired
d. asleep

25. formidable
a. of discouraging difficulty
b. inactive
c. apathetic
d. open

26. mundane
a. healthy
b. ordinary
c. uncaring
d. friendly

27. nostalgic
a. nosy
b. homesick
c. friendly
d. noticeable

28. pessimist
a. one who is a pest
b. one who is sad
c. one who is gloomy
d. one who is cheerful

29. optimist
a. one who is bad
b. one who is friendly
c. relating to
d. one who is cheerful

30. sentimental
a. lacking feeling
b. sentence
c. emotional
d. friendly

TRUE/FALSE TEST 1

Directions: This is a true/false test on Exercises 1–30. Read each sentence carefully. Decide whether it is true or false. Put a *T* for *true* or an *F* for *false* in the blank. The number after the sentence tells you if the word is from Exercise 1, 2, or 3.

_______ 1. *Integrate* and *segregate* are antonyms. 1

_______ 2. When you frustrate someone, you stop him or her from doing something he or she wants to do. 1

_________ 3. A naive person is sophisticated. 1

_________ 4. A biography would be fictitious. 2

_________ 5. An inquisitive person would be considered a curious person. 1

_________ 6. When someone sustains something, he or she wants to get rid of it. 1

_________ 7. Something overt would be out of view. 2

_________ 8. To curtail your allowance would be to increase it. 2

_________ 9. A formidable task would be easy to achieve. 3

10. Something covert would be open to all. 2

11. A listless person would be a spiritless person. 1

12. An affluent person would have an abundance of goods or riches. 2

13. *Optimist* and *pessimist* are antonyms. 3

14. Mundane things are spiritual or high-minded things. 3

15. Persons who are nostalgic look to the future. 3

16. A sentimental person would be apathetic. 3

17. A pessimist looks on the gloomy side of things. 3

18. When you have an alternative, you have no choice. 3

STOP. Check answers for both tests at the end of Chapter Two (p. 43).

SCORING OF TESTS

Multiple-Choice Vocabulary Test

Number Wrong	*Score*
0–2	Excellent
3–5	Good
6–8	Weak
Above 8	Poor

Score _______

True/False Test

Number Wrong	*Score*
0–1	Excellent
2–3	Good
4–5	Weak
Above 5	Poor

Score _______

1. If you scored in the excellent or good range on *both tests,* you are doing well. Go on to Chapter Three.

2. If you scored in the weak or poor range on either test, turn to the next page and follow directions for Additional Practice. Note that the words on the tests are arranged so that you can tell in which exercise to find them. This will help you if you need additional practice.

ADDITIONAL PRACTICE SETS

A. Directions: Write the words you missed on the tests from the three exercises in the space provided. Note that the tests are presented so that you can tell to which exercises the words belong.

Exercise 1 Words Missed

1. ____________	6. ____________
2. ____________	7. ____________
3. ____________	8. ____________
4. ____________	9. ____________
5. ____________	10. ____________

Exercise 2 Words Missed

1. ____________	6. ____________
2. ____________	7. ____________
3. ____________	8. ____________
4. ____________	9. ____________
5. ____________	10. ____________

Exercise 3 Words Missed

1. ____________	6. ____________
2. ____________	7. ____________
3. ____________	8. ____________
4. ____________	9. ____________
5. ____________	10. ____________

B. Directions: Restudy the words that you have written down on this page. Do Step I and Step II for those you missed. Note that Step I and Step II are on the following pages:

Exercise 1–pp. 11–13.

Exercise 2–pp. 16–18.

Exercise 3–pp. 22–24.

C. Directions: Do Additional Practice 1 on p. 38 if you missed words from Exercise 1. Do Additional Practice 2 on pp. 38–39 if you missed words from Exercise 2. Do Additional Practice 3 on p. 39 if you missed words from Exercise 3. Now go on to Chapter Three.

Additional Practice 1 for Exercise 1

Directions: Ten sentences follow. Define the underlined word.

1. Sometimes it's best not to be so candid because people often don't want to hear the truth. ______________________
2. Because I don't like nosy questions, I wish you wouldn't be so inquisitive. ______________________
3. How could you be so naive as to believe that he wanted you to go to his apartment to look at his pictures? ______________________
4. Many school districts are trying to integrate their schools by combining groups of students from different neighborhoods. ______________________
5. At the party, try not to go off in a corner and segregate yourself from everyone else. ______________________
6. I don't know how we will be able to sustain ourselves on the salary that we have. ______________________
7. No one said anything, but there was a tacit agreement on what to do. ______________________
8. Remember to be terse when you give the report so that we can leave early. ______________________
9. After working so hard on that plan, I am frustrated to learn that it has been defeated. ______________________
10. Some speakers are so verbose that they can go on for hours. ______________________

STOP. Check answers at the end of Chapter Two (p. 43).

Additional Practice 2 for Exercise 2

Directions: Ten sentences that contain the meanings of vocabulary presented in Exercise 2 follow. Choose the word that *best* fits the word or phrase underlined in the sentence.

Word List

overt, fatal, covert, affluent, relevant, lethal, hostile, fictitious, amnesty, curtail.

1. As John is so wealthy, money means nothing to him. ______________________
2. The secret activities of the government spies were finally uncovered. ______________________
3. All my business deals have to be open and aboveboard. ______________________

4. We knew that the decisive hour would arrive soon. ____________________
5. As children, my friend and I used to make up lots of imaginary stories to tell to each other. ____________________
6. A pardon was given to a former spy who helped the government capture other spies. ____________________
7. If you cut off any more of my funds, we won't have enough to live on. ____________________
8. Why are some people so unfriendly? ____________________
9. He accidentally drank a deadly dose of poison. ____________________
10. When you write your report, make sure that everything you put in it is related to your topic. ____________________

STOP. Check answers at the end of Chapter Two (p. 44).

Additional Practice 3 for Exercise 3

Directions: Ten sentences follow. Define the underlined word.

1. We had no alternative but to concede that we were beaten. ____________________
2. When you give your answers on the final, be concise and to the point. ____________________
3. The task seemed so formidable to her that she didn't know whether she should undertake it. ____________________
4. We are famished because we haven't eaten for almost twenty-four hours. ____________________
5. I'm so fatigued that I feel as though I could sleep for a week. ____________________
6. Every day I have the same old mundane things to do. ____________________
7. When he saw his newborn child, he felt very sentimental. ____________________
8. Because I'm an optimist, I predict that we'll have a sunny day for our picnic tomorrow. ____________________
9. Because Jim is a pessimist, he predicted that it will rain for our picnic tomorrow. ____________________
10. Every year during the spring I become nostalgic about my former home with its garden and large lawn. ____________________

STOP. Check answers at the end of Chapter Two (p. 44).

ANSWERS: Chapter Two

Exercise 1 (pp. 11-16)

Practice A

(1) segregate, (2) naive, (3) candid, (4) inquisitive, (5) frustrate, (6) verbose, (7) tacit, (8) terse, (9) sustain, (10) integrate.

Practice B

(1) sustain, (2) naive, (3) frustrate, (4) inquisitive, (5) candid, (6) tacit, (7) verbose, (8) integrate, (9) terse, (10) segregate.

Practice C

(1) d, (2) g, (3) b, (4) i, (5) c, (6) j, (7) a, (8) e, (9) f, (10) h.

Additional Words (pp. 15-16)

1. **listless.** Spiritless; indifferent; inactive; apathetic.
2. **ecstasy.** Great joy.
3. **peruse.** To read carefully; to inspect closely.
4. **terminate.** To end.
5. **tentative.** Done on trial or experimentally; not final; uncertain.

Practice for Additional Words (p. 16)

A. (1) c, (2) d, (3) e, (4) a, (5) b.
B. (1) terminate, (2) tentative, (3) ecstasy, (4) listless, (5) peruse.

Exercise 2 (pp. 16-22)

Practice A

(1) lethal, (2) curtail, (3) hostile, (4) amnesty, (5) relevant, (6) affluent, (7) fatal, (8) overt, (9) fictitious, (10) covert.

Practice B

(1) verbose, (2) covert, (3) lethal, (4) amnesty, (5) overt, (6) curtail, (7) hostile, (8) naive, (9) candid, (10) relevant, (11) fictitious, (12) affluent, (13) tacit.

Practice C

(1) wealthy, (2) deadly, (3) imaginary, (4) deadly, (5) unfriendly, (6) cut off, (7) secret, (8) pardon, (9) suitable, (10) open.

Additional Words (pp. 20-21)

1. **crafty**. Sly; skillful in deceiving; cunning.
2. **versatile**. Changeable; turning with ease from one thing to another; many-sided.
3. **tenure**. The right to hold or possess something; length of time something is held; status assuring an employee of permanence in his or her position or employment (tenure protects an employee such as a teacher from being dismissed except for serious misconduct or incompetence).
4. **temerity**. Rash boldness; foolhardiness.
5. **tenet**. Any opinion, doctrine, principle, dogma, and the like held as true; belief.

Practice for Additional Words (pp. 21-22)

A. (1) b, (2) d, (3) e, (4) a, (5) c.
B. (1) tenure, (2) temerity, (3) listless, (4) crafty, (5) tenet, (6) versatile, (7) terminate.

Exercise 3 (pp. 22-29)

Practice A

(1) emotional, (2) very hungry, (3) ordinary, (4) gloomy person, (5) homesick, (6) brief, (7) choice, (8) cheerful person, (9) weariness, (10) awesome.

Practice B

(1) none–affluent, (2) concise, (3) famish, (4) nostalgic, (5) none–sentimental, (6) pessimist, (7) mundane, (8) fatal, (9) none–hostile, (10) optimist, (11) none–formidable, (12) fatigue, (13) none–alternative, (14) candid, (15) covert, (16) overt, (17) naive.

Word Rectangle (p. 25)

N	O	S	T	A	L	G	I	C
O	P	T	I	M	I	S	T	O
F	E	D	P	U	L	M	A	V
A	S	C	O	N	C	I	S	E
M	S	I	F	D	A	N	T	R
I	I	T	A	A	N	A	E	T
S	M	A	T	N	D	I	R	A
H	I	X	A	E	I	V	S	I
E	S	I	L	R	D	E	E	T
R	T	F	A	T	I	G	U	E

Practice C

(1) sentimental, (2) fatigued, (3) formidable, (4) famished, (5) optimist, (6) pessimist, (7) mundane, (8) alternative, (9) concise, (10) nostalgic.

Additional Words (p. 27)

1. **tactful.** Considerate; conscientiously inoffensive; skillful in dealing with people or difficult situations.
2. **expedite.** To hasten; to speed up the progress of; to ease the progress of.
3. **obfuscate.** To darken; to confuse; to obscure.
4. **constraint.** Confinement; the act of restricting; a restriction; the act of using force; force; compulsion; coercion.
5. **variable.** Changeable; something that may or does vary.

Practice for Additional Words (pp. 27-29)

A. (1) d, (2) c, (3) e, (4) b, (5) a.
B. (1) tentative, (2) variable, (3) tactful, (4) ecstasy, (5) expedite, (6) peruse, (7) constraint, (8) temerity, (9) crafty, (10) obfuscate.

Crossword Puzzle 1 (pp. 30–31)

Word Scramble 1 (p. 32)

(1) candid, (2) frustrate, (3) integrate, (4) segregate, (5) tacit, (6) terse, (7) sustain, (8) affluent, (9) covert, (10) amnesty, (11) curtail, (12) hostile, (13) relevant, (14) alternative, (15) famished, (16) formidable, (17) mundane, (18) nostalgic, (19) pessimist, (20) optimist.

Analogies 1 (pp. 32–33)

(1) naive, (2) integrate, (3) famished, (4) defeat, (5) obfuscate, (6) mundane, (7) steady, (8) concise, (9) spiritless, (10) optimist, (11) ecstasy, (12) temerity, (13) posterior, (14) terminate, (15) amnesty, (16) tenet, (17) prying, (18) vociferous, (19) curtail, (20) tacit.

Multiple-Choice Vocabulary Test 1 (pp. 33–35)

Exercise 1

(1) b, (2) a, (3) b, (4) a, (5) c, (6) d, (7) b, (8) c, (9) b, (10) c.

Exercise 2

(11) b, (12) c, (13) c, (14) b, (15) d, (16) c, (17) b, (18) d, (19) a, (20) d.

Exercise 3

(21) b, (22) d, (23) c, (24) c, (25) a, (26) b, (27) b, (28) c, (29) d, (30) c.

True/False Test 1 (pp. 35–36)

(1) T, (2) T, (3) F, (4) F, (5) T, (6) F, (7) F, (8) F, (9) F, (10) F, (11) T, (12) T, (13) T, (14) F, (15) F, (16) F,[1] (17) T, (18) F.

STOP. Turn to page 36 for the scoring of the tests

Additional Practice Sets (pp. 37–39)

Additional Practice 1

(1) honest, (2) prying, (3) unsophisticated, (4) unite, (5) separate, (6) maintain, (7) unspoken, (8) brief, (9) filled with a sense of discouragement, (10) wordy.

---

[1] As a sentimental person is filled with emotion, he or she would not be apathetic. An apathetic person is without feelings.

Additional Practice 2

(1) affluent, (2) covert, (3) overt, (4) fatal, (5) fictitious, (6) amnesty, (7) curtail, (8) hostile, (9) lethal, (10) relevant.

Additional Practice 3

(1) choice, (2) brief, (3) discouragingly difficult, (4) starved, (5) tired, (6) ordinary, (7) filled with tenderness, emotional, (8) person who looks at the bright side of things, (9) person who looks at the bad or gloomy side of things, (10) homesick.

CHAPTER THREE

Exercises 4–6

Crossword Puzzle 2

Word Scramble 2

Analogies 2

Multiple-Choice Vocabulary Test 2

True/False Test 2

Scoring of Tests

Additional Practice Sets

Answers

EXERCISE 4

Step I. Vocabulary Words in Sentences

Directions: Sentences using the ten vocabulary words from Exercise 4 follow. See whether you can figure out the meanings of the underlined words from the clues in the sentences. Blanks are provided for your estimates of the definitions. Check your meanings with those in Step II.

1. I have always been a very <u>diligent</u> worker. It makes no difference if its a formidable task or not, because I will apply myself to it and persist until I have succeeded. ____________________

2. Last week, I met my friend in the library, and by <u>coincidence</u> we had both chosen equivalent topics to write on for our anthropology course. It seemed incredible that by chance we should both have chosen the same tribe of people about which to write. ____________________

3. It was a unique tribe, which centuries ago had <u>isolated</u> itself from all contact with civilization. It lived alone, never integrating with any other tribes. ____________________

4. Although there were not many references about this tribe, I was able to find enough with pertinent information. The references were relevant and applied exactly to my topic. ____________________

5. Even though my report was rather long, I wouldn't delete one word. I left every word in. ____________________

6. However, I had a dilemma. Everyone was supposed to be writing on different topics, and the paper was due the next day; so I didn't have time to do another. ____________________

7. My friend said that he would affirm that we had not planned it together. After all, we were telling the truth. ____________________

8. Concerning the tribe, when the anthropologists discovered it, the tribespeople seemed to regard the scientists with disdain. Perhaps they looked upon them as unworthy because the scientists looked so different and might be a threat to them. ____________________

9. The tribespeople, who were a haughty group, took great pride in themselves. ____________________

10. They had been able to survive for so long by eradicating anyone that came upon their land. On the basis of these facts, why did this tribe allow these anthropologists to live? ____________________

Step II. Vocabulary Words

1. **affirm** (af̸ · firm′) *v.* To declare or state positively; to say or maintain that something is true. *The auditor examined the bank accounts and **affirmed** that they were all in order with positively no problems.*

2. **coincidence** (co · in · ci · dence) (kō · in′ si · dense̸) *n.* The occurrence of things or events at the same time by chance. *What a **coincidence** to find Jim in Paris at the same time that I was there.*

3. **delete** (de · lēte̸′) *v.* To take out or remove a letter, word, and so on; to cross out; to erase. *After Ms. Jones had dictated the letter to her secretary, she asked her to **delete** the whole last paragraph because it was not worded properly.*

4. **dilemma** (di · lem′ m̸a) *n.* Any situation that necessitates a choice between equally unfavorable or equally unpleasant alternatives; an argument that presents two equally unfavorable alternatives. *Mr. Morton's **dilemma** is a serious one because, if he agrees to the transplant, he might die during the operation or from the effects of it; but if he doesn't have one, he might die also.*

5. **diligent** (dil · i · gent) (dil′ i · jent) *adj.* Applying oneself in whatever is

undertaken; working in a constant effort to accomplish something; industrious. *He worked in such a **diligent** manner to complete his project that he didn't even stop for a break.*

6. **disdain** (dis · dā̸i̸n') *v.* To regard as unworthy; to despise. *n.* The feeling of scorn or of despisal; expression of scorn (contempt). *Jane was looked at with great **disdain** by all her fellow workers when they found that she had been giving covert information about them to the boss.*
7. **eradicate** (e · rad · i · cate) (e · rad' i · kāte̸) *n.* To destroy completely; to pull out by the roots; to wipe out; to exterminate. *The engineers wanted to **eradicate** all possible errors from their calculations before attempting to construct their new machine.*
8. **haughty** (haugh · ty) (haw' tē) *adj.* Having or showing great pride in oneself and contempt (disrespect) or scorn for others; overbearing; snobbish; arrogant. *Many **haughty** people are so egocentric and overbearing that they make others feel hostile toward them.*
9. **isolate** (ī' so · lāte̸') *v.* To set apart from others; to place alone; to separate. *In the hospital, doctors **isolate** patients with contagious (catching) diseases in rooms by themselves so that they will not spread their germs to others.*
10. **pertinent** (per' ti · nent) *adj.* Relevant; relating to or bearing upon the matter in hand; being to the point. *The witness said that he had **pertinent** information that was relevant to the case.*

Step III. Practice

A. Directions: Each sentence has a missing word. Choose the word that *best* completes the sentence.

Word List

diligent, haughty, eradicate, coincidence, pertinent, isolate, dilemma, affirm, delete, disdain.

1. It was a remarkable ____________________ that two scientists working separately in different countries discovered a cure for a disease at exactly the same time.
2. You face a terrible ____________________ because either choice you make will have unfortunate consequences.
3. Make sure you report only ____________________ information and leave out anything not relevant.
4. We can both ____________________ that the evidence you have given is truthful.

5. ________________ people, who are filled with pride and show disrespect toward others, are not well liked.

6. Because I had a contagious disease, the hospital had to ________________ me from the other patients.

7. In order to ________________ all the rats in the building, the exterminator used toxic materials that were lethal only to rats and other rodents.

8. A number of times censors ________________ words from television programs because they feel that the words should not be presented to a family audience.

9. He looked with ________________ at the man who was responsible for so many deaths because of his reckless driving.

10. As a(n) ________________ worker, I always apply myself to whatever I do.

STOP. Check answers at the end of Chapter Three (p. 77).

B. Directions: Ten sentences containing the meanings of vocabulary presented in Exercise 4 follow. Choose the word that *best* fits the meaning of the word or phrase underlined in the sentence.

Word List

diligent, haughty, eradicate, coincidence, pertinent, isolate, dilemma, affirm, delete, disdain.

1. The doctors said that they could completely wipe out certain diseases if they had enough money to support the scientific research.

   ____

2. People don't like an overbearing person. ________________

3. The club members had feelings of scorn for Mike because he told nonmembers about their covert doings. ________________

4. He is such a success because he is an industrious worker.

   ____

5. The material you collected for the report is all relevant.

   ____

6. Try not to set yourself apart from everyone at the gathering.

   ____

7. I had to take out a number of words from my report because it was too long. ________________

8. John and I couldn't get each other on the phone because by chance we were phoning each other at the same time. ________________

9. "Let me state positively that I feel that my client is innocent," said the lawyer. ____________________

10. When we found ourselves with an equally bad pair of alternatives, we didn't know what to do. ____________________

STOP. Check answers at the end of Chapter Three (p. 77).

C. Directions: The words from Exercise 4 follow. Match each word with the *best* definition.

_________	1. coincidence	a. applying oneself in whatever is undertaken
_________	2. delete	b. to destroy completely
_________	3. affirm	c. a choice between two equally unpleasant things
_________	4. dilemma	d. the feeling of scorn or despisal
_________	5. haughty	e. to erase; to cross out
_________	6. diligent	f. occurrence of events at the same time by chance
_________	7. pertinent	g. showing great pride in oneself; overbearing
_________	8. disdain	h. to set apart from others
_________	9. eradicate	i. relevant
_________	10. isolate	j. to declare positively

STOP. Check answers at the end of Chapter Three (p. 78).

EXTRA WORD POWER

ante. Before. *Ante* is placed in front of many words and means "before." *Anti,* means "against." Do not confuse *ante* with *anti.* Examples: *antebellum*—before the war; *anteroom*—waiting room, a lobby; *antedate*—to date before; *antemeridian*—before noon (the abbreviation is A.M.); *antecedent*—going before; *antiwar*—against war.

Additional Words

From your ability to use context clues, can you figure out the meanings of the following words?

1. **arrogant** (ar′ r̸o · gant) *adj. He is so* ***arrogant*** *that people try to avoid being in his presence because it's no fun being with someone who thinks he's so great.*

   ____

2. **thrifty** (thrif · ty) (thrif′ tē) *adj. When you have a limited amount of money and many expenses, you have to be* ***thrifty.***

   ____

3. **replete** (re · plēte̸′) *adj. His words were* ***replete*** *with praise for his colleague, whom he admired.*

   ____

4. **replenish** (re · plen′ ish) *v. Unless they* ***replenished*** *their stock immediately, they would run out of everything.*

   ____

5. **vestige** (ves · tige) (ves′ tije̸) *n. There was no* ***vestige*** *of woodland in this area, which had once been replete with trees.*

   ____

STOP. Check answers at the end of Chapter Three (p. 78).

Practice for Additional Words

A. Directions: Match each word with the *best* definition.

________	1. arrogant	a. clever at managing money
________	2. thrifty	b. a trace
________	3. replete	c. to supply again
________	4. replenish	d. full of pride
________	5. vestige	e. well filled

STOP. Check answers at the end of Chapter Three (p. 78).

B. Directions: Each sentence has a nonsense word. Choose the word that *best* replaces the nonsense word. Some of the words are from previous exercises.

Word List

expedite, variable, constraint, arrogant, vestige, replete, thrifty, crafty, replenish, peruse.

1. I usually read questions on exams very quickly, but I should geroit them instead. ____________________
2. A major froit is that the salary is too low. ____________________
3. When the police arrived, no breit of any violence was visible. ____________________
4. The captain said that they would be in a lot of trouble unless they were able to creible the water supply soon. ____________________
5. The weather is so martible in our area that we have difficulty determining what to wear in the morning. ____________________
6. Our finances are at a disaster level, so from now on we will have to be more nift. ____________________
7. I always feel uncomfortable in Bill's presence because his remarks and comments are usually greible with sarcasm. ____________________
8. My boss phoned our supplier and told him to try to drep the shipment of our order. ____________________
9. Sharon left the party because she preferred the company of modest and unassuming persons rather than of such larent ones. ____________________
10. The con man was so riet that no one knew that he or she had been swindled until after the con man had left town. ____________________

STOP. Check answers at the end of Chapter Three (p. 78).

EXERCISE 5

Step I. Vocabulary Words in Sentences

Directions: Sentences using the ten vocabulary words from Exercise 5 follow. See whether you can figure out the meanings of the underlined words from the clues in the sentences. Blanks are provided for your estimates of the definitions. Check your meanings with those in Step II.

1. The saying "Turn the other cheek," which comes to us from the Scripture, is sometimes very difficult to follow. Let me tell you a tale for which I'm sure there are many precedents; that is, I'm sure you, too, can give similar examples. ____________________

2. At the end of last semester, right after finals, some of my colleagues and I decided to combine our efforts to try to get a research grant from the federal government. As my fellow workers are very diligent, I like to work with them. ____________________

3. Being reliable individuals, if they say that they will persevere until something is completed, they will persist until the task is done. That's how dependable they are. ____________________; ____________________

4. Well, we spent what seemed like an infinite amount of time and energy developing an intricate research design with which we finally were all pleased. ____________________

5. Antecedent to this complex research plan, we had been involved in a very sophisticated project concerning hypertension. ____________________

6. We felt that we had made a significant breakthrough in the area of high blood pressure, which is known as the "silent killer." Although we felt the breakthrough was important and meaningful, we felt that we needed to do some more research before we released our results to others.

   ____

7. We were reluctant to reveal our results because we felt that more study was needed. As we were unwilling to release our results, a man, whom I'll call Dr. X, decided to steal our findings and do his own research with them. ____________________

8. Dr. X made an adaptation of our plan, called it his own, and submitted it to Washington, D.C., for a grant. Actually, it wasn't even an adaptation, for so few changes were made. ____________________

9. You can imagine our surprise when a federal agency called us to Washington, D.C., and started to interrogate us about our research. When they questioned us, they acted as though we had done something illegal. It wasn't until much later that we learned about Dr. X and what he had done. ____________________

Step II. Vocabulary Words

1. **adaptation** (ad · ap · ta · tion) (ad · ap · tā′ shun) *n.* The act of fitting or suiting one thing to another; an adjusting to fit new conditions; a modification (a partial or slight change) for a new use. *As the story was too long for the kindergarten children, the teacher made an* ***adaptation*** *of it to suit the children's attention span.*

2. **antecedent** (an · te · ced · ent) (an · te · sēd′ ent) *adj.* Going before in time; prior; preceding; previous. *n.* The word, phrase or clause to which a pronoun refers. *In writing you must be careful that your pronoun refers to a definite* ***antecedent.***

3. **colleague** (col · league) (kol′ ēg) *n.* A fellow worker in the same profession. *My* ***colleagues*** *and I feel that our vocation needs more members who are diligent workers.*

4. **intricate** (in · tri · cate) (in′ tri · kit) *adj.* Complicated; difficult to follow or understand; complex. *The plan was so* ***intricate*** *that we needed many meetings in order to be able to understand it.*

5. **interrogate** (in · ter′ r̸o · gāte̸) *v.* To ask questions of formally; to examine by questioning. *The police said that they would* ***interrogate*** *everyone who was anywhere near the location of the homicide to try to get some answers.*

6. **persevere** (per · se · vēre̸′) *v.* To persist; to continue doing something in spite of difficulty. *Despite all hardships, some people are able to* ***persevere*** *and succeed in achieving their objectives.*

7. **precedent** (prec · e · dent) (pres′ e · dent) *n.* Something done or said that may serve as an example; in law, a legal decision serving as an authoritative rule in future similar cases. *adj.* Preceding; anterior; going before. *By doing that, you may have set a* ***precedent*** *for other people to follow.*

8. **reliable** (re · li · a · ble) (re · lī′ a · bul) *adj.* Dependable; trustworthy. *As Arthur is so* ***reliable*** *I know that we can depend on his doing the job diligently and well.*

9. **reluctant** (re · luc · tant) (re · luk′ tant) *adj.* Unwilling; opposed. *We were all* ***reluctant*** *to say that we would buy tickets to the show until we had more information about the cost.*

10. **significant** (sig · nif · i · cant) (sig · nif′ i · kant) *adj.* Having or expressing meaning; full of meaning; important. *The test results were so* ***significant*** *that the scientists knew that they had made a great breakthrough in medicine.*

Special Notes

1. **precedent** *n.* Something done or said that may serve as an example. Note that the noun *precedent* presented in this exercise comes from the combining form *ced,* meaning "go" or "yield," and *pre,* meaning "before."

2. **antecedent** *adj.* Going before in time. *n.* Word, phrase, or clause to which a pronoun refers. Note that *antecedent* is derived from the combining form *ced,* meaning "go" or "yield," and *ante,* meaning "before." You have probably met the term *antecedent* in your English course. The word, phrase, or clause to which a pronoun refers is called the *antecedent.* For example, in the sentence "John Smith was the judge who made that important decision," *judge* is the antecedent of *who.* In other words, *who* refers to *judge.* In "Jack lost his hat," *Jack* is the antecedent of *his.*

Step III. Practice

A. Directions: Each sentence has a missing word. Choose the word that *best* completes the sentence.

Word List

intricate, antecedent, adaptation, interrogate, significant, reliable, colleague, reluctant, precedent, persevere.

1. My ____________________ s and I held our biannual professional conference at the biologists' convention.

2. As there were no ____________________ s to go by, the lawyers knew that they were dealing in a new legal area.

3. The mountain climbers said that they would allow nothing to get in the way of achieving their formidable task, and they would ____________________ at all costs.

4. Only the most ____________________ federal agents, who could be trusted, were used to guard former criminals who were giving evidence against top crime figures.

5. When we lost our passports in Europe, we were told by customs officials that they would have to ____________________ us to determine if they had been stolen or lost.

6. I am always ____________________ to sign anything that I haven't first read.

7. The man in the commercial was trying to affirm that there was a(n)

________________ difference between his product and another similar product produced by another manufacturer.

8. The directions to get to the picnic grounds were so ________________ that we all had difficulty following them.
9. ________________ to this exercise, you worked on Exercise 4.
10. Have you ever seen a(n) ________________ of an old movie in which the main story line is kept the same, but the period in which the story takes place is changed?

STOP. Check answers at the end of Chapter Three (p. 78).

B. Directions: Ten sentences follow. Define the underlined word.

1. The judge's decision will serve as a precedent in future similar cases.
____
2. That event was antecedent to the war and may have been the cause of it.
____
3. Only reliable men were chosen for the mission because they had to be trusted with very secret information. ________________
4. The stockholders were reluctant to vote a pay increase for the company executives because the company was losing money. ________________
5. Is the study you are working on so significant that it will make a difference in the way things will be done in the future? ________________
6. Professor Jones said that he was meeting a number of his colleagues at their annual professional convention. ________________
7. Some of the methods that are used to interrogate persons are quite cruel.
____
8. The intricate dress pattern was too complicated for me; so I asked my friend, a professional dressmaker, to help me. ________________
9. A new television show, which is an adaptation of a former radio program, is well suited for a contemporary audience. ________________
10. When people become frustrated, they tend to give up rather than to persevere. ________________

STOP. Check answers at the end of Chapter Three (p. 78).

C. Directions: In the Word Square there are eight words from Exercise 5. Find the words in the square and match them with their correct meanings. Note that there are *more* meanings than words. If there is no word in the square for a meaning, write *none*, and give the word.

WORD SQUARE

L	A	D	A	P	T	A	T	I	O	N
O	M	O	N	T	P	U	S	R	S	P
A	I	M	T	E	E	I	I	N	M	R
I	N	T	E	R	R	O	G	A	T	E
I	T	M	C	E	S	A	N	S	R	C
J	R	O	E	L	E	R	I	W	E	E
R	I	N	D	I	V	S	F	I	L	D
S	C	S	E	A	E	O	I	C	U	E
Q	A	R	N	B	R	M	C	O	C	N
U	T	A	T	L	E	U	A	I	R	T
S	E	A	R	E	S	E	N	L	E	O
C	O	L	L	E	A	G	T	U	L	M

Meanings	*Words*
1. Complicated	______________
2. Important	______________
3. Act of fitting one thing to another	______________
4. Going before	______________
5. Fellow worker	______________
6. To question	______________
7. To persist	______________
8. Example	______________
9. Dependable	______________
10. Unwilling	______________

STOP. Check answers at the end of Chapter Three (pp. 78-79).

EXTRA WORD POWER

> **ship.** State, condition, or quality of; office, rank, or dignity; art or skill. *Ship* is added to the end of many nouns. For example: *kingship*—dignity or rank of king; *governorship*—rank or office of governor; *lordship*—rank of a lord; *dictatorship*—office or rank of a head of government who has absolute control of the government; *citizenship*—state or quality of being a citizen; *friendship*—state of being a friend; *penmanship*—art or skill of handwriting; *leadership*—skill as a leader. How many more words with *ship* can you supply?

Additional Words

From your ability to use context clues, can you figure out the meanings of the following words?

1. **procrastinate** (pro • cras • ti • nate) (prō • kras′ ti • nātɇ) *v. If you **procrastinate** all the time, you will never accomplish anything. You can put off doing things for just so long.*

   ____

2. **prudent** (prū′ dent) *adj. On the contrary, John was always **prudent** rather than rash in dealing with difficult matters.*

   ____

3. **virile** (vir′ ilɇ) *adj. **Virile** men usually don't have to prove their masculinity to anyone.*

   ____

4. **vindictive** (vin • dic • tive) (vin • dik′ tivɇ) *adj. It's difficult not to want **vindictive** punishment for killers who have murdered your loved ones.*

   ____

5. **satiate** (sa • ti • ate) (sā′ shē • ātɇ) *v. Everyone was able to **satiate** his or her appetite at the banquet.*

   ____

STOP. Check answers at the end of Chapter Three (p. 79).

Practice for Additional Words

A. Directions: Match each word with the *best* definition.

________	1. procrastinate	a. revengeful
________	2. prudent	b. to overindulge
________	3. virile	c. sensible
________	4. vindictive	d. to put off doing
________	5. satiate	e. manly

STOP. Check answers at the end of Chapter Three (p. 79).

B. Directions: Each sentence has a missing word. Choose the word that *best* completes the sentence. There are more words in the list than you need.

Word List

procrastinate, satiate, crafty, temerity, peruse, tentative, vindictive, virile, prudent, variable, expedite, versatile.

1. She is an extremely ________________ actress who can play many different roles equally well.
2. He could never ________________ his appetite for fishing and boating.
3. If he were a(n) ________________ person, he would have demanded similar punishment for them.
4. The stuntmen in the film have such ________________ that they drive their cars through flames and then jump off a cliff.
5. Her personality is as ________________ as the weather.
6. We were surprised that someone as ________________ as Jane would do something so foolhardy.
7. Jim and Jane's house is in complete disrepair because they tend to ________________ about everything that they have to do.
8. A ________________ man need not be 200 pounds, 6 feet tall, and muscular.

STOP. Check answers at the end of Chapter Three (p. 79).

EXERCISE 6

Step I. Vocabulary Words in Sentences

Directions: Sentences using the ten vocabulary words from Exercise 6 follow. See whether you can figure out the meanings of the underlined words from the clues in the sentences. Blanks are provided for your estimates of the definitions. Check your meanings with those in Step II.

1. In my high school class there were a number of students who had many liabilities. These students had no fathers, no mothers, no one who took an interest in them, and no money. They had many disadvantages.
   ____

2. The only asset that some of these students had was their desire to persist, to persevere, to make something of themselves. This asset proved to be a very valuable thing to have. ____________________

3. A decade later I met one of these students at a high school reunion, but I didn't recognize him because not only had his appearance changed, but he had also modified his manner of speaking and way of acting.
   ____

4. When I learned about how successful he had become, I asked him how he had achieved it. He said that instead of coveting or desiring what others had, he went after what he wanted. ____________________

5. He said that he was very frugal. He spent money only for necessities.
   ____

6. He said that he had learned to economize. He didn't know what it was to have anything extra. ____________________

7. Throughout college, he said that he allotted himself a certain amount of time for study, a certain amount of time for work, and very little time for leisure. ____________________

8. Upon talking to some other former high school buddies whom I hadn't seen before the reunion, I found that they had greatly changed their views on life. Many conservative students, who didn't want change in anything, were now broad-minded. Many liberal students, who had been broad-minded, were now conservatives. ____________________;
   ____

9. From my high school reunion, I learned that people are not like stagnant water, which remains in one place, but are dynamic, active beings who can control their lives. ____________________

1. **allot** (al̸ · lot′) *v.* To divide or distribute by lot; to distribute or parcel out in portions; to appoint. *The State Department of Education said that it would* ***allot*** *the money to school districts on the basis of a new formula, so that the money would be equally divided.*

2. **asset** (as′ s̸et) *n.* Anything owned that has value; any valuable or desirable thing that serves as an advantage. *Instead of being a problem and undesirable, he turned out to be an enormous* ***asset*** *to us.*

3. **conservative** (con · ser · va · tive) (kon · ser′ va · tive̸) *adj.* Tending to maintain established traditions and to resist or oppose any change in these; cautious, moderate; traditional in style or manner; avoiding showiness. *n.* One who clings to traditional or long-standing methods, views, ideas, and so on. *A* ***conservative*** *person is reluctant to see any change.*

4. **covet** (cov · et) (kov′ et) v. To desire very much what another has; to crave; to long for. *In the Scriptures it says that you should not* ***covet*** *another's wife.*

5. **economize** (e · con · o · mize) (e · kon′ o · mīze̸) *v.* To use or manage with thrift or prudence; to avoid waste or needless spending; to reduce expenses. *With everything costing so much, we will have to* ***economize*** *and curtail our spending.*

6. **frugal** (frū′ gal) *adj.* Thrifty; not spending freely; avoiding waste. *When you have a fixed and limited income and when the price of everything is high, you must be* ***frugal.***

7. **liability** (li · a · bil · i · ity) (lī · a · bil′ i · tē) *n.* Something that is owed; a debt; legal obligation to make good any loss or damage that occurs in a transaction (a business deal); something that works to a person's disadvantage. *The officers of the corporation realized that the new company they had acquired was a* ***liability*** *to them because of its large losses.*

8. **liberal** (lib′ er · al) *adj.* Giving freely; generous; large or plentiful; tolerant of views differing from one's own; broad-minded; favoring reform or progress; *n.* A person who is open-minded or broad-minded. *As a very* ***liberal-****minded person, he is for reform and a great amount of personal freedom for individuals.*

9. **modify** (mod · i · fy) (mod′ i · fī) *v.* To change slightly or make minor changes in character, form, and so on; to change or alter; to limit or reduce; in grammar, to limit or restrict a meaning. *Persons usually* ***modify*** *their views as they get older because their ways of seeing things change.*

10. **stagnant** (stag′ nant) *adj.* Lacking motion or current; not flowing or moving; foul (dirty and bad-smelling) from lack of movement; lacking in

activity; sluggish; dull. *The **stagnant** pond had a terribly bad odor because many of the aquatic plants in it were decaying.*

Special Notes

1. *Asset* has a special meaning when used in the plural, *assets.* The term *assets* is used in accounting to mean all the items on a balance sheet that show the property or resources (what an individual has) of a person or business, such as inventory (list of all goods in stock), cash, real estate, equipment, accounts and notes receivable, and so on.
2. When *liability* is used in the plural, it usually is referring to a debt such as accounts payable, capital stock, losses, and so on. Accounts payable, losses, and capital stock are *liabilities* of a corporation.
3. When *modify* is used in grammar, it means "to limit or restrict in meaning." In the sentence "That is a huge dormitory," *huge* modifies *dormitory.* Adding the word *huge* to *dormitory* limits or restricts *dormitory.* You know that it is not a small dormitory. If *co-ed* is added to *huge dormitory,* you are limiting the meaning of *dormitory* even more. Words that limit or restrict another word are describing the word. That is, *huge* and *co-ed* are describing *dormitory.*

Step III. Practice

A. Directions: Each of the following sentences has a missing word. Choose the word that *best* completes the sentence.

Word List

allot, asset, liability, frugal, stagnant, modify, conservative, liberal, economize, covet.

1. The ____________________ pond was completely still.
2. We usually ____________________ our views in college because our experiences cause us to make some changes in the way we think or feel.
3. Because I'm paying my own way through school, I must be very ____________________.
4. Fortunately, I don't have even one ____________________, because at this moment I couldn't afford to owe anyone anything.
5. The ____________________ group was opposed to the changes that were being proposed.
6. Rather than ____________________ what affluent people have, why don't you try to do something with your own potential?

7. Make the most of your ____________________ s, and play down your faults when you go on the job interview.

8. He is very ____________________ with money because he is so affluent and generous.

9. Even though I am quite affluent now, I still ____________________ because I can't stand waste.

10. Did you ____________________ each person an equivalent portion?

STOP. Check answers at the end of Chapter Three (p. 80).

B. Directions: Ten sentences follow. Define the underlined word.

1. If you don't start to <u>economize</u> now, you won't have any money left at the end of the week. ____________________

2. My views are always contrary to my parents' views, and because they like everything to remain the same, I'm a <u>liberal</u>. ____________________

3. Mary is so <u>frugal</u> that absolutely nothing is ever wasted by her.
____

4. As a young child, John was ridiculed about being so tall, but at college his height was an <u>asset</u> for the basketball team. ____________________

5. I <u>allot</u> myself a certain amount of time each week to spend in reading books other than those assigned in class. ____________________

6. One of the political parties in our township is so <u>conservative</u> that it won't even let you change a meeting time. ____________________

7. I saw a film in which you know that conflict is going to take place because in the opening scene a young cowhand wanders in, looks at the wife of the rancher, and immediately you know he <u>covets</u> her. ____________________

8. The <u>stagnant</u> pond water smelled as bad as a sewer. ____________________

9. The city council members found that they would have to <u>modify</u> their plan if they wanted it to be accepted. ____________________

10. As a successful model, Jane found her height was an advantage to her rather than a <u>liability</u>. ____________________

STOP. Check answers at the end of Chapter Three (p. 80).

C. Directions: In the Word Square there are seventeen words from Exercises 4, 5, 6, and some previous exercises. Find the words in the square and match them with their correct meanings. Note that there are *more* meanings than words. If there is no word in the square for a meaning, write *none,* and give the word.

WORD SQUARE

E	C	O	N	O	M	I	Z	E	S	E	R
A	L	L	O	T	P	R	E	D	U	A	L
R	I	F	R	U	G	A	L	E	P	M	U
E	A	S	S	E	T	C	I	L	E	N	A
L	B	I	T	M	A	A	B	E	R	E	L
U	I	S	A	O	C	N	E	T	V	S	A
C	L	O	G	D	I	D	R	E	I	T	U
T	I	L	N	I	T	I	A	C	T	Y	D
A	T	A	A	F	O	D	L	O	A	A	I
N	Y	T	N	Y	M	A	O	V	L	E	B
T	O	E	T	O	E	E	U	E	S	D	L
C	O	N	S	E	R	V	A	T	I	V	E

Meanings — *Words*

1. Frank ____________
2. Able to be heard ____________
3. A pardon ____________
4. The occurrence of events at the same time ____________
5. To divide or distribute ____________
6. Unspoken ____________
7. To separate from; to place apart from ____________
8. Thrifty ____________
9. Unwilling ____________
10. A valuable thing to have ____________
11. To take out ____________
12. To desire what others have ____________
13. To state positively ____________
14. Tending to maintain established traditions ____________
15. Giving freely; broad-minded ____________

16. To avoid waste ________________

17. A debt ________________

18. To change slightly ________________

19. Lacking motion ________________

20. Difficult choice because both are disagreeable ________________

STOP. Check answers at the end of Chapter Three (p. 80).

EXTRA WORD POWER

super. Above in position; over; above or beyond; greater than or superior to; extra; in the highest degree; in excessive degree. *Super* is found at the beginning of many words. You have probably met *super* in words like *superior,* meaning "of higher degree"; *superb,* meaning "of the highest quality"; and *superlative,* meaning "of the highest degree." Following is a list of words in which *super* is added to the beginning of the word and changes the word meaning to include "in excessive degree" or "in the highest degree." *supercritical*—highly critical; *supersafe*—safe in the highest degree; *supersweet*—sweet in the highest degree; *superabundance*—abundance in excess; *superacid*—excessively acid. Following is a list of words in which *super* is found at the beginning of the word, and it is a necessary part of the word; that is, if *super* were deleted from the word, the word would lose its meaning. *supervision*— the act of overseeing others; *superintendent*—one who has charge of a department, building, institution, and the like; *superstititous*—having beliefs that are not consistent with the known laws of science. How many more words with *super* can you supply? Check your dictionary for a long list of *super* words.

Additional Words

From your ability to use context clues, can you figure out the meanings of the following words?

1. **vital** (vi • tal) (vī' tul) *adj. The doctor said that the operation was so* ***vital*** *that not having it would be fatal.*

____

2. **laudable** (laud • a • ble) (laud′ a • bul) *adj. What the group has done is highly* ***laudable****, and it should be praised for its efforts. Not many students would give up their free time to help others.*

____

3. **vindicate** (vin • di • cate) (vin′ di • kāte̸) *v. Although she was completely* ***vindicated*** *by the trial, some people treated her as though she were guilty.*

____

4. **sedate** (se • dāte̸′) *adj. v. The sedative calmed him down so much that it was hard to believe that this* **sedate** *person had been belligerent a few moments ago.*

____

5. **castigate** (cas • ti • gate) (kas′ ti • gāte̸) *v. The judge* ***castigated*** *the parents for their behavior toward their children and warned them that next time he would take the children away from them.*

____

STOP. Check answers at the end of Chapter Three (pp. 80–81).

Practice for Additional Words

A. Directions: Match each word with the *best* definition.

______ 1. vital	a. worthy of praise
______ 2. laudable	b. calm; composed
______ 3. vindicate	c. necessary to life
______ 4. sedate	d. to correct or subdue by punishing
______ 5. castigate	e. to clear from criticism

STOP. Check answers at the end of Chapter Three (p. 81).

B. Directions: Here are five sentences that contain the meanings of the additional words presented in this exercise. Choose the word that *best* fits the underlined word or phrase in the sentence.

Word List

vital, laudable, vindicate, sedate, castigate.

1. Foreign trade is <u>essential</u> to the welfare of nations. ______________
2. The men tried to <u>quiet</u> the wild dogs with tranquilizer guns.
____

3. It is commendable of you to spend so much of your time at the hospital reading to children. ____________________

4. It's difficult to rebuke terrorists because they will not accept criticism. ____________________

5. The witness was able to clear the defendant. ____________________

STOP. Check answers at the end of Chapter Three (p. 81).

Some People Have Different Opinions on What Is *Vital*

Reprinted by permission of NEA, Inc.

CROSSWORD PUZZLE 2

Directions: The meanings of a number of the words from Exercises 4–6 follow. Your knowledge of these words will help you to solve this crossword puzzle. Note that *combining form* is abbreviated as *comb. f.*

Across

1. Way of saying *father*
3. Broad-minded
6. Sixth letter of the alphabet
7. An indefinite article
8. Dependable
13. In favor of something
15. Opposite of *down* (pl.)
18. When your heart stops beating, you are ___
19. Thrifty
22. Same as #1 Down
25. When your heart stops beating you have ___
27. Homonym of *sew*
28. Abbreviation for *for example*
29. Homonym of *two*
30. Same as #2 Down
31. In opposition to something
32. Abbreviation for *Rhode Island*
33. Abbreviation for *East*
34. Abbreviation for *South Carolina*
35. Sound you make when you laugh
37. A beverage
38. Same as #10 Down
39. Foul from not moving
43. The basic metric unit of length
46. Your dog or cat is your ___
47. Same as #9 Down
48. Part of your face
49. To wipe out completely
52. Choice between two equally bad alternatives
55. To question formally
58. Another way of referring to God
60. Same as #2 Down
61. To give food to
62. A verb ending
63. Same as #62 Across
64. Opposite of *gain*
65. Applying oneself to whatever is undertaken
68. Same as #66 Down
69. Slang for *Communists*

Down

1. A friend
2. Mohammed ___
3. Worthy of praise
4. Used for the comparative degree of adjectives
5. Contraction of *are*
6. Lots of water vapor on the ground causes ___, which makes it difficult to see
9. *Much ___ About Nothing*
10. Homonym of *bee*
11. Musical syllable
12. Ending for the past tense of regular verbs
13. Example
14. This goes on the floor
16. ___ needles, which come from an evergreen tree
17. ___ the table
19. Same as #6 Across
20. Rhymes with *cat*
21. ___ and behold; means *see*
22. A light blow
23. A fermented beverage
24. A debt; disadvantage
26. To despise; scorn
27. Important; full of meaning
32. Abbreviation for *rear admiral*
33. Christian holiday around March 21
34. California is a ___
35. Masculine pronoun
36. Same as #20 Down
40. Same as #29 Across
41. Without any; nothing left
42. Past tense of something necessary
43. Abbreviation of girl's name, *Margaret*
44. Time period
45. Same as #32 Across
46. To persist
47. Rhymes with *ham*

71. Sound made when laughing
72. Comb. f. for *in*
73. Something that tastes good is ___
75. Same as #7 Across
76. Comb. f. for *together; with*
78. You ___ your *i* and put this at the end of a sentence
79. Same as #20 Down
80. Referring to *voice*
82. Same as #77 Down
83. Comb. f. for *having; full of*
84. Unwilling
88. Opposite of *she*
89. Grows in ground, is eaten, and has a strong, sharp smell and taste
90. Opposite of *near*
91. Refers to a small child
92. To desire very much what others have
93. Form of the verb *to be*
94. Same as #5 Down

50. To divide or portion off
51. Homonym of *two*
52. Way of saying *father* (pl.)
53. ___ of the valley; a flower
54. ___ shot; slang for picture of face
56. You do this when you are fatigued
57. Opposite of *off*
59. Comb. f. for *people*
66. Pronoun referring to *me*
67. Unspoken
70. To carry out; to perform
71. Same as #35 Across
73. Same as #29 Across
74. Indefinite article
77. Opposite of *off*
81. Same as #7 Across
84. Same as #32 Down
85. Same as #21 Down
86. Comb f. for *not*
87. Same as #51 Down
88. To own
90. Previous; former; earlier
92. You drive this

STOP. Check answers at the end of Chapter Three (p. 81).

WORD SCRAMBLE 2

Directions: Word Scramble 2 is based on words from Exercises 4–6. The meanings are your clues to arranging the letters in correct order.

1.	diiccnocene	____________	the occurrence of things at the same time by chance
2.	eeeltd	____________	to take out
3.	riffma	____________	to state positively
4.	melmaid	____________	a situation that presents two equally disagreeable choices
5.	gentilid	____________	applying oneself
6.	tentrepin	____________	relevant

7. aaadoitnpt ____________________ act of fitting or suiting one thing to another

8. centdeanet ____________________ going before

9. nitiraetc ____________________ complicated

10. guelolaec ____________________ fellow worker

11. tingerorate ____________________ to question

12. servereep ____________________ to persist

13. eelblair ____________________ dependable

14. cansignfiti ____________________ important

15. tsase ____________________ something of value

16. tagstnna ____________________ without motion

17. altol ____________________ to divide or distribute by lot

18. gufrla ____________________ thrifty

19. toevc ____________________ to desire what others have

20. domyfi ____________________ to alter

STOP. Check answers at the end of Chapter Three (p. 81).

ANALOGIES 2

Directions: Find the word from the following list that *best* completes each analogy. There are more words in the list than you need.

Word List

sensible, timid, fearful, blast, persevere, scorn, temerity, think, bold, eradicate, manly, decisive, diligent, vital, save, frugal, replenish, replete, satiate, affirm, associate, isolate, contagious, commendable, rebuke, build, alter, delete, omission, reply, question, postpone, broad-minded, conservative, sophisticated, covet, covert, overt, buy, intricate.

1. Frank : candid :: virile : ____________________.
2. Positive : definite :: disdain : ____________________.
3. Parade : procession :: interrogate : ____________________.
4. Hostile : friendly :: liberal : ____________________.
5. Haughty : arrogant :: resupply : ____________________.

6. Stale : fresh :: deny : ____________________.

7. Dependable : reliable :: persist : ____________________.

8. Synonym : antonym :: simple : ____________________.

9. Frustrated : defeated :: colleague : ____________________.

10. Castigate : rebuke :: segregate : ____________________.

11. Thrifty : frugal :: laudable : ____________________.

12. Inferior : superior :: insert : ____________________.

13. Hate : animosity :: desire : ____________________.

14. Provisions : supplies :: prudent : ____________________.

15. Plump : corpulent :: modify : ____________________.

16. Pertinent : relevant :: industrious : ____________________.

17. Tepid : lukewarm :: essential : ____________________.

18. Modest : shy :: procrastinate : ____________________.

19. Alarm : warn :: bomb : ____________________.

20. Blanket : cover :: economize : ____________________.

STOP. Check answers at the end of Chapter Three (p. 81).

MULTIPLE-CHOICE VOCABULARY TEST 2

Directions: This is a test on words in Exercises 4–6. Words are presented according to exercises. *Do all exercises before checking answers.* Underline the meaning that *best* fits the word.

Exercise 4

1. coincidence
   a. something that happens
   b. a chance happening
   c. occurrence of things at the same time by chance
   d. a happening

2. delete
   a. to put in
   b. to take out
   c. to write
   d. to allow

3. affirm
   a. to deny
   b. to ask
   c. to question
   d. to state positively

4. dilemma
   a. a problem
   b. an argument
   c. something unpleasant
   d. a choice between two equally disagreeable things

5. diligent
   a. a choice
   b. a choice between equally disagreeable things
   c. applying oneself
   d. an argument

6. disdain
   a. a disagreement
   b. unequal choices
   c. to regard as unworthy
   d. to apply onself

7. eradicate
   a. to take a word away
   b. to wipe out completely
   c. to despise
   d. to disagree with

8. haughty
   a. having a lot of pride in oneself
   b. applying oneself
   c. disagreeable
   d. hostile

9. isolate
   a. to harm
   b. to help
   c. to set apart
   d. to stay together

10. pertinent
   a. unrelated
   b. not appropriate
   c. appropriate
   d. set apart

Exercise 5

11. adaptation
   a. act of adjusting to old situations
   b. a fitting outcome
   c. refers to adoption
   d. act of fitting one thing to another

12. antecedent
   a. going against
   b. going after
   c. going before
   d. going first

13. intricate
   a. complicated
   b. simple
   c. presenting a problem
   d. helpful

14. colleague
   a. a college buddy
   b. a friend
   c. an enemy
   d. a fellow worker in a profession

15. interrogate
   a. to speak
   b. to state
   c. to question
   d. to make a choice

16. persevere
   a. to help
   b. to persist
   c. to move
   d. to be active

17. precedent
   a. something that serves as an example
   b. an offense
   c. something unnecessary
   d. something that comes after

18. reliable
   a. helpful
   b. dependable
   c. hostile
   d. presenting an example

19. reluctant
   a. willing
   b. helping
   c. unwilling
   d. hostile

20. significant
a. a sign
b. a meaning
c. helpful
d. full of meaning

Exercise 6

21. allot
a. to donate
b. to state an opinion
c. to sell a lot
d. to divide

22. asset
a. to assess
b. happy
c. a valuable thing
d. an opinion

23. conservative
a. tending to like change
b. tending to like differences
c. tending to be broad-minded
d. tending to like things to remain the same

24. covet
a. to like things
b. to dislike things
c. to desire greatly things that others have
d. to hope

25. frugal
a. spending freely
b. wise
c. spends often
d. thrifty

26. liability
a. a gift
b. legal
c. a debt
d. a feeling

27. economize
a. to spend freely
b. to spend money
c. refers to economics
d. to avoid waste

28. liberal
a. big
b. broad-minded
c. remain the same
d. helpful

29. modify
a. to change slightly
b. to move
c. to dress
d. to be mod

30. stagnant
a. lacking movement
b. moving
c. healthful
d. refers to running water

TRUE/FALSE TEST 2

Directions: This is true/false test on Exercises 4–6. Read each sentence carefully. Decide whether it is true or false. Put a *T* for *true* or an *F* for *false* in the blank. The number after the sentence tells you if the word is from Exercise 4, 5, or 6.

________ 1. Someone who economizes would be a frugal person. 6

________ 2. All assets are good to have. 6

________ 3. *Frugal* and *thrifty* are antonyms. 6

_______ 4. When you allot something to someone, you give him a lot. 6

_______ 5. A dilemma is easy to solve. 4

_______ 6. When someone is held in disdain, he is scorned. 4

_______ 7. When something is eradicated, it is partially wiped out. 4

_______ 8. *Liability* and *asset* are antonyms. 6

_______ 9. When something is stagnant, it is still. 6

_______ 10. In the sentence "Mother is a wonderful woman, who is a great cook," *woman* is the antecedent of *who.* 5

_______ 11. A precedent comes to us from the past and serves as a guide or example. 5

_______ 12. A diligent worker is a lazy person. 4

_______ 13. Pertinent information is information that doesn't apply. 4

_______ 14. When something happens by coincidence, it is planned. 4

_______ 15. An adaptation of a plan is a plan that has been changed to suit the new situation. 5

_______ 16. A significant result in a study is a doubtful finding. 5

_______ 17. A conservative person resists change. 6

_______ 18. When you delete a sentence, you are modifying it. 4, 6

_______ 19. A colleague refers to a friendly fellow. 5

_______ 20. An intricate plan is a simple plan. 5

STOP. Check answers for both tests at the end of Chapter Three (p. 82).

SCORING OF TESTS

Multiple-Choice Test

Number Wrong	*Score*
0–2	Excellent
3–5	Good
6–8	Weak
Above 8	Poor

Score _______

True/False Test

Number Wrong	*Score*
0–1	Excellent
2–3	Good
4–5	Weak
Above 5	Poor

Score _______

1. If you scored in the excellent or good range on *both tests,* you are doing well. Go on to Chapter Four.

2. If you scored in the weak or poor range on either test, look below and follow directions for Additional Practice. Note that the words on the tests are arranged so that you can tell in which exercise to find them. This will help you if you need additional practice.

ADDITIONAL PRACTICE SETS

A. Directions: Write the words you missed on the tests from the three exercises in the space provided. Note that the tests are presented so that you can tell to which exercises the words belong.

Exercise 4 Words Missed

1. ______________ 6. ______________
2. ______________ 7. ______________
3. ______________ 8. ______________
4. ______________ 9. ______________
5. ______________ 10. ______________

Exercise 5 Words Missed

1. ______________ 6. ______________
2. ______________ 7. ______________
3. ______________ 8. ______________
4. ______________ 9. ______________
5. ______________ 10. ______________

Exercise 6 Words Missed

1. ______________ 6. ______________
2. ______________ 7. ______________
3. ______________ 8. ______________
4. ______________ 9. ______________
5. ______________ 10. ______________

B. Directions: Restudy the words that you have written down on this page. Do Step I and Step II for those you missed. Note that Step I and Step II are on the following pages:

Exercise 4—pp. 45–47.

Exercise 5—pp. 51–54.

Exercise 6—pp. 59–61.

C. Directions: Do Additional Practice 1 on this page if you missed words from Exercise 4. Do Additional Practice 2 on p. 76 if you missed words from Exercise 5. Do Additional Practice 3 on pp. 76–77 if you missed words from Exercise 6. Now go on to Chapter Four.

Additional Practice 1 for Exercise 4

Directions: Ten sentences with missing words follow. Underline the word that *best* fits the sentence. Two choices are given for each sentence.

1. Because he is such a (pertinent, diligent) worker, he will finish the job on time.
2. What a (dilemma, coincidence) to have to choose between two equally bad things.
3. My essay was too long, so I decided to (affirm, delete) some words.
4. Hitler tried to (eradicate, isolate) a whole group of people by murdering all of them.
5. This statement must be left in because it is (diligent, pertinent) to the report.
6. Because nations depend upon one another, it is difficult in contemporary times for nations to (affirm, isolate) themselves from others.
7. The witness said that he would again (affirm, delete) the statement he made before because it was correct and important.
8. What a (coincidence, dilemma) to have both of us doing the same thing at the same time.
9. I do not like to be with (diligent, haughty) people because they think that they are so great and they look down on others.
10. When they heard that Ms. Jones had betrayed their confidence, she was held in great (dilemma, disdain).

STOP. Check answers at the end of Chapter Three (p. 82).

Additional Practice 2 for Exercise 5

Directions: Ten sentences containing the meanings of vocabulary presented in Exercise 5 follow. Choose the word that *best* fits the word or phrase underlined in the sentence.

Word List

intricate, interrogate, antecedent, adaptation, colleagues, significant, reliable, precedent, persevere, reluctant.

1. This play, which is based on a famous novel, is a perfect modification suited to the contemporary scene. ____________________
2. The plan we developed is so involved and complicated that it will probably take some time for the others to understand it. ____________________
3. The findings from your research are so important and full of meaning that they should be shared with the world. ____________________
4. My fellow professional associates are joining me at a special convention. ____________________
5. Ms. Smith was unwilling to go along with the rest of the committee because the idea did not sound workable to her. ____________________
6. As he is a very dependable and trustworthy person, many people will vote for him. ____________________
7. The judge used a former case as an example on which to make his decision. ____________________
8. As a policewoman, she must always tell persons of their rights before she can formally question them. ____________________
9. When I have a hard job to do, I persist until I have finished it. ____________________
10. The invention of the train was prior to that of the airplane. ____________________

STOP. Check answers at the end of Chapter Three (p. 82).

Additional Practice 3 for Exercise 6

Directions: Ten sentences containing the meanings of vocabulary presented in Exercise 6 follow. Choose the word that *best* fits the word or phrase underlined in the sentence.

Word List

conservative, stagnant, allot, frugal, covet, liberal, asset, liability, economize, modify.

1. Under the terms of the will, they will divide the money equally among the children. ____________
2. A pleasant smile is a valuable and desirable thing to have. ____________
3. We are traditional persons reluctant to have any change, and our group will oppose any changes that you attempt to make. ____________
4. Seth is a thrifty person. ____________
5. Anthony and Donna spend their money wisely to avoid waste. ____________
6. The major debt I have is my school loan. ____________
7. Some people only desire what other people have. ____________
8. When lake water is without motion, it can begin to have a bad smell. ____________
9. My broad-minded friends are all very interested in reform and progress. ____________
10. I am going to change my speech slightly so that it will appeal to more people. ____________

STOP. Check answers at the end of Chapter Three (p. 82).

ANSWERS: Chapter Three

Exercise 4 (pp. 45–51)

Practice A

(1) coincidence, (2) dilemma, (3) pertinent, (4) affirm, (5) Haughty, (6) isolate, (7) eradicate, (8) delete, (9) disdain, (10) diligent.

Practice B

(1) eradicate, (2) haughty, (3) disdain, (4) diligent, (5) pertinent, (6) isolate, (7) delete, (8) coincidence, (9) affirm, (10) dilemma.

Practice C

(1) f, (2) e, (3) j, (4) c, (5) g, (6) a, (7) i, (8) d, (9) b, (10) h.

Additional Words (p. 50)

1. **arrogant.** Full of pride and self-importance; overbearing; haughty.
2. **thrifty.** Clever at managing one's money; economical; not spending money unnecessarily.
3. **replete.** Well filled or supplied.
4. **replenish.** To supply or fill again.
5. **vestige.** A trace, mark, or sign of something that once existed but doesn't anymore.

Practice for Additional Words (pp. 50-51)

A. (1) d, (2) a, (3) e, (4) c, (5) b.
B. (1) peruse, (2) constraint, (3) vestige, (4) replenish, (5) variable, (6) thrifty, (7) replete, (8) expedite, (9) arrogant, (10) crafty.

Exercise 5 (pp. 51-58)

Practice A

(1) colleague, (2) precedent, (3) persevere, (4) reliable, (5) interrogate, (6) reluctant, (7) significant, (8) intricate, (9) Antecedent, (10) adaptation.

Practice B

(1) example, (2) prior, (3) dependable, (4) unwilling, (5) important, (6) fellow workers in a profession, (7) question, (8) complicated, (9) modification for a new use, (10) persist.

Practice C

(1) intricate, (2) significant, (3) adaptation, (4) antecedent, (5) none—colleague, (6) interrogate, (7) persevere, (8) precedent, (9) reliable, (10) none—reluctant.

WORD SQUARE

L	A	D	A	P	T	A	T	I	O	N
O	M	O	N	T	P	U	S	R	S	P
A	I	M	T	E	E	I	I	N	M	R
I	N	T	E	R	R	O	G	A	T	E
I	T	M	C	E	S	A	N	S	R	C
J	R	O	E	L	E	R	I	W	E	E
R	I	N	D	I	V	S	F	I	L	D
S	C	S	E	A	E	O	I	C	U	E
Q	A	R	N	B	R	M	C	O	C	N
U	T	A	T	L	E	U	A	I	R	T
S	E	A	R	E	S	E	N	L	E	O
C	O	L	L	E	A	G	T	U	L	M

Additional Words (p. 57)

1. **procrastinate.** To put off doing something until a future time; to postpone taking action.
2. **prudent.** Capable of using sound judgment in practical matters; wisely cautious; sensible; not rash.
3. **virile.** Manly; masculine; forceful; able to procreate (to produce or reproduce).
4. **vindictive.** Revengeful in spirit; spiteful.
5. **satiate.** To fill; to satisfy the appetite completely; to supply with anything to excess; to glut (overindulge). (*Satiate* used to mean only "to satisfy completely," but the term is now usually used to mean "to overindulge to the point that there is no longer any pleasure.")

Practice for Additional Words (p. 58)

A. (1) d, (2) c, (3) e, (4) a, (5) b.
B. (1) versatile, (2) satiate, (3) vindictive, (4) temerity, (5) variable, (6) prudent, (7) procrastinate, (8) virile.

Exercise 6 (pp. 59-66)

Practice A

(1) stagnant, (2) modify, (3) frugal, (4) liability, (5) conservative, (6) covet, (7) asset, (8) liberal, (9) economize, (10) allot.

Practice B

(1) avoid waste, (2) a person who is open-minded, (3) thrifty, (4) something of value, (5) parcel out or set aside, (6) opposed to change, (7) longs for, (8) foul from not moving, (9) alter, (10) disadvantage.

Practice C

(1) candid, (2) audible, (3) amnesty, (4) none–coincidence, (5) allot, (6) tacit, (7) isolate, (8) frugal, (9) reluctant, (10) asset, (11) delete, (12) covet, (13) none–affirm, (14) conservative, (15) liberal, (16) economize, (17) liability, (18) modify, (19) stagnant, (20) none–dilemma.

WORD SQUARE

E	C	O	N	O	M	I	Z	E	S	E	R
A	L	L	O	T	P	R	E	D	U	A	L
R	I	F	R	U	G	A	L	E	P	M	U
E	A	S	S	E	T	C	I	L	E	N	A
L	B	I	T	M	A	A	B	E	R	E	L
U	I	S	A	O	C	N	E	T	V	S	A
C	L	O	G	D	I	D	R	E	I	T	U
T	I	L	N	I	T	I	A	C	T	Y	D
A	T	A	A	F	O	D	L	O	A	A	I
N	Y	T	N	Y	M	A	O	V	L	E	B
T	O	E	T	O	E	E	U	E	S	D	L
C	O	N	S	E	R	V	A	T	I	V	E

Additional Words (pp. 64-65)

1. **vital.** Necessary to life; essential; energetic.
2. **laudable.** Worthy of praise; commendable.
3. **vindicate.** To clear from criticism, accusation, or suspicion.

4. **sedate.** Calm; composed; quiet; serene; sober; to put under sedation.
5. **castigate.** To correct or subdue by punishing; to criticize with drastic severity; to rebuke.

Practice for Additional Words (pp. 65-66)

A. (1) c, (2) a, (3) e, (4) b, (5) d.
B. (1) vital, (2) sedate, (3) laudable, (4) castigate, (5) vindicate.

Crossword Puzzle 2 (pp. 66-68)

Word Scramble 2 (pp. 68-69)

(1) coincidence, (2) delete, (3) affirm, (4) dilemma, (5) diligent, (6) pertinent, (7) adaptation, (8) antecedent, (9) intricate, (10) colleague, (11) interrogate, (12) persevere, (13) reliable, (14) significant, (15) asset, (16) stagnant, (17) allot, (18) frugal, (19) covet, (20) modify.

Analogies 2 (pp. 69-70)

(1) manly, (2) scorn, (3) question, (4) conservative, (5) replenish, (6) affirm, (7) persevere, (8) intricate, (9) associate, (10) isolate, (11) commendable, (12) delete, (13) covet, (14) sensible, (15) alter, (16) diligent, (17) vital, (18) postpone, (19) eradicate, (20) save.

Multiple-Choice Vocabulary Test 2 (pp. 70–72)

Exercise 4

(1) c, (2) b, (3) d, (4) d, (5) c, (6) c, (7) b, (8) a, (9) c, (10) c.

Exercise 5

(11) d, (12) c, (13) a, (14) d, (15) c, (16) b, (17) a, (18) b, (19) c, (20) d.

Exercise 6

(21) d, (22) c, (23) d, (24) c, (25) d, (26) c, (27) d, (28) b, (29) a, (30) a.

True/False Test 2 (pp. 72–73)

(1) T, (2) T, (3) F, (4) F, (5) F, (6) T, (7) F, (8) T, (9) T, (10) T, (11) T, (12) F, (13) F, (14) F, (15) T, (16) F, (17) T, (18) F, (19) F, (20) F.

STOP. Turn to p. 73 for the scoring of the tests.

Additional Practice Sets (pp. 74–77)

Additional Practice 1

(1) diligent, (2) dilemma, (3) delete, (4) eradicate, (5) pertinent, (6) isolate, (7) affirm, (8) coincidence, (9) haughty, (10) disdain.

Additional Practice 2

(1) adaptation, (2) intricate, (3) significant, (4) colleagues, (5) reluctant, (6) reliable, (7) precedent, (8) interrogate, (9) persevere, (10) antecedent.

Additional Practice 3

(1) allot, (2) asset, (3) conservative, (4) frugal, (5) economize, (6) liability, (7) covet, (8) stagnant, (9) liberal, (10) modify.

CHAPTER FOUR

Exercises 7–9

Crossword Puzzle 3

Word Scramble 3

Analogies 3

Multiple-Choice Vocabulary Test 3

True/False Test 3

Scoring of Tests

Additional Practice Sets

Answers

EXERCISE 7

Step I. Vocabulary Words in Sentences

Directions: Sentences using the ten vocabulary words from Exercise 7 follow. See whether you can figure out the meanings of the underlined words from the clues in the sentences. Blanks are provided for your estimates of the definitions. Check your meanings with those in Step II.

1. Jeffrey James was a young man who had strong artistic <u>inclinations.</u> As a young child, he used to isolate himself from others and spend all his time drawing and painting. ____________________
2. While at school, he didn't pay attention to anything except what he considered <u>aesthetic</u> things, such as art and beauty. ____________________
3. His teachers didn't understand his feelings or <u>attitudes</u> toward art.

   ____
4. His behavior and opinions <u>antagonized</u> them. Rather than help him to develop his artistic potential, they frustrated his efforts to paint.

   ____

5. The teachers had felt that it was an affront to them that Jeffrey wouldn't do anything but draw. They were insulted because they felt that what they were presenting in school was more important for Jeffrey than his drawing. ____________________

6. As a result, they sometimes made derogatory remarks about his paintings. Soon Jeffrey was ridiculed by students also. ____________________

7. Fortunately for Jeffrey, one of his special characteristics was being able to survive despite formidable odds. ____________________

8. He was not easily intimidated. The more the students made fun of him, the more he drew. He was not afraid. ____________________

9. It's interesting to note what hypocrites many of Jeffrey James's former classmates are. When Jeffrey became famous, they said that they knew all along how good he was. ____________________

10. However, while in school, they didn't even use any euphemisms to tell Jeffrey how they felt. They just came right out and said distasteful things to him. ____________________

Step II. Vocabulary Words

1. **aesthetic** (aes · thet · ic) (a̸es · thet′ ik) *adj.* Referring to beauty; sensitive to art and beauty; showing good taste; artistic. *Sharon has a highly developed **aesthetic** sense because she is so sensitive to art and beauty.*

2. **affront** (af̸ · front′) *v.* To insult. *n.* An insult; an open and intentional insult. *That was a definite **affront** to me because I was the only one in the class not invited.*

3. **antagonize** (an · tag′ o · nīze̸) *v.* To make unfriendly; to make an enemy of; to oppose; to act against. *If you persist in behaving in this way, you will **antagonize** your boss and make him hostile toward you.*

4. **attitude** (at′ t̸i · tūde̸) *n.* A way of feeling, acting, or thinking that shows one's disposition (one's frame of mind) or opinion; the feeling itself; posture. *It is very difficult to change **attitudes** because the way we feel about things comes to us from our past experiences and has been with us for some time.*

5. **characteristic** (char · ac · ter · is · tic) (kar · ak · ter · is′ tik) *adj.* Marking the peculiar quality or qualities of a person or thing; distinctive; special. *n.* A special trait, feature, or quality; individuality. *All mammals have certain **characteristics** in common.*

6. **derogatory** (de · rog · a · to · ry) (de · rog′ a · tor · ē) *adj.* Tending to make less well regarded; tending to belittle someone or something; dis-

paraging; belittling. *The **derogatory** remarks were supposed to make us think less of Mr. Jones, but on the contrary, they made us think less of the person who made them.*

7. **euphemism** (eu • phe • mism) (ȼū′ fe • miz • um) *n.* The substitution of a word or phrase that is less direct, milder, or vaguer for one thought to be harsh, offensive, or blunt; a word or phrase considered less distasteful or less offensive than another. *"They are in their final resting place" is a **euphemism** for "They are dead."*

8. hypocrite (hyp • o • crite) (hip′ o • kritȼ) *n.* A person who pretends to be what he or she is not; one who pretends to be better than he or she really is. *He is a **hypocrite** because he made us all feel guilty about asking for our share of the profits when he had already pocketed his share a long time ago.*

9. **inclination** (in • cli • na • tion) (in • kli • nā′ shun) *n.* A personal leaning or bent; a liking; a bending, slanting, or sloping surface; a slope. *Whatever your **inclinations** are in this matter, you must try to be fair and not allow your personal leanings to get in the way of your decision.*

10. **intimidate** (in • tim′ i • dātȼ) *v.* To make timid; to cause fear; to scare; to discourage by threats or violence. *The reason many big crime figures are not convicted is that they **intimidate** witnesses so that the witnesses are afraid to say anything against them.*

Special Notes

1. Note that *posture* and *attitude* are synonyms. Posture can mean "a mental position or frame of mind." Also, the way that one carries himself or herself or the position of the body can show an individual's attitude.
2. The phrase *strike an attitude* means "to assume a posture or pose for effect."

Step III. Practice

A. Directions: Each sentence has a missing word. Choose the word that *best* completes the sentence.

Word List

affront, aesthetic, attitude, characteristic, inclination, hypocrite, derogatory, euphemism, intimidate, antagonize.

1. You can usually tell what a person's ____________________ toward something is by the way he or she behaves.
2. Because some people have a more developed ____________________ sense than others, they are more sensitive to art and beauty.

3. When you are insulted by someone you count as a friend, the _________________ is even more painful.

4. The doctor asked the mother of the child if she noticed any special _________________ s that the child had.

5. As I don't like to have people hostile toward me, I try not to _________________ others.

6. The hill's _________________ was so steep that I had difficulty walking up the slope.

7. "She is pleasingly plump" is a(n) _________________ for "She is fat."

8. Mary is a(n) _________________ because she had us believing that she was going to help us when all along she had no intention of doing this.

9. They tried to _________________ us by using threats and insults, but we wouldn't change our story.

10. Politicians usually make _________________ remarks about their opponents because they want to belittle them.

STOP. Check answers at the end of Chapter Four (p. 114).

B. Directions: Ten sentences follow. Define the underlined word.

1. His <u>characteristic</u> way of greeting someone makes him more distinctive. _________________

2. We were very upset by the <u>derogatory</u> statements made about our friend by someone trying to belittle her. _________________

3. When a visiting diplomat was not invited to a state dinner recently, it was regarded as a direct <u>affront</u> to the diplomat and the country he represented. _________________

4. Presidents' wives seem to be interested in art and become involved in <u>aesthetic</u> functions. _________________

5. I always use a <u>euphemism</u> when I don't want to come right out and say something that might be distasteful. _________________

6. He is a <u>hypocrite</u> to act so moral when he has been more immoral than anyone else. _________________

7. She seems to have an <u>inclination</u> to help persons who are in trouble. _________________

8. From the way he behaved, it was difficult to tell what his <u>attitude</u> toward the speaker's comments was. _________________

9. When the judge learned that an attempt to <u>intimidate</u> jurors had been

made, he asked the police to arrest the persons who were trying to frighten the jurors. ____________________

10. The insulting remarks did antagonize the witness, so that he became hostile to the lawyer. ____________________

STOP. Check answers at the end of Chapter Four (pp. 114–115).

C. Directions: The words from Exercise 7 follow. Match the word with the meaning that *best* fits.

	Words	*Meanings*
________	1. antagonize	a. an insult
________	2. attitude	b. tending to belittle; belittling
________	3. aesthetic	c. one's feeling
________	4. affront	d. to make an enemy of
________	5. characteristic	e. a less distasteful word or phrase to describe something
________	6. derogatory	f. referring to beauty
________	7. euphemism	g. a personal leaning or bent
________	8. hypocrite	h. to make timid
________	9. intimidate	i. one who pretends to be what he or she is not
________	10. inclination	j. peculiar quality

STOP. Check answers at the end of Chapter Four (p. 115).

EXTRA WORD POWER

age. Condition; state of; action; collection of; place for. When *age* is added to the end of a word, it can mean "condition," "state of," "act of," "collection of," or "place for." For example: *haulage*—act of hauling; *marriage*—state of being wed; *passage*—act of passing; *wastage*—amount wasted; *dosage*—amount to be given; *acreage*—collection of acres; *orphanage*—place for orphans or collection of orphans; *outage*—state of being interrupted; *wattage*—amount of electric power; total number of watts needed; *shrinkage*—act of shrinking; amount of decrease; *spillage*—amount spilled; the act of spilling. How many more words can you supply that end in *age*?

ure. Act; result of an action; agent of action; state of. *Ure* is found at the end of many nouns. For example: *legislature*—body of lawmakers; *exposure*—state of being exposed or laid open; *posture*—state of carriage (how one carries oneself); *rupture*—the act of something breaking apart; *torture*—act of causing severe pain; *temperature*—degree of hotness or coldness of something. How many more words that end in *ure* can you supply?

Additional Words

From your ability to use context clues, can you figure out the meanings of the following words?

1. **exonerate** (ex • on • er • ate) (eg • zon′ e • rāte) *v. He was granted an amnesty by the government and* ***exonerated*** *of all charges made against him.*

   ____

2. **jeopardy** (jeop • ar • dy) (jeop′ ar • dē) *n.* (*pl.* **ies**) *When the witness testified against a major crime figure, he knew that he was putting his life in* ***jeopardy****.*

   ____

3. **temperate** (tem • per • ate) (tem′ per • et) *adj. As Arthur is* ***temperate*** *in everything he does, you would not expect him to overeat or overdrink.*

   ____

4. **corroborate** (cor • rob • o • rate) (kor • rob′ o • rāte) *v. He* ***corroborated*** *our suspicions concerning her guilt when he testified that she tried to sell him the stolen goods.*

   ____

5. **repent** (re • pent′) *v. He* ***repented*** *the fact that he had not been kinder to his mother while she was still alive.*

   ____

STOP. Check answers at the end of Chapter Four (p. 115).

Practice for Additional Words

A. Directions: Match each word with the *best* definition.

________	1. exonerate	a. danger
________	2. jeopardy	b. to feel regret
________	3. temperate	c. to confirm
________	4. corroborate	d. to clear of guilt
________	5. repent	e. moderate

STOP. Check answers at the end of Chapter Four (p. 115).

B. Directions: Here are five sentences. Define the underlined word.

1. After the mobster testified against the key man in the organization, his life was in jeopardy, so the authorities helped him to start a new life with a new identity. ____________

2. The mobster's testimony was corroborated by other witnesses.

   ____

3. The mobster said that from now on he would live a more temperate life and avoid extremes. ____________

4. The mobster said that he repented the life that he had led and that he would try to make up for it in his new existence. ____________

5. The mobster was exonerated of all the charges against him because he had agreed to testify against the key man in the organization.

   ____

STOP. Check answers at the end of Chapter Four (p. 115).

EXERCISE 8

Step I. Vocabulary Words in Sentences

Directions: Sentences using the ten vocabulary words from Exercise 8 follow. See whether you can figure out the meanings of the underlined words from the clues in the sentences. Blanks are provided for your estimates of the definitions. Check your meanings with those in Step II.

1. By the time he was twenty, John ("Baby Face") Malloy was infamous. Baby Face was known throughout the country for his bank robberies.

   ____

2. All bank presidents and employees were apprehensive about their banks being robbed by Baby Face. They feared that they would be next.

   ____

3. In discussing Baby Face, some persons claimed that he was bland and mild-mannered. Others claimed he was violent and vicious.

   ____

4. Some said that as long as the people being robbed were docile, they were not harmed. Others stated that even if persons in the bank were obedient, Baby Face would beat them. ____________________

5. Some claimed he took a miscellaneous collection of bills from the banks. Others said that he took only large bills, not several kinds. ____________________

6. It was obvious from the contradictory statements that there was no unanimous agreement on Baby Face's characteristics. ____________________

7. In order to capture Baby Face, a new operation was initiated called Operation Baby Face. ____________________

8. Everyone on this mission was very discreet or careful in what he or she said or did. ____________________

9. The members of the mission were all sure that their plan was foolproof and that no omissions had been made. Nothing was left to chance or left out.

   ____

10. They had scrutinized every possible problem that could arise. At no time in the police chiefs' memories could they remember such a careful investigation. ____________________

Step II. Vocabulary Words

1. **apprehensive** (ap • ~~p~~re • hen′ siv~~e~~) *adj.* Fearful; expecting evil, danger, or harm; anxious. *The frightened witness was so **apprehensive** about his life that he refused to give evidence.*

2. **bland** (bland) *adj.* Mild; soft; gentle; balmy; kindly; soothing. *You should eat only **bland** foods after you have had an upset stomach because they are very gentle.*

3. **discreet** (dis • creet) (dis • krē~~e~~t′) *adj.* Careful about what one says or does; prudent; cautious. *The President's relatives should be **discreet** because if they are not careful about what they do or say, it can embarrass the President.*

4. **docile** (doc • ile) (dos′ ul) *adj.* Easy to teach; easy to discipline; obedient. *Teachers like to have* ***docile*** *students in their classes because they are easy to teach.*

5. **infamous** (in′ fa • møus) *adj.* Having a bad reputation; notorious. *Al Capone was* ***infamous*** *because he was well known for his bad actions.*

6. **initiate** (in • i • ti • ate) (i • nish′ ē • atɇ) *v.* To introduce by doing or using first; to bring into use or practice; to admit as a member into a fraternity, sorority, club, and so on, especially through the use of a secret ceremony. *I will* ***initiate*** *the program by having everyone introduce himself or herself to everyone else.*

7. **miscellaneous** (mis • cel • la • ne • ous) (mis • uł • lā′ nē • øus) *adj.* Mixed; consisting of several kinds; various. *The box contained a number of* ***miscellaneous*** *items, which were different things I had collected through the years.*

8. **omission** (o • mis • sion) (o • mish′ un) *n.* Anything left out or not done; failure to include. *When it was discovered that the main speaker's name was left out of the program, an investigation was started to determine who was responsible for the* ***omission.***

9. **scrutinize** (scru • ti • nize) (skrū′ ti • nīzɇ) *v.* To observe closely; to examine or inquire into critically; to investigate. *The police said that they would* ***scrutinize*** *the evidence very carefully to make sure that nothing escaped investigation.*

10. **unanimous** (ū • nan′ i • møus) *adj.* Agreeing completely; united in opinion; being of one mind; being in complete agreement. *As everyone was in agreement, the vote was* ***unanimous.***

Step III. Practice

A. Directions: Each sentence has a missing word. Choose the word that *best* completes the sentence.

Word List

infamous, bland, discreet, docile, apprehensive, unanimous, scrutinize, omission, miscellaneous, initiate.

1. Spies must be ____________________ about what they do because they never know who is watching or listening to them.

2. People are ____________________ about walking alone late at night because it is so dangerous.

3. Not every school has students who are so ____________________ and obedient.

4. Although you are well known when you are ____________________, you are known because of the bad things that you have done.

5. I am on a(n) ____________________ diet because of my ulcer.

6. I am going to ____________________ that situation very carefully because it looks to me as if something is wrong.

7. Whenever a(n) ____________________ is made, we try to determine whether the item was left out on purpose or not.

8. At our meetings it's almost impossible to get everyone to agree on anything, so we never have ____________________ agreements.

9. The ____________________ items were put on sale because the several things that were left were all one of a kind.

10. The fraternity decided not to ____________________ any members this year because of the fatal accident that occurred last year.

STOP. Check answers at the end of Chapter Four (p. 115).

B. Directions: Ten sentences containing the meanings of vocabulary presented in Exercise 8 follow. Choose the word that *best* fits the word or phrase underlined in the sentence.

Word List

infamous, discreet, initiate, bland, unanimous, scrutinize, miscellaneous, docile, apprehensive, omission.

1. His gentle personality is a relief after going with Jeff, who was always ready to explode. ____________________

2. Please be careful about what you say and do because we are being watched.
____

3. I am so fearful about the exam results. ____________________

4. All of us were in complete agreement that we go to the shore for our class picnic. ____________________

5. Hitler was notorious. ____________________

6. After the auction, only a few different items were left for sale.
____

7. The leaving out of my name from the report was merely a mistake.
____

8. At our college we decided to start a class on the art of cooking and choosing wines. ____________________

9. In our biology class, we had to observe carefully cells under the microscope to determine whether they were moving or not. ____________________

10. The children were so obedient that they were very easy to teach.

____

STOP. Check answers at the end of Chapter Four (p. 115).

C. Directions: In the Word Square there are eleven words that you have met. Find the words in the square and match them with their correct meanings. Note that there are *more* meanings than words. If there is no word in the square for a meaning, write *none,* and give the word. Some words in the square are from preceding exercises.

WORD SQUARE

I	N	I	T	I	A	T	E	O
A	D	I	S	C	R	E	E	T
C	O	D	E	L	E	T	E	A
I	C	O	V	E	T	R	T	S
M	I	N	F	A	M	O	U	S
B	L	A	N	D	U	O	S	E
O	E	F	R	U	G	A	L	T
U	N	A	N	I	M	O	U	S
O	M	I	S	S	I	O	N	E

Meanings	*Words*
1. To desire what others have	____________
2. To introduce by doing or using first	____________
3. Anything left out	____________
4. Agreeing completely	____________
5. Mixed; consisting of several kinds	____________
6. To take out	____________
7. To observe closely	____________
8. Thrifty	____________
9. Careful about what one does	____________
10. Something valuable	____________
11. Mild	____________
12. Fearful	____________
13. Easy to teach	____________
14. Having a bad reputation	

STOP. Check answers at the end of Chapter Four (pp. 115–116).

EXTRA WORD POWER

ism. Act of, practice of, or result of; condition of being; action or quality of. *Ism* is used at the end of a great number of words. For example: *terrorism*—practice of terror; the use of fear to frighten or intimidate; *barbarism*—the condition of being primitive or brutal; *pauperism*—the condition of being very poor; *patriotism*—quality of being a patriot; *Americanism*—practice of values characteristic of Americans; *socialism*—the principle whereby the ownership and operation of the means of production are by society or the community rather than by private individuals, with all members of the community sharing in the work and products; *nationalism*—devotion to one's nation. How many other words with *ism* can you supply?

ive. Of; relating to; belonging to; having the nature or quality of; tending to. *Ive* is added to the end of many words. For example: *legislative*—relating to the body of lawmakers; *affirmative*—having the quality of a positive statement; *derogative*—tending to belittle; *native*—belonging to a country by birth; *creative*—tending to be able to create; *destructive*—tending to cause destruction or the tearing down of things; *massive*—having the quality of being very large. How many more words with *ive* can you supply?

Additional Words

From your ability to use context clues, can you figure out the meanings of the following words?

1. **futile** (fu • tile) (fū′ tul) *adj. The doctor's efforts to save the child who had consumed the toxic liquid were* ***futile****, because the dose consumed was a lethal one.*

   ____

2. **criterion** (cri • te • ri • on) (krī • tir′ ē • un) *n.* (*pl.* **criteria**) (krī • tir′ ē • a) *The journal's staff decided on the* ***criteria*** *they would use to judge whether papers were acceptable for publication in their journal.*

   ____

3. **valid** (val′ id) *adj. After the judge ruled that the will was* ***valid****, the lawyer for the estate called all the beneficiaries together for a reading of it.*

   ____

4. **datum** (dā′ tum) *n.* (*pl.* **data**) (dā′ ta) (Plural form usually used.) *Because of insufficient **data**, the problem could not be solved.*

____

5. **invincible** (in • vin • ci • ble) (in • vin′ si • bul) *adj.* *The **invincible** army won every battle.*

____

STOP. Check answers at the end of Chapter Four (p. 116).

Practice for Additional Words

A. Directions: Match each word with the *best* definition.

________	1. futile	a. not able to be conquered
________	2. invincible	b. information given
________	3. criterion	c. a standard of judging
________	4. valid	d. useless
________	5. data	e. sound in principle

STOP. Check answers at the end of Chapter Four (p. 116)

B. Directions: Here are five sentences. Define the underlined word.

1. Her reasons for wanting to go are valid ones, so I think we should fund her trip. ____

____

2. The data that she will bring back from her trip will be important for our research. ____

____

3. It's too bad that some people have to learn the hard way that they are not invincible. ____

____

4. It's futile to try to reason with fanatics or terrorists. ____________

____

5. What criteria did you use to judge the papers that were submitted? ____________

____

STOP. Check answers at the end of Chapter Four (p. 116).

EXERCISE 9

Step I. Vocabulary Words in Sentences

Directions: Sentences using the ten vocabulary words from Exercise 9 follow. See whether you can figure out the meanings of the underlined words from the clues in the sentences. Blanks are provided for your estimates of the definitions. Check your meanings with those in Step II.

1. The acquisition of vocabulary is the objective of this book. If you are acquiring knowledge of words and their meanings, this intention is being realized. ____________
2. By this time you should be more adept at figuring out words, using context clues. As you have seen, to become an expert at something, you have to work diligently and persevere. ____________
3. The words that are being presented in this book are neither exotic nor trite; that is, the words are neither so strange that you will hardly meet them nor so commonplace that they are used with almost no meaning.

   ____________ : ____________
4. If you are a gregarious person who likes to be with a lot of people, you will find that being adept in vocabulary will help you in telling anecdotes. The more skilled you are in vocabulary, the more able you will be to make your stories exciting, interesting, and entertaining. ____________;

   ____
5. You will find also that you will become more active rather than passive in discussions. ____________
6. With your skill in words, you would probably be able to overcome your opponent in a debate. Persons would be reluctant to oppose you because of your verbal ability. ____________
7. No more would your stomach be in a turmoil because you had to give a

speech in a particular class. There is no need for feeling disturbed when you have "word power." ____________________

8. It is hoped that learning new vocabulary words will become a contagious "disease" from which you will not be cured. Not only will you continue acquiring new words, but you will spread this enthusiasm for words to others. ____________________

Step II. Vocabulary Words

1. **acquisition** (ac • qui • si • tion) (ak • wi • zish′ un) *n.* The act of obtaining or acquiring; something obtained or gained as property, knowledge, and so on. *When the school population increased, the **acquisition** of another building was necessary to house all the students.*

2. **adept** (a • dept′) *adj.* Highly skilled; proficient; expert. *I would call him an expert golfer because he is so **adept** at it.*

3. **anecdote** (an • ec • dote) (an′ ek • dōte̸) *n.* A short, entertaining account of some happening, usually personal or biographical. *The sailor told us many interesting **anecdotes** about his sea adventures.*

4. **contagious** (con • ta • gious) (kon • tā′ jus) *adj.* Spreading by contact; spreading or tending to spread from person to person. *Some diseases are very **contagious** and you can catch them from persons if they sneeze or cough near you.*

5. **exotic** (ex • ot • ic) (eg • zot′ ik) *adj.* Foreign; not native; introduced from a foreign country; having the charm of the unfamiliar; strangely beautiful. *The florist imported some **exotic** plants from another country for one of his special customers.*

6. **gregarious** (gre • gar • i • ous) (gre • gar′ ē • o̸us) *adj.* Fond of the company of others; sociable; characteristic of a flock, herd, or crowd. ***Gregarious** people usually enjoy being in the company of other people.*

7. **opponent** (op̸ • pō′ nent) *n.* One who opposes another, as in battle or debate; one who acts against something or another; adversary; antagonist. *When you play a game, the person whom you are playing against is your **opponent**.*

8. **passive** (pas̸′ sive̸) *adj.* Not acting; acted upon; unresisting; not opposing; unenthusiastic; inactive. *When you have no interest in something, you behave in a very **passive** manner.*

9. **trite** (trīte̸) *adj.* Used so often as to be too common; made commonplace by repetition; lacking freshness or originality. *It is easier to use **trite** phrases, which are ready-made and common, than to think of a more original way to say something.*

10. **turmoil** (tur′ moil) *n.* Confused motion or state; disturbance; tumult. *There was so much* ***turmoil*** *in the stores during the Christmas rush, with everyone rushing around in all different directions that I became confused.*

Special Notes

1. The word *contagious* usually refers to the spreading of disease, but it can also refer to the spreading of other things, such as laughter, sadness, and so on. For example:
   a. The *contagious* laughter spread throughout the whole class, and before long everyone was aching from laughing so much.
   b. The child's crying was so *contagious* that soon all the children in the kindergarten were crying.
2. The term *opponent,* meaning "one who opposes another," is derived from the combining form *pos, pon,* meaning "place" or "set."

Step III. Practice

A. Directions: Each sentence has a missing word. Choose the word that *best* completes the sentence.

Word List

contagious, adept, turmoil, acquisition, trite, anecdote, exotic, opponent, passive, gregarious.

1. The ____________________ of knowledge is necessary for anyone who wishes to enter some profession or trade.
2. The ____________________ laughter spread throughout the room.
3. There was such a(n) ____________________ after the robbery that no one knew what anyone was doing.
4. As that is such a(n) ____________________ saying, can't you come up with something more original?
5. He is so ____________________ at so many things that we call him Mr. General Expert.
6. If you continue to be so ____________________, we will have to ask you to go, because we want more active people on this job.

7. Opposites must attract, because George is so shy and his girlfriend, Karen, is so ____________________.

8. Do you know who your ____________________ will be in the chess game?

9. Every night she tells her children a delightful ____________________ about something that happened to her during the day.

10. We are going on a trip to a(n) ____________________ country that is far away and strangely beautiful.

STOP. Check answers at the end of Chapter Four (p. 116).

B. Directions: Ten sentences follow. Define the underlined word.

1. The heavyweight champion's opponent was a very strong man who would give the champion a good fight. ____________________

2. Why don't you play a more active role in the convention elections rather than such a passive one? ____________________

3. As my brother can't stand any disturbances, we avoid any turmoil. ____________________

4. *Gross* is a trite word because it is used too often. ____________________

5. A Southern politician was known for the anecdotes he would tell concerning funny things that had happened to him. ____________________

6. When a number of people had a contagious disease, the doctors isolated these patients in a special wing of the hospital. ____________________

7. I like exotic things because they are rare. ____________________

8. As Jack and Herb are very gregarious, they shine when they are with lots of people. ____________________

9. When the store ran out of necessary supplies, the manager was upset to learn that his order for the acquisition of new supplies had not yet been sent out. ____________________

10. A good secretary should be adept at typing and shorthand. ____________________

STOP. Check answers at the end of Chapter Four (p. 117).

C. Directions: The words from Exercise 9 follow. Match each word with the *best* definition.

Words		*Meanings*
________	1. acquisition	a. foreign; not native
________	2. adept	b. act of obtaining something
________	3. anecdote	c. one who acts against something or another
________	4. contagious	d. highly skilled
________	5. exotic	e. confused motion
________	6. gregarious	f. used so often as to be commonplace
________	7. opponent	g. fond of the company of others
________	8. passive	h. spreading by contact
________	9. trite	i. inactive
________	10. turmoil	j. a short, entertaining account of some happening

STOP. Check answers at the end of Chapter Four (p. 117).

EXTRA WORD POWER

ish. Belonging to; like or characteristic of; tending to; somewhat or rather; about. Many words end in *ish.* For example: *Spanish*—belonging to Spain; *Irish*—belonging to Ireland; *Danish*—belonging to Denmark; *devilish*—like or characteristic of a devil; *boyish*—like or characteristic of a boy; *bookish*—inclined to books; involved with books; *tallish*—rather tall; *bluish*—rather blue; *thirtyish*—about thirty. How many words with *ish* can you supply?

ic. Relating to; like. *Ic* is added to the end of a great number of words. For example: *hyperbolic*—relating to a hyperbole or a great exaggeration; *heroic*—like a hero; *poetic*—like poetry; *tragic*—like a tragedy, in which something is very sad or there is disaster; *public*—relating to the public or people at large; *euphemistic*—relating to euphemism or a milder way of saying something; *enthusiastic*—relating to enthusiasm or a lively interest in something; *majestic*—like royalty; *realistic*—like reality;

scientific—relating to science; *historic*—relating to history, which is an account of what has happened; famous in history. How many words with *ic* can you supply?

Additional Words

From your ability to use context clues, can you figure out the meanings of the following words?

1. **attrition** (at • tri • tion) (a • trish′ un) *n.* *When employees retired or quit their jobs, no new persons were hired to take their places. The employers were not firing anyone; they were just letting the workforce become smaller through* ***attrition****.*

   ____

2. **abridge** (a • bridge) (a • brij′) *v.* *The kindergarten teachers decided to* ***abridge*** *some of the longer stories so that they would suit the younger children's attention spans.*

   ____

3. **imminent** (im′ mi • nent) *adj.* *The people were warned that an earthquake was* ***imminent****, so that they would have to leave their homes immediately.*

   ____

4. **paradox** (par • a • dox) (par′ a • doks) *n.* *It is a* ***paradox*** *to say that you are here and not here at the same time.*

   ____

5. **phenomenon** (phe • nom • e • non) (fe • nom′ e • non) *n.* (*pl.* **phenomena**) *An eclipse is a* ***phenomenon*** *of astronomy that has been observed and scientifically described.*

   ____

STOP. Check answers at the end of Chapter Four (p. 117).

Practice for Additional Words

A. Directions: Match each word with the *best* definition.

________	1. attrition	a. a scientifically described fact
________	2. abridge	b. contradiction
________	3. imminent	c. a gradual wearing down
________	4. paradox	d. about to happen
________	5. phenomenon	e. to curtail

STOP. Check words at the end of Chapter Four (p. 117).

B. Directions: Here are five sentences. Define the underlined word.

1. I prefer to read the complete book rather than an abridged version of it.
____

2. The captors said that the hostages' lives were in grave danger and that their deaths were imminent. _______________

3. At our college the attrition of instructors has been very high because of so many retirements. _______________

4. It's a paradox that something good can also be something bad.
____

5. There are many phenomena of nature that are destructive.
____

STOP. Check answers at the end of Chapter Four (p. 117).

CROSSWORD PUZZLE 3

Directions: The meanings of a number of the words from Exercises 7–9 follow. Your knowledge of these words will help you to solve this crossword puzzle. Note that *combining form* is abbreviated as *comb. f.*

Across

1. Sound of surprise
4. You ___ the bell
6. Respectful address to men
7. Abbreviation for *distance*
10. A pronoun
11. Same as #8 Down
12. To stay or fall behind
13. He ___ with his eyes
15. Holds back water
18. Texas is a ___
21. Abbreviation for *South Carolina*
22. Able to be taught
24. Belittling; disparaging
27. Opposite of *he*
28. A pronoun
29. A conjunction
30. A ___ of film
32. An indefinite article
33. Rhymes with *cat*
34. Same as #14 Down
36. Exam
37. Faster than *walk*
39. To make an opening with a knife

Down

1. Abbreviation for *Arkansas*
2. Opposite of *hers*
3. To make lively; to make alive
5. Sociable
7. Careful about what you say or do
8. Anger
9. You plant this
12. A drug that makes you erratic
14. Code signal for *help*
15. When your heart stops, you ___
16. Abbreviation for *Alabama*
17. Homonym of *meat*
19. Homonym of *two*
20. The self
21. Feeling out of ___
23. Special trait
25. Same as #1 Down
26. Opposite of *no*
31. Abbreviation for *lieutenant*
33. Indefinite article—rhymes with *man*
34. Synonym of *intimidate*

40. Opposite of *present*
42. Past tense of *is*
43. A game called ___ ball
44. Same as #33 Down
45. You roll these in games of chance
46. Abbreviation for *period*
47. Something of value
50. Slang for *is not*
51. Comb. f. for *condition; state of*
52. Mixed; variety
55. Girl's name
56. Used to form the comparative degree of adjectives
57. Opposite of *yes*
58. Referring to *voice*
60. Abbreviation for *Rhode Island*
61. Sound made when you laugh
63. Abbreviation for *Elizabeth*
64. Same as #32 Across
65. A person involved in covert activities
68. In games of chance you place ___
70. Too commonplace
73. Flower ___
76. Same as #28 Across
77. Homonym for *sea*
78. Known for bad actions
82. Referring to beauty
87. Mohammed ___
88. Same as #57 Across
89. A girl's name
90. Same as #83 Down
91. Iron ___ is found in a mine
93. Outer covering of a body
94. Opposite of *subtract*
95. A woman devoted to the religious life
96. Same as #2 Down
99. She is ___ good ___ he
101. You commit a ___ when you break a religious law
103. To scare
107. Opposite of *woman*

35. What you get when something is boiling
38. Employ
40. Opposite of *active*
41. A short, entertaining story
42. Opposite of *loser*
43. To ask for charity in a humble way
45. Abbreviation for *diameter*
46. Way of saying *father*
48. *Yes* in Spanish
49. *Docile* means "easy to ___"
50. Same as #16 Down
53. Comb. f. for *not*
54. Homonym of *sew*
59. Opposite of *early*
61. Opposite of *she*
62. Same as #33 Across
66. You write with this
67. Comb. f. for *having; full of*
68. Soft; mild; kindly
69. Opposite of *stand*
71. Comb f. for *again; back*
72. Same as #28 Across
73. A friend is a ___
74. The act of leaving out
75. Same as #19 Down
77. To observe carefully
79. Musical sound
80. Comb. f. for *one*
81. Male child
83. A verb ending
84. Same as #61 Down
85. Same as #83 Down
86. Electrically charged atom
89. Abbreviation of *advertisement*
92. Same as #83 Down
94. Same as #32 Across
96. Same as #2 Down
97. A leaning
98. Same as #18 Across
99. Rhymes with *ham*
100. To state something is not true
101. Opposite of *dangerous*

108. Same as #45 Down
110. Slang for *go away*
111. Same as #95 Across
112. An insult
113. Same as #31 Down
114. Same as #83 Down
115. To attempt
116. Same as #61 Down
118. An aquanaut travels under the ___
119. A man wears this on his shirt
120. Same as #15 Down
121. Same as #32 Across
122. A precious stone is called a ___
123. Skillful
126. Same as #10 Across
128. Opposite of *off*
129. The sun is this
131. Girl's name
132. A waitress takes your ___
134. A word for what you call yourself
136. A long poem telling a tale of some deed
138. Same as #83 Down
139. You go to a doctor to help ___ you of an illness
140. Manner of feeling
143. ___ *and behold*; look
144. Same as #14 Down
145. Neither this ___ that
148. Rhymes with *sit*
149. Meaning of *non*
150. Same as #128 Across
151. Same as #71 Down
152. You build a house on a ___
153. Same as #33 Down

102. Same as #78 Across
104. Rhymes with *sit*
105. Comb. f. for *before*
106. Disturbance; confused motion
107. Used to support sails on a ship
108. You ___ your *i*
109. When you were famished, you ___
114. You ___ when you are hungry
116. To own
117. The garden where Adam and Eve first lived
120. Contraction for *do not*
122. To welcome
124. Same as #56 Across
125. Same as #46 Down
127. To make a mistake
129. To place with care
130. Same as #32 Across
133. The hiding place of a wild animal; lair
135. Slang for a *baseball glove*
137. Comb. f. for *together*
139. Swindle
140. Same as #32 Across
141. Same as #53 Down
142. To perform
144. Same as #54 Down
146. Same as #29 Across
147. Same as #71 Down
152. Musical syllable

STOP. Check answers at the end of Chapter Four (p. 118).

WORD SCRAMBLE 3

Directions: Word Scramble 3 is based on words from Exercises 7–9. The meanings are your clues to arranging the letters in correct order.

		Meanings
1. goanitanez	______________	to make unfriendly
2. roffant	______________	insult
3. actactherisicr	______________	peculiar quality
4. meehpumsi	______________	a milder word or phrase
5. datinimite	______________	to frighten
6. tioninainlc	______________	a leaning or bent
7. adnlb	______________	mild; soft
8. seetcird	______________	careful about what one does or says
9. clodie	______________	easy to teach
10. nofamuis	______________	known for bad actions
11. itinatei	______________	to begin; to bring into practice
12. imissono	______________	anything left out
13. initscurez	______________	to observe closely
14. minonusua	______________	being in complete agreement
15. petad	______________	skillful
16. gatnocsuoi	______________	spreading by contact
17. coeitx	______________	foreign; strangely beautiful
18. veissap	______________	not acting
19. reitt	______________	used so often as to be commonplace
20. oilturm	______________	disturbance

STOP. Check answers at the end of Chapter Four (p. 118).

ANALOGIES 3

Directions: Find the word from the following list that *best* completes each analogy. There are more words in the list than you need.

Word List

exonerate, risk, insult, careful, compliment, bland, feeling, gregarious, inclination, commonplace, exotic, active, scrutinize, passive, common, commence, notorious, overindulgent, standard, characteristic, ally, expert, euphemism, spreading, undisputed, fearful, imminent, aesthetic, jeopardy, unskilled, skilled, unmanageable, terminate, disturbance.

1. Convenient : unsuitable :: affront : ________________.
2. Error : mistake :: apprehensive : ________________.
3. Isolate : integrate :: initiate : ________________.
4. Tenacious : stubborn :: trite : ________________.
5. Corroborate : deny :: adept : ________________.
6. Inanimate : alive :: opponent : ________________.
7. Conceited : egotistical :: criterion : ________________.
8. Custom : habit :: leaning : ________________.
9. Boundary : limit :: contagious : ________________.
10. Concede : resist :: docile : ________________.
11. Attitude : feeling :: turmoil : ________________.
12. Innate : inborn :: vindicate : ________________.
13. Confuse : obfuscate :: mild : ________________.
14. Abridge : curtail :: infamous : ________________.
15. Temerity : discreet :: domestic : ________________.
16. Repentant : remorseful :: inactive : ________________.
17. Lush : barren :: indiscreet : ________________.
18. Inward : shy :: outgoing : ________________.
19. Drizzle : downpour :: observe : ________________.
20. Simmer : boil :: temperate : ________________.

STOP. Check answers at the end of Chapter Four (p. 119).

MULTIPLE-CHOICE VOCABULARY TEST 3

Directions: This is a test on words in Exercises 7–9. Words are presented according to exercises. *Do all exercises before checking answers.* Underline the meaning that *best* fits the word.

Exercise 7

1. aesthetic
   a. referring to being poor
   b. likes food
   c. referring to beauty
   d. a feeling

2. affront
a. an insult
b. a front
c. friendly
d. not friendly

3. antagonize
a. helpful
b. friendly
c. to make an enemy of
d. feeling

4. attitude
a. manner of feeling
b. unfriendly feeling
c. friendly feeling
d. happy feeling

5. characteristic
a. person
b. play
c. special trait
d. feeling

6. derogatory
a. a lot of
b. tending to belittle
c. helpful
d. talkative

7. euphemism
a. a wise saying
b. hold back
c. a saying
d. a less distasteful description of something

8. hypocrite
a. to frighten
b. to be friendly
c. to lean
d. one who pretends to be what he or she is not

9. inclination
a. insult
b. a leaning
c. frighten
d. a saying

10. intimidate
a. to scare
b. to lean
c. to insult
d. to make unfriendly

Exercise 8

11. apprehensive
a. mild
b. fearful
c. helpful
d. cheerful

12. bland
a. refers to sadness
b. friendly
c. mild
d. evil

13. discreet
a. fearful
b. friendly
c. evil
d. careful

14. docile
a. active
b. easy to teach
c. noisy
d. frightened

15. infamous
a. well known
b. happy
c. a crook
d. having a bad reputation

16. initiate
a. to party
b. to start
c. to insult
d. to frighten

17. miscellaneous	a. mixed b. most	c. one d. wrong
18. omission	a. task b. skill	c. trip d. anything left out
19. scrutinize	a. able to see b. to watch someone	c. to observe very closely d. to help
20. unanimous	a. agreeing completely b. some	c. several d. not any

Exercise 9

21. acquisition	a. curious b. inquisitive	c. quiet d. the obtaining of something
22. adept	a. helpful b. friendly	c. skillful d. changing
23. anecdote	a. something funny b. a note	c. a joke d. a short, entertaining account of a happening
24. contagious	a. germs b. referring to contact	c. spreading from person to person d. unhealthy
25. exotic	a. native b. foreign	c. far away d. pretty
26. gregarious	a. hostile b. helpful	c. sociable d. strange
27. opponent	a. friend b. enemy	c. one who opposes another d. hostile
28. passive	a. enthusiastic b. lively	c. unresisting d. active
29. trite	a. important b. meaningful	c. different d. commonplace
30. turmoil	a. movement b. confused motion	c. spirit d. lively

TRUE/FALSE TEST 3

Directions: This is a true/false test on Exercises 7–9. Read each sentence carefully. Decide whether it is true or false. Put a *T* for *true* or an *F* for *false* in the blank. The number after the sentence tells you if the word is from Exercise 7, 8, or 9.

_________ 1. A characteristic would be a special individual trait of a person. 7

_________ 2. To affront someone is to insult him or her intentionally. 7

_________ 3. An artistic person would not have any aesthetic sense. 7

_________ 4. When you have a miscellaneous group of things, you have an assortment of things. 8

_________ 5. Persons who are apprehensive are not fearful or anxious about something. 8

_________ 6. Someone with bland manners is usually very rude. 8

_________ 7. When detectives scrutinize evidence, they examine it very carefully. 8

_________ 8. Something exotic is usually something mundane. 9

_________ 9. Gregarious people like to isolate themselves. 9

_________ 10. An omission is never an error. 8

_________ 11. In a unanimous decision, not everyone must agree. 8

_________ 12. "He is underprivileged" is a euphemism for "He is poor." 7

_________ 13. When someone says something in a derogatory manner, he or she is being kind. 7

_________ 14. *Passive* and *dormant* are antonyms. 9

_________ 15. An acquisition of something means the selling of something. 9

_________ 16. An anecdote is a biography. 9

_________ 17. "He is mature" can be a euphemism for "He is old." 7

_________ 18. To be adept at something is to be skillful at it. 9

_________ 19. An infamous person is a famous celebrity known for good deeds. 8

_________ 20. A discreet person tells his or her secrets to anyone who will listen. 8

STOP. Check answers for both tests at the end of Chapter Four (p. 119).

SCORING OF TESTS

Multiple-Choice Test

Number Wrong	*Score*
0–2	Excellent
3–5	Good
6–8	Weak
Above 8	Poor

Score ________

True/False Test

Number Wrong	*Score*
0–1	Excellent
2–3	Good
4–5	Weak
Above 5	Poor

Score ________

1. If you scored in the excellent or good range on *both tests,* you arc doing well. Go on to Chapter Five.
2. If you scored in the weak or poor range on either test, look below and follow directions for Additional Practice. Note that the words on the tests are arranged so that you can tell in which exercise to find them. This will help you if you need additional practice.

ADDITIONAL PRACTICE SETS

A. Directions: Write the words you missed on the tests from the three exercises in the space provided. Note that the tests are presented so that you can tell to which exercises the words belong.

Exercise 7 Words Missed

1. ________ 6. ________
2. ________ 7. ________
3. ________ 8. ________
4. ________ 9. ________
5. ________ 10. ________

Exercise 8 Words Missed

1. ________ 6. ________
2. ________ 7. ________
3. ________ 8. ________
4. ________ 9. ________
5. ________ 10. ________

Exercise 9 Words Missed

1. ____________________ 6. ____________________
2. ____________________ 7. ____________________
3. ____________________ 8. ____________________
4. ____________________ 9. ____________________
5. ____________________ 10. ____________________

B. Directions: Restudy the words that you have written down on p. 111 and this page. Do Step I and Step II for those you missed. Note that Step I and Step II are on the following pages:

Exercise 7–pp. 83–85.

Exercise 8–pp. 89–91.

Exercise 9–pp. 96–98.

C. Directions: Do Additional Practice 1 on this page and the next if you missed words from Exercise 7. Do Additional Practice 2 on p. 113 if you missed words from Exercise 8. Do Additional Practice 3 on p. 114 if you missed words from Exercise 9.

Additional Practice 1 for Exercise 7

Directions: Ten sentences containing the meanings of vocabulary presented in Exercise 7 follow. Choose the word that *best* fits the meaning of the word or phrase underlined in the sentence.

Word List

characteristic, inclination, attitude, affront, derogatory, hypocrites, euphemism, antagonize, intimidate, aesthetic.

1. What an insult it was not to shake my hand in front of all my friends. ____________________
2. A person's way of feeling is very difficult to change. ____________________
3. Can you think of a milder phrase for "the economy is terrible"? ____________________
4. If anyone tries to frighten you so that you will not tell your story, go to the police. ____________________
5. Jennifer has a certain leaning toward music. ____________________
6. Every person should have at least one good trait. ____________________

7. I dislike those who pretend to be virtuous but who are not. ____________

8. John doesn't like to make an enemy of anyone. ________________

9. You have an artistic appreciation of nature. ________________

10. No one is allowed to make belittling remarks about my friends in my presence. ________________

STOP. Check answers at the end of Chapter Four (p. 119).

Additional Practice 2 for Exercise 8

Directions: Ten sentences containing the meanings of vocabulary presented in Exercise 8 follow. Choose the word that *best* fits the meaning of the word or phrase underlined in the sentence.

Word List

apprehensive, discreet, bland, unanimous, scrutinize, docile, miscellaneous, omission, infamous, initiate.

1. The act of leaving out his name from the guest list caused us a lot of embarrassment. ________________

2. Seth is such a mild and kindly gentlemen. ________________

3. There were various items from which I could choose what I wanted. ________________

4. Our art teacher taught us to observe very carefully the subjects that we were painting. ________________

5. Everyone was in complete agreement that the meeting should have convened an hour ago. ________________

6. Throughout the land, he is known for his bad actions. ________________

7. Teachers enjoy having obedient children in their classes. ________________

8. He decided to introduce a new game among his friends. ________________

9. Try to be careful about what you say because I don't want anyone to know that I'm seeing you. ________________

10. I am rather fearful about telling my parents about what happened in school today. ________________

STOP. Check answers at the end of Chapter Four (p. 119).

Additional Practice 3 for Exercise 9

Directions: Ten sentences containing the meanings of vocabulary presented in Exercise 9 follow. Choose the word that *best* fits the meaning of the word or phrase underlined in the sentence.

Word List

passive, acquisition, trite, anecdote, opponent, turmoil, contagious, adept, exotic, gregarious.

1. You always seem to use commonplace phrases rather than original ones. ____________
2. The disturbance at the factory was due to the strike. ____________
3. His adversary was very skillful. ____________
4. Why are you always so unenthusiastic? ____________
5. The disease was spreading from person to person so rapidly that the doctors feared there would soon be an epidemic. ____________
6. Carol is a very sociable person. ____________
7. Arthur is very skillful in fixing anything in the house. ____________
8. The act of obtaining knowledge is not easy. ____________
9. Some of the birds I saw in Africa were strangely beautiful. ____________
10. The short, entertaining story told by Sharon was very funny. ____________

STOP. Check answers at the end of Chapter Four (p. 119).

ANSWERS: Chapter Four

Exercise 7 (pp. 83-89)

Practice A

(1) attitude, (2) aesthetic, (3) affront, (4) characteristic, (5) antagonize, (6) inclination, (7) euphemism, (8) hypocrite, (9) intimidate, (10) derogatory.

Practice B

(1) special, (2) belittling or disparaging, (3) insult, (4) artistic, (5) a less direct way of saying something, (6) one who pretends to be better or other

than he or she is, (7) leaning, liking, (8) opinion, (9) scare, (10) make unfriendly.

Practice C

(1) d, (2) c, (3) f, (4) a, (5) j, (6) b, (7) e, (8) i, (9) h, (10) g.

Additional Words (p. 88)

1. **exonerate.** To relieve, as of a charge or blame resting on one; to clear of a charge of guilt; to declare or prove blameless; to relieve of a debt or duty.
2. **jeopardy.** Risk; danger; peril.
3. **temperate.** Moderate in everything; avoiding extremes or excesses.
4. **corroborate.** To confirm (to strengthen; to make firm; to affirm); to make more certain.
5. **repent.** To feel pain, sorrow, or regret for something left undone or done; to feel remorse.

Practice for Additional Words (p. 89)

A. (1) d, (2) a, (3) e, (4) c, (5) b.
B. (1) danger, (2) confirmed, (3) moderate, (4) felt regret, (5) cleared.

Exercise 8 (pp. 89–96)

Practice A

(1) discreet, (2) apprehensive, (3) docile, (4) infamous, (5) bland, (6) scrutinize, (7) omission, (8) unanimous, (9) miscellaneous, (10) initiate.

Practice B

(1) bland, (2) discreet, (3) apprehensive, (4) unanimous, (5) infamous, (6) miscellaneous, (7) omission, (8) initiate, (9) scrutinize, (10) docile.

Practice C

(1) covet, (2) initiate, (3) omission, (4) unanimous, (5) none–miscellaneous, (6) delete, (7) none–scrutinize, (8) frugal, (9) discreet, (10) asset, (11) bland, (12) none–apprehensive, (13) docile, (14) infamous.

WORD SQUARE

I	N	I	T	I	A	T	E	O
A	D	I	S	C	R	E	E	T
C	O	D	E	L	E	T	E	A
I	C	O	V	E	T	R	T	S
M	I	N	F	A	M	O	U	S
B	L	A	N	D	U	O	S	E
O	E	F	R	U	G	A	L	T
U	N	A	N	I	M	O	U	S
O	M	I	S	S	I	O	N	E

Additional Words (pp. 94-95)

1. **futile.** Useless; vain; ineffectual; trifling; unimportant.
2. **criterion.** A standard of judging; any established law, rule, or principle by which a correct judgment may be formed.
3. **valid.** Sound; well grounded on principles or evidence; having legal force.
4. **datum.** Information given; a premise upon which something can be argued; material used as a basis for calculations. (*Data* [the plural form] is often used in a singular construction.)
5. **invincible.** Impossible to overcome; not able to be conquered.

Practice for Additional Words (pp. 95-96)

A. (1) d, (2) a, (3) c, (4) e, (5) b.
B. (1) sound, (2) information, (3) impossible to overcome, (4) useless, (5) standards.

Exercise 9 (pp. 96-102)

Practice A

(1) acquisition, (2) contagious, (3) turmoil, (4) trite, (5) adept, (6) passive, (7) gregarious, (8) opponent, (9) anecdote, (10) exotic.

Practice B

(1) adversary, (2) unenthusiastic or inactive, (3) disturbance, (4) commonplace, (5) short, entertaining accounts of some happenings, (6) spreading by contact, (7) foreign or strange, (8) fond of the company of others, (9) act of obtaining something, (10) highly skilled.

Practice C

(1) b, (2) d, (3) j, (4) h, (5) a, (6) g, (7) c, (8) i, (9) f, (10) e.

Additional Words (p. 101)

1. **attrition.** A gradual wearing down or weakening; a rubbing out or grinding down.
2. **abridge.** To shorten; to curtail; to give the substance of in fewer words.
3. **imminent.** About to happen; threatening (said especially of danger).
4. **paradox.** Contradiction; a self-contradictory statement that is false; a statement that seems absurd, contradictory, or unbelievable but may be true.
5. **phenomenon.** Any fact, circumstance, or experience that is apparent to the senses and that can be scientifically described; something extremely unusual.

Practice for Additional Words (pp. 101-102)

A. (1) c, (2) e, (3) d, (4) b, (5) a.
B. (1) shortened, (2) about to happen, (3) gradual wearing away, (4) contradiction, (5) circumstances that can be scientifically described.

Crossword Puzzle 3 (pp. 102–105)

Word Scramble 3 (pp. 105–106)

(1) antagonize, (2) affront, (3) characteristic, (4) euphemism, (5) intimidate, (6) inclination, (7) bland, (8) discreet, (9) docile, (10) infamous, (11) initiate, (12) omission, (13) scrutinize, (14) unanimous, (15) adept, (16) contagious, (17) exotic, (18) passive, (19) trite, (20) turmoil.

Analogies (pp. 106–107)

(1) compliment, (2) fearful, (3) terminate, (4) commonplace, (5) unskilled, (6) ally, (7) standard, (8) inclination, (9) spreading, (10) unmanageable, (11) disturbance, (12) exonerate, (13) bland, (14) notorious, (15) exotic, (16) passive, (17) careful, (18) gregarious, (19) scrutinize, (20) overindulgent.

Multiple-Choice Vocabulary Test 3 (pp. 107–109)

Exercise 7

(1) c, (2) a, (3) c, (4) a, (5) c, (6) b, (7) d, (8) d, (9) b, (10) a.

Exercise 8

(11) b, (12) c, (13) d, (14) b, (15) d, (16) b, (17) a, (18) d, (19) c, (20) a.

Exercise 9

(21) d, (22) c, (23) d, (24) c, (25) b, (26) c, (27) c,[1] (28) c, (29) d, (30) b.

True/False Test 3 (p. 110)

(1) T, (2) T, (3) F, (4) T, (5) F, (6) F, (7) T, (8) F, (9) F, (10) F, (11) F, (12) T, (13) F, (14) F, (15) F, (16) F, (17) T, (18) T, (19) F, (20) F.

STOP. Turn to p. 111 for the scoring of the tests.

Additional Practice Sets (pp. 111–114)

Additional Practice 1

(1) affront, (2) attitude, (3) euphemism, (4) intimidate, (5) inclination, (6) characteristic, (7) hypocrites, (8) antagonize, (9) aesthetic, (10) derogatory.

Additional Practice 2

(1) omission, (2) bland, (3) miscellaneous, (4) scrutinize, (5) unanimous, (6) infamous, (7) docile, (8) initiate, (9) discreet, (10) apprehensive.

Additional Practice 3

(1) trite, (2) turmoil, (3) opponent, (4) passive, (5) contagious, (6) gregarious, (7) adept, (8) acquisition, (9) exotic, (10) anecdote.

[1] Choice *c* is a better answer than *b* because not all opponents are enemies. Your opponent in a game would not be your enemy.

CHAPTER FIVE

Exercises 10–12

Crossword Puzzle 4

Word Scramble 4

Analogies 4

Multiple-Choice Vocabulary Test 4

True/False Test 4

Scoring of Tests

Additional Practice Sets

Answers

EXERCISE 10

Step I. Vocabulary Words in Sentences

Directions: Sentences using the ten vocabulary words from Exercise 10 follow. See whether you can figure out the meanings of the underlined words from the clues in the sentences. Blanks are provided for your estimates of the definitions. Check your meanings with those in Step II.

1. My friend George says that his younger brother tries to <u>emulate</u> everything he does. At times George feels that he is seeing a replay of his life. ____________________

2. It is difficult for some people who are very independent to <u>conform</u> to certain rules that we have at our company, but those persons who want to stay do. ____________________

3. Our company is such a <u>traditional</u> one that I'm amazed that the management is actually installing a computer system because our way of doing things hasn't changed since the company started over a hundred years ago. ____________________

4. Mr. Brown was fired when it was learned that he had obtained his job

under some false pretense. Mr. Brown had told his employer that he had worked for a certain firm, but he never had. ____________________

5. The plaintiff in the lawsuit said that she had been severely hurt in the automobile accident. The lawyer for the defense was trying to prove that the complaining party was not hurt. ____________________

6. Politicians try to avoid discussing controversial issues in an election year. They try to avoid any disputes, and, when they discuss a topic that might lend itself to controversy, they usually "talk out of both sides of their mouths." ____________________

7. The strike lasted for over six weeks because neither one of the sides would compromise. Neither the workers nor the employers would give in even a little on their demands. ____________________

8. We couldn't believe how the strike affected some of the people. Persons who used to be very polite became curt and abrupt, and persons who used to be sensitive and considerate of others became crass and uncaring.

____

9. It's difficult to appraise the value of a strike because different persons judge it differently based on their position. ____________________

Step II. Vocabulary Words

1. **appraise** (ap • praise) (ap̸ • prāze̸′) *v.* To set a value on; to estimate the worth of; to estimate the quantity of; to give an expert judgment of; to evaluate. *The insurance company told me that it would not insure my ring until I had it* ***appraised.***

2. **compromise** (com • pro • mise) (kom′ pro • mīze̸) *n.* A settlement of differences in which each side gives up some demands. *v.* To settle differences by mutual concessions. *If a* ***compromise*** *is not reached soon in the strike, the city will be paralyzed.*

3. **conform** (con • form) (kon • form′) *v.* To give the same shape, form, or character to; to make like; to be similar or identical; to be in agreement; to adapt oneself to; to act in accordance with rules, customs, and so on. *I had a lot of difficulty* ***conforming*** *to the rules and regulations of army life.*

4. ***controversy*** (con • tro • ver • sy) (kon′ tro • ver • sē) *n.* (*pl.* **sies**) A discussion in which there are opposing views; a dispute; a quarrel. *We couldn't believe that a friendly discussion could end in such a* ***controversy*** *that police had to be called to quiet down the opposing parties.*

5. **crass** (krass) *adj.* Insensitive; thick; coarse; lacking delicacy; gross; unfeeling; stupid. *The* ***crass*** *person approached the widow and asked her how she felt about her husband's murder.*

6. **curt** (kurt) *adj.* Marked by rude or abrupt shortness of words. *I was surprised that a firm would hire a receptionist who spoke in such a* ***curt*** *manner to all visitors.*

7. **emulate** (em′ ū • lāt~~e~~) *v.* To attempt to equal or excel; to imitate. *All my life I have tried to* ***emulate*** *my brother in everything, so I am going to the same college as he, and I am also going to be a lawyer.*

8. **plaintiff** (plā~~i~~n′ tif~~f~~) *n.* The complaining party in a lawsuit. *After the* ***plaintiff*** *told how she had been beaten and assaulted, she started to cry.*

9. **pretense** (prē • tens~~e~~′) *n.* A false claim; a claim not supported by fact; make believe; deception by showing what is false and hiding what is real. *When we play with my baby sister, we make a* ***pretense*** *of looking for her, even though she is in the room.*

10. **traditional** (tra • di • tion • al) (tra • dish′ on • al) *adj.* Handed down by custom or convention; conventional; customary. *In many European schools, it is* ***traditional*** *for students to rise when the teacher enters the room.*

Special Note

Compromise also means "to give up one's interest in something, to endanger the interests, to give in to something shameful, or to lay oneself open to something shameful." Examples: When he was young, he never *compromised* his principles, but as he got older he found it easier and easier to do so. One day it was a *compromise* of his principles and the next of his soul.

Step III. Practice

A. Directions: Each sentence has a missing word. Choose the word that *best* completes the sentence.

Word List

traditional, conform, emulate, pretense, plaintiff, appraise, compromise, curt, crass, controversy.

1. In my town on July Fourth, it is ____________________ for the townspeople to put on colonial costumes and parade down Main Street.

2. There is an instructor who enjoys ____________________ so much that he will actually begin one by choosing an unpopular position and defending it against all arguments.

3. The bank officer told us that the bank would have to send someone to ____________________ our house before the bank could approve any mortgage for it.

4. How can you be so ______________ and think of money at a time like this?

5. Three days after the trial had begun, the ______________ decided to drop the charges.

6. It's amusing to watch my sister trying to ______________ the characteristics of famous stars.

7. Unless the heads of state stop behaving in such an unyielding manner and ______________, a lot of lives will be lost.

8. The robber had made some ______________ of looking for his car keys while people were in the bank.

9. Persons who are polite rather than ______________ are more pleasant to be with.

10. Jim found it hard to ______________ to a 9 to 5 job after having been a free agent for so many years.

STOP. Check answers at the end of Chapter Five (p. 152).

B. Directions: In the Word Square there are ten words that you have met. The words may or may not be from this exercise. Find the words in the square and match them with their correct meanings. Note that there are *more* meanings than words. If there is no word in the square for a meaning, write *none*, and give the word.

WORD SQUARE

N	A	P	R	E	T	E	N	S	E
O	P	R	E	A	D	E	P	T	D
T	P	E	T	R	I	T	E	V	O
C	R	A	S	S	S	T	U	I	C
E	A	S	R	S	C	U	R	T	I
L	I	U	T	U	R	M	O	I	L
M	S	I	P	R	E	Q	L	M	E
A	E	L	M	O	E	P	M	E	O
E	M	U	L	A	T	E	O	A	P
C	O	M	P	R	O	M	I	S	E

Meanings	*Words*
1. To set a value on	________________
2. To act in accordance with rules	________________
3. A settlement of differences in which each side gives up some demands	________________
4. To imitate	________________
5. Something done or said that may serve as an example	________________
6. Make-believe	________________
7. To separate	________________
8. The complaining party in a lawsuit	________________
9. Insensitive	________________
10. Conventional	________________
11. Highly efficient	________________
12. Lacking freshness or originality	________________
13. Tumult	________________
14. Careful	________________
15. Obedient	________________
16. Abrupt shortness of words	________________
17. Very hungry	________________

STOP. Check answers at the end of Chapter Five (p. 152).

C. Directions: A number of sentences with missing words follows. Underline the word that *best* fits the sentence. Three choices are given for each sentence.

1. His (pretense, controversy, compromise) was such an obvious one that even a very young child could see through it.
2. Everything we do is (unanimous, crass, traditional) rather than modern and progressive.
3. When I was young I tried to (scrutinize, compromise, emulate) my fourth-grade teacher because I admired her so much.
4. Everyone agreed that the person we wanted to represent us should be a sensitive individual rather than a(n) (indiscreet, crass, docile) one.

5. I told them that I would rather resign than (emulate, conform, compromise) my principles.

6. Although we knew that the (pretense, affront, controversy) was hurting the reputation of our school, we didn't know how to get the opposing sides together to settle their differences.

7. When we learned that someone had been fired because she had not (corroborated, appraised, conformed) to certain rules of the company, we were enraged.

8. The jeweler said that he could not (compromise, segregate, appraise) my silver dish because the price of silver was too unstable at the moment.

STOP. Check answers at the end of Chapter Five (p. 152).

EXTRA WORD POWER

al. Of; relating to; belonging to; characterized by; like; the act of. When *al* is added to the end of a noun, it usually changes the noun into an adjective. For example: *fiction, fictional*—relating to fiction; *nature, natural*; *function, functional*; *nation, national*; *direction, directional*; tribe, tribal; *condition, conditional*; *tradition, traditional.* When *al* is added to the end of a verb, it usually changes the verb into a noun, and *al* generally means "the act of." For example: *refuse, refusal*—the act of refusing; *acquit, acquittal*—the act of acquitting or clearing; *rehearse, rehearsal*—the act of rehearsing; *arrive*; *arrival*—the act of arriving.

ity, ty. Quality of being; state of; condition of; degree. When *ity* or *ty* is added to the end of a word, it usually changes the word into a noun. For example: *nobility*—the state or quality of being noble; *complexity*—the state of being complex; *sovereignty*; *activity*; *reality*; *sincerity*; *alkalinity*; *brutality*; *absurdity*; *hostility*; *frugality*; *artificiality*; *cordiality*; *fraternity*; *civility*; *jollity*; *unity*; *safety*; *liberty.*

Special Note

When *ty* is found at the end of numerals such as *twenty, thirty, forty, fifty,* and so on, *ty* means "tens; times ten." For example, twenty is two times ten, and thirty is three times ten.

Additional Words

From your ability to use context clues, can you figure out the meanings of the following words?

1. **awe** (awe̸) *n.* *When the guerrilla leader entered a room, everyone stood in **awe** of him.* ____________________
2. **apt** (apt) *adj. v.* *If you are not careful, he is just as **apt** to insult you as to compliment you.* ____________________
3. **redundant** (re • dun′ dant) *adj.* *What Charles says tends to be so **redundant** that he repeats the same thing ten times.* ____________________
4. **waive** (wāi̸ve̸) *v.* *The defendant said that she would **waive** her right to a jury trial for a lesser charge.* ____________________
5. **amend** (a • mend′) *v.* *After leading a life of crime, he said that he would try to **amend** his way of living and be a law-abiding citizen.*

   ____

STOP. Check answers at the end of Chapter Five (pp. 152–153).

Practice for Additional Words

A. Directions: Match each word with the *best* definition.

________	1. apt	a. to give up a right
________	2. awe	b. characterized by repetition
________	3. amend	c. inclined to
________	4. redundant	d. dread
________	5. waive	e. to change for the better

STOP. Check answers at the end of Chapter Five (p. 153).

B. Directions: Each sentence has a missing word. Choose the word that *best* completes the sentence. There are more words in the list than you need.

Word List

apt, awe, affront, intimidate, euphemism, waive, amend, redundant, disdain, haughty, affirm, delete, dilemma, diligent.

1. We worked for days trying to ____________________ our former proposal, but every change we made seemed to bring more criticism rather than less.
2. You can count on my friend who is ____________________ to finish the report on time.

3. We considered it a(n) ____________________ when the host did not ask us to stay for dinner.

4. I told my buddies that I couldn't represent them at the debating contest because I was ____________________ to become tongue-tied in the middle of it.

5. What you say is too ____________________ ; try to be more brief and to the point, and less repetitious.

6. If you sign that contract, you will probably ____________________ all your rights concerning future decisions.

7. I am in such ____________________ of him that when I am in his presence I behave like a nincompoop.

8. My instructor told me that my paper was too long and that I needed to ____________________ parts of it if I wanted it to be considered for publication in the school magazine.

STOP. Check answers at the end of Chapter Five (p. 153).

EXERCISE 11

Step I. Vocabulary Words in Sentences

Directions: Sentences using the ten vocabulary words from Exercise 11 follow. See whether you can figure out the meanings of the underlined words from the clues in the sentences. Blanks are provided for your estimates of the definitions. Check your meanings with those in Step II.

1. Income rather than <u>infidelity</u> is the major cause of divorce among persons who marry young. However, in films, whenever there is a divorce, it is usually due to the unfaithfulness of one of the <u>spouses</u>. ____________________

2. When the husband or wife is being unfaithful, the other spouse is often shown to be very <u>gullible</u> and is easily fooled or deceived.
____

3. The most interesting parts of films that deal with divorce have to do with how the person having the affair tries to <u>extricate</u> himself or herself from either the marriage or from the affair. Some very funny films have been made showing how a spouse tries hard to get himself or herself out of some difficulty. ____________________

4. It's <u>inevitable</u> that the other spouse will eventually find out about the affair. ____________________

5. Sooner or later, the other spouse has to recognize that something is awry or amiss. ____________________

6. Today when we go to see a film concerning divorce, we have no assurance as to how it will turn out. Years ago, we could guarantee that somehow the spouses would work out their problems. ____________________

7. Films have changed drastically in the past decade, and you can no longer make the assumption that the person wanting the divorce or having the affair is the male. ____________________

8. In many of the films the persons are so busy expending their energies trying to have a good time that it's a wonder they are such successes professionally. They seem to be using up all their energies in other directions.

____

9. Years ago, in the movies, when a husband or wife was unfaithful, the unfaithful partner usually felt some kind of remorse. In today's films, you usually do not see the unfaithful spouse feeling guilty. ____________________

Step II. Vocabulary Words

1. **assumption** (as • sump • tion) (as̸ • sump′ shun) *n.* The act of taking for granted without proof; a taking to or upon oneself; a supposition. *When the police found Jim standing over the body of the murdered man, they made the* ***assumption*** *that he was the murderer.*

2. **assurance** (as • sur • ance) (as̸ • shur′ anse̸) *n.* The act of making sure or certain; security; certainty; confidence; guarantee. *Nobody doubted him because he acted with such* ***assurance.***

3. **awry** (a • wry) (a • w̸rī′) *adj. adv.* With a turn or twist to one side; away from the expected or hoped for direction; wrong. *Everything seemed to be going smoothly until the last day when everything went* ***awry.***

4. **expend** (ex • pend) (ek • spend′) *v.* To use up; to spend. *It's a shame that he did not win the prize because he* ***expended*** *so much energy on his project.*

5. **extricate** (ex • tri • cate) (ek′ stra • kāte̸) *v.* To free or release from difficulties, entanglements, embarrassing situations, and so on. *He knew that the longer he waited, the more difficult it would be to* ***extricate*** *himself from the situation he was in, but he seemed powerless to act.*

6. **gullible** (gul • li • ble) (gul′ l̸i • bul) *adj.* Easily deceived or cheated. *Everyong seems to take advantage of my friend Frank because he is so* ***gullible.***

7. **inevitable** (in • ev • i • ta • ble) (in • ev′ i • ta • bul) *adj.* Not able to be avoided or escaped; sure to happen; certain. *He led such a dangerous existence that it was **inevitable** he would die violently.*

8. **infidelity** (in • fi • del • i • ty) (in • fi • del′ i • tē) *n.* (*pl.* **ties**) Unfaithfulness; a disloyal act; adultery. *In the film the **infidelity** of the husband did not seem to bother the wife because she too was unfaithful to her husband.*

9. **remorse** (re • mors~~e~~) *n.* Painful and deep regret for wrongdoing; a strong anguish arising from regret for past misdeeds. *Throughout the trial the defendant said that he felt no **remorse** for his crimes.*

10. **spouse** (spouz) *n.* A husband or a wife; either member of a married pair. *To make ends meet, both **spouses** usually work.*

Step III. Practice

A. Directions: Choose the word from the word list that *best* fits the definition.

Word List

gullible, spouse, extricate, assumption, awry, expend, remorse, assurance, infidelity, inevitable.

1. Away from the expected direction ____________
2. To use up ____________
3. A husband or a wife ____________
4. To free or release from difficulty ____________
5. The act of making sure ____________
6. Unfaithfulness ____________
7. Painful and deep regret for wrongdoing ____________
8. The act of taking for granted without proof ____________
9. Certain ____________
10. Easily deceived ____________

STOP. Check answers at the end of Chapter Five (p. 153).

B. Directions: Ten sentences follow. Define the underlined word.

1. In many homes today both spouses seem to share equally in making decisions. ____________________

2. We have no assurance that you will not again allow minors to enter the premises; therefore we will not grant you a permit to reopen. ____________________

3. I can't afford to expend any more of my time or energy on this project. ____________________

4. When the driver learned that, while driving under the influence of liquor, he had hit and crippled a small child, he felt great remorse and said that he would never touch alcohol again. ____________________

5. Each day he seemed to get deeper and deeper in debt to the loan sharks; soon he would find it impossible to extricate himself from their clutches. ____________________

6. The officer at the bank refused to speak to the person because he was under the assumption that the poorly dressed man was not very important; however, the poorly dressed man turned out to be one of the bank's most important accounts. ____________________

7. It is certainly a shock to learn about the infidelity of your spouse. ____________________

8. When things go awry for me, I try to stop and think why things did not go as they should have. ____________________

9. The two things that are inevitable in life are death and taxes. ____________________

10. My friend Frank is so gullible that he now holds shares in two dry oil wells, a piece of swamp property, and a nonexistent company. ____________________

STOP. Check answers at the end of Chapter Five (p. 153).

C. Directions: There are seven words in the Word Square from this exercise. Find the seven words and define each one.

WORD SQUARE

L	O	T	A	M	E	I	U	I	A
A	E	O	W	A	O	N	N	N	S
E	X	T	R	I	C	A	T	E	S
P	P	E	Y	N	O	C	I	V	U
R	E	M	O	R	S	E	E	I	M
O	N	O	U	T	P	L	L	T	P
S	D	T	R	U	O	E	M	A	T
E	R	H	E	O	U	V	O	B	I
D	A	A	L	V	S	E	R	L	O
R	O	V	E	L	E	N	E	E	N

Words *Meanings*

1. ____________________
2. ____________________
3. ____________________
4. ____________________
5. ____________________
6. ____________________
7. ____________________

STOP. Check answers at the end of Chapter Five (p. 153).

EXTRA WORD POWER

ab, abs. From; away; away from; off. *Abs.* is used before words beginning with *c* and *t.* Examples: *abscond*—to go away hurriedly and secretly; *abstain*—to do without something voluntarily. Here are some examples of words that have *ab* at the beginning of them. Examples: *abduct*—to carry off; *abortive*—coming to nothing; *abrupt*—sudden; *absent*—away; *absorb*—to take in or up; *abuse*—to use wrongly.

ment. The act of; the result of; the state of. When *ment* is added to the end of a verb, it usually changes the verb into a noun. Examples: *amaze, amazement*—the state of being amazed; *develop, development*—the act or result of developing; *enjoy, enjoyment*; *advance, advancement*; *improve, improvement*; *pave, pavement*; *measure, measurement*; *entangle, entanglement.* How many more words can you think of that have *ment* at the end of them?

Additional Words

From your ability to use context clues, can you figure out the meanings of the following words?

1. **abortion** (a • bor • tion) (a • bor′ shun) *n. In the film, a woman with two married children found out that she was pregnant, and she had to decide whether to get an* ***abortion*** *or to have the child.*

   ____

2. **celibacy** (cel • i • ba • cy) (sel′ i • ba • sē) *n.* (*pl.* **cies**) *My friend doesn't understand how monks and priests can lead a life of* ***celibacy*** *because he can't be away from women for more than a day or two.*

   ____

3. **esoteric** (es • o • ter • ic) (es • o • ter′ ik) *adj. In the film, the secret club had* ***esoteric*** *customs that its members had to adhere to, and no outsider was ever allowed to observe the ceremony or to enter the special room where the ceremony was held.*

   ____

4. **query** (que • ry) (kwer′ ē) *n.* (*pl.* **ries**) *v. All reporters seemed to have the same* ***query****; that is, they wanted to know when the hostages would be released.*

   ____

5. **improvise** (im • pro • vise) (im′ pro • vīz~~e~~) *v. When one of our performers became ill, I was called upon to* ***improvise*** *some kind of act that would entertain the audience.*

   ____

STOP. Check answers at the end of Chapter Five (p. 154).

Practice for Additional Words

A. Directions: Match each word with the *best* definition.

________	1. celibacy	a. question
________	2. abortion	b. to make up something on the spur of the moment
________	3. esoteric	c. induced termination of a pregnancy
________	4. improvise	d. the state of being unmarried
________	5. query	e. understood only by a select few

STOP. Check answers at the end of Chapter Five (p. 154).

B. Directions: Each sentence has a missing word. Choose the word from the word list that *best* completes the sentence. Some of the words are from previous exercises.

Word List

query, improvise, affluent, overt, covet, esoteric, apt, awry, abortion, celibacy, naive, lethal, assumption, extricate, gullible, awe, waive, redundant, amend.

1. Although she is ________________ and can buy anything she wants, she is usually very frugal.
2. Did you want to ________________ him further on that or are you satisfied with his answers?
3. I never thought that Mike would be the one to take an oath of ________________ and retreat to the mountains.
4. The police said that they did not operate in a covert manner and that everything they did was ________________ and aboveboard.
5. Every spring I am ________________ to fall in love.
6. It's a good thing that I am able to ________________, because I am always called on to perform at the last moment.
7. The doctors were unable to save her life because she had taken a(n) ________________ dose of the poison.
8. He behaved in such a(n) ________________ manner that some of us began to wonder whether there was something wrong.
9. There is a great deal of controversy surrounding the topic of ________________ between pro-life groups and groups that feel that

women should have the right to make their own decision concerning their own bodies.

10. The instructor said that I tend to be __________________ and that I should try to be less wordy when I speak and write.

STOP. Check answers at the end of Chapter Five (p. 154).

EXERCISE 12

Step I. Vocabulary Words in Sentences

Directions: Sentences using the ten vocabulary words from Exercise 12 follow. See whether you can figure out the meanings of the underlined words from the clues in the sentences. Blanks are provided for your estimates of the definitions. Check your meanings with those in Step II.

1. I have been working at one job or another since I have been about ten years old, and it looks as though I will be working for the duration of my life. __________________
2. I don't anticipate inheriting any fortune, and I don't expect to find a pot of gold at the end of the rainbow. __________________
3. I'm not worried because I'm highly motivated, and I'm able to cope with any problems that arise. I don't want to sound arrogant, but I've always had a lot of drive, and I've always been able to solve my problems based on reality. __________________; __________________; __________________
4. I may go into politics because I'm told that I have a lot of charisma. Last year when our club needed funds, I was elected to make the appeals speech because I seem to be able to get persons enthused about things. __________________
5. I don't like tedious work. I get bored very easily if I have to do the same thing over and over again. __________________
6. Since I am a realist rather than an idealist, I tend to be skeptical about things. I tend not to believe things until I see them. __________________; __________________
7. I am rather astute about financial matters because I have been on my own for so long. Persons have been trying to con me out of my money for as long as I can remember; fortunately for me, I am not easily taken in. __________________

Step II. Vocabulary Words

1. **anticipate** (an • tic • i • pate) (an • tis′ i • pāte̸) *v.* To expect; to look forward to; to foresee; to act, use, or make in advance. *From the candidate's answers, you could tell that he had* ***anticipated*** *exactly what questions the reporters would ask.*

2. **astute** (a • stūte̸′) *adj.* Shrewd; ingenious; clever; crafty. *The* ***astute*** *lawyer was able to win every argument.*

3. **charisma** (cha • ris • ma) (ka • riz′ ma) *n.* A rare power or personal magic of leadership that an individual possesses that arouses special enthusiasm or loyalty; a special magnetic charm or appeal. *He had such great* ***charisma*** *that his followers would gladly go to their deaths for him.*

4. **cope** (kōpe̸) *v.* To struggle or fight with on fairly even terms or with some degree of success (usually followed by *with*); to deal with and attempt to overcome problems and difficulties (usually used with *with*). *George was very anxious about his promotion because he did not know if he could* ***cope*** *with all the responsibilities that he would have if he were promoted.*

5. **duration** (du • ra • tion) (du • rā′ shun) *n.* Persistence or continuance in time; the time during which something exists or lasts. *For the* ***duration*** *of the strike people had to find alternate means of transportation.*

6. **idealist** (i • de • al • ist) (ī • dē′ a • list) *n.* A person who acts according to high ideals, that is, one who conforms to ultimate perfection or excellence; one who is unrealistic and impractical; one who believes in something that exists only in the mind. *People can't understand how I can be an* ***idealist*** *in a world filled with imperfection, but I am.*

7. **motivate** (mō′ ti • vāte̸) *v.* To stimulate to action; to provide with an incentive; to set in motion or arouse. *Even though a person may have a lot of ability, unless that person is* ***motivated*** *to achieve, he or she will not.*

8. **reality** (re • al • i • ty) (rē • al′ i • tē) *n.* (*pl.* **ties**) The state of being real, actual, or true; what actually exists or is. *Some people distort* ***reality*** *in order to solve their problems because they cannot cope with the situation as it really is.*

9. **skeptical** (skep • ti • cal) (skep′ ti • kal) *adj.* Inclined to doubt; not believing easily; questioning the truth of theories or of facts. *I am very* ***skeptical*** *about someone who says that he is going to make me wealthy overnight if I follow his advice.*

10. **tedious** (te • di • ous) (tē′ dē • øus) *adj.* Tiresome or uninteresting because of extreme length or slowness; boring; monotonous; wearisome. *I can't understand how someone who loves adventure and excitement could work at such a* ***tedious*** *job.*

Step III. Practice

A. Directions: Here are ten definitions. Write the word from this exercise that *best* fits the definition.

1. To stimulate to action ____________
2. Inclined to doubt ____________
3. One who is impractical and unrealistic ____________
4. The time during which something exists or lasts ____________
5. Shrewd ____________
6. Tiresome because of extreme length ____________
7. To expect ____________
8. A special magnetic charm or appeal ____________
9. The state of being actual ____________
10. To deal with and attempt to overcome difficulties ____________

STOP. Check answers at the end of Chapter Five (p. 154).

B. Directions: Each sentence has a missing word. Choose the word that *best* completes the sentence.

Word List

duration, charisma, cope, reality, skeptical, motivate, astute, anticipate, idealist, tedious.

1. Working in a political campaign may seem exciting to outsiders, but it is actually very ____________ work for most of us because all we do is stuff envelopes and answer the phone.
2. One of the candidates had to withdraw from the race because he had a number of problems, and he just could not ____________ with them.
3. I don't ____________ any problems on my new job, but you never know.
4. Her ____________ is so strong that she can get you to do practically anything.
5. After all the things that have happened in your life, how can you still be such a(n) ____________.

6. The ____________________ gentleman knew that he would have to remain calm and not panic in order to get out of the situation alive.
7. For the ____________________ of my stay in school, I intend to do my assignments on time.
8. My friends are very ____________________ about my keeping up with all my assignments.
9. This semester I am living in ____________________, so I see things as they really are rather than as I would like them to be.
10. No one can ____________________ you to do anything because the drive or energy must come from within you.

STOP. Check answers at the end of Chapter Five (p. 154).

C. Directions: Each of the following sentences has a word that is underlined. Write a synonym for each of the underlined words. The synonym should be a word from the exercises in this book.

1. It pays to be very doubtful about anyone who promises miracles.
____
2. It is certain that you will win the election because all the delegates have said that they are voting for you. ____________________
3. My husband and I have decided to separate. ____________________
4. I could not stand his unfaithfulness any longer. ____________________
5. My brother is a very shrewd person, but he has a lot of problems that prevent him from succeeding. ____________________
6. Because of his magnetism, his subjects followed him to their deaths.
____
7. Persons who are highly stimulated to achieve usually do.
____
8. Everyone says that a perfectionist cannot survive in the real world.
____
9. After she was betrayed by her friends, she had great difficulty in dealing with situations that involved trust. ____________________
10. We never expected that we would run into so much opposition and so many problems. ____________________

STOP. Check answers at the end of Chapter Five (p. 154).

EXTRA WORD POWER

ary. Relating to; connected with. When *ary* is found at the end of a word, the word is either a noun or an adjective. Examples of nouns: *dietary*—relating to diet; *military*—relating to soldiers, arms, or war; *parliamentary*; *reactionary*; *boundary.* Examples of adjectives: *voluntary*; *honorary*; *budgetary*; *secondary*; *supplementary.*

ery. Refers to a place of doing, keeping, producing, or selling; refers to practice; refers to a collection or class of things; refers to certain characteristics, behavior, conditions, or status. When *ery* is found at the end of a word, the word is generally a noun. Examples: *bakery*; *hatchery*; *fishery*; *archery*; *cannery*; *grocery*; *pottery*; *nunnery*; *trickery*—the practice of underhand tricks to deceive; *finery*—a collection of fine clothing; *slavery*—the condition of being a slave; *witchery*—the practice of witchcraft.

Additional Words

From your ability to use context clues, can you figure out the meanings of the following words?

1. **morale** (mor • al¢′) *n.* *After having lost five games in a row, the team's **morale** was very low.*

   ____

2. **compensate** (com • pen • sate) (kom′ pen • sāt¢) *v.* The woman, crying hysterically, told the lawyer that no amount of money could ***compensate*** for the loss of her son in the accident.

   ____

3. **delve** (delv¢) *v.* *We didn't want to **delve** any further into the mystery because we were afraid of what we might find.*

   ____

4. **deprecate** (dep • re • cate) (dep′ re • kāt¢) *v.* *During the campaign the politicians expressed strong disapproval of further taxes, but after the campaign was over, the winner stopped **deprecating** the need for more taxes.*

   ____

5. **austere** (aus • tere) (au • stēr$\not{e}$′) *adj.* *I still remember my **austere** third-grade teacher, who could frighten us with just one glance.*

____

STOP. Check answers at the end of Chapter Five (p. 154).

Practice for Additional Words

A. Directions: Match each word with the *best* definition.

________	1. delve	a. stern
________	2. austere	b. to search deeply
________	3. deprecate	c. to be equivalent to
________	4. morale	d. to express disapproval of
________	5. compensate	e. the mental or emotional condition of a person or group

STOP. Check answers at the end of Chapter Five (p. 155).

B. Directions: Each sentence has a nonsense word. Choose a word from the word list to replace the nonsense word. There are more words in the list than you need.

Word List

delved, austere, deprecated, morale, compensate, apt, awe, amend, waived, redundant, abortion, celibacy, esoteric, query, improvised.

1. During the war many actors and actresses went overseas to try to raise the flooble of our soldiers. ________________
2. The entertainers bleebed many shows in which soldiers from the audience would be called on stage to be part of the show. ________________
3. Even the most clubert general seemed to enjoy the show and seemed to mellow a bit. ________________
4. One show that we saw was so nerobic that no one understood it.

   ____
5. It seemed odd that my friend who had erherted violence all his life should become involved with a band of robbers. ________________
6. The manager of the store said that he would mercant us for our trouble.

   ____
7. The more we getered into the subject, the more confused we became.

   ____
8. The wester from the audience seemed to paralyze the speaker, and for a moment he was at a loss for words. ________________

9. Our speech professor told us that many of us tend to repeat ourselves and to be norbit. ____________________

10. My friend is more leter than me to be successful because she is very highly motivated, whereas I am not motivated at all to succeed. ________________

STOP. Check answers at the end of Chapter Five (p. 155).

CROSSWORD PUZZLE 4

Directions: The meanings of a number of the words from Exercises 10–12 follow. Your knowledge of these words will help you to solve this crossword puzzle. Note that *combining form* is abbreviated as *comb. f.*

Across

1. Roman numeral *one hundred*
2. To join to another
5. An indefinite article
6. The foot of a horse
9. To use up
11. To adapt oneself to
13. Interjection for *behold*
14. Contraction for *do not*
15. Abbreviation for *East*
16. Antonym of *down*
18. Abbreviation for *venereal disease*

Down

1. Relating to a dispute
2. A cutting tool
3. Abbreviation for *displaced person*
4. To make a detailed search for information
5. Abbreviation for *Anno Domini*
6. Glory
7. A function word
8. Enemy
9. One who imitates another

19. In addition to those used
21. Part of a knife
23. Same as #1 Across
24. To rouse
25. An overwhelming feeling of admiration
26. The eighth letter of the alphabet
27. Abbreviation for *Britain*
28. Roman numeral *five*
29. Exactly suitable
31. An appeal
34. The central part
36. In favor of
37. A lion does this
38. To damage or spoil
39. Having keenness of insight
43. Antonym of *delete*
45. Same as #1 Across
46. A number
47. Form of the verb *to be*
48. Same as #47 Down
49. Occurring in the air
53. Roman numeral *one thousand*
54. Rubbing out
57. The body of law contained in Jewish Scripture
60. A girl
61. To unite by stitches
62. Same as #5 Across
63. You do this to a banana

10. To make a downward motion of the head
11. The settlement of differences by each side giving in a little
12. Symbol used for a motion picture rating
17. The foot of an animal
20. The past tense ending for regular verbs
22. To express disapproval
23. A special charm
27. Abbreviation for *Before Christ*
29. To estimate
30. A false claim
32. To cut off branches from
33. You do this when you are hungry
35. Past tense of *run*
40. Same as #1 Across
41. Roman numeral *six*
42. Comb. f. for *out of*
44. Same as #15 Across
47. A pronoun
50. Abbreviation for *right guard*
51. Same as #47 Down
52. Humble in character
55. Same as #12 Down
56. Flows from a tree
58. Same as #12 Down
59. An exclamation of surprise or joy
61. Makes nouns plural

STOP. Check answers at the end of Chapter Five (p. 155).

WORD SCRAMBLE 4

Directions: Word Scramble 4 is based on words from Exercise 10–12. The meanings are your clues to arranging the letters in correct order.

		Meanings
1. iaserpap	________________	to estimate the worth of
2. nocrfmo	________________	to make like

3.	teacniipta	________________	to expect
4.	sscar	________________	insensitive
5.	ustiode	________________	monotonous
6.	repsente	________________	a false claim
7.	eiasckptl	________________	inclined to doubt
8.	iisdalet	________________	one who is unrealistic and impractical
9.	oepc	________________	to deal with and attempt to overcome problems
10.	lateume	________________	to imitate
11.	llilgueb	________________	able to be easily fooled
12.	tacexetri	________________	to free or release from difficulties
13.	eepdxn	________________	to use up
14.	ssepou	________________	a husband or wife
15.	yarw	________________	with a turn or twist to one side
16.	ttusae	________________	shrewd
17.	eermsor	________________	painful and deep regret for wrongdoing
18.	maahcrsi	________________	a special magnetic charm
19.	truc	________________	marked by rude or abrupt shortness of words
20.	ttmeaoiv	________________	to stimulate to action

STOP. Check answers at the end of Chapter Five (p. 155).

ANALOGIES 4

Directions: Find the word from the following list that *best* completes each analogy. There are more words in the list than you need.

Word List

practical, curt, traditional, esoteric, wife, austere, complete, emulate, infidelity, actuality, supposition, charisma, sister, crass, hateful, impractical, speech, pay, evaluate, spouse, relative, sympathetic, awe, awful, controversy, remorseful, gloomy, plaintiff, extra, assurance, yielding.

1. Brother : sibling :: husband : ____________________.
2. Former : latter :: polite : ____________________.
3. Infamous : notorious :: repentant : ____________________.
4. Accused : complainant :: defendant : ____________________.
5. Optimist : cheerful :: pessimist : ____________________.
6. Pertinent : relevant :: conventional : ____________________.
7. Haughty : arrogant :: insensitive : ____________________.
8. Whisper : shout :: misunderstanding : ____________________.
9. Verbose : terse :: uncertainty : ____________________.
10. Siren : warn :: appraisal : ____________________.
11. Assistance : helping :: compromise : ____________________.
12. Apprehensive : anxious :: dread : ____________________.
13. Disdain : despise :: assumption : ____________________.
14. Insert : delete :: faithfulness : ____________________.
15. Concise : less :: redundant : ____________________.
16. Affront : compliment :: lenient : ____________________.
17. Mundane : commonplace :: imitate : ____________________.
18. Fantasy : imagination :: reality : ____________________.
19. Skeptic : doubting :: idealist : ____________________.
20. Actor : talent :: leader : ____________________.

STOP. Check answers at the end of Chapter Five (p. 155).

MULTIPLE-CHOICE VOCABULARY TEST 4

Directions: This is a test on words in Exercises 10–12. Words are presented according to exercises. *Do all exercises before checking answers.* Underline the meaning that *best* fits the word.

Exercise 10

1. appraise
   a. to praise
   b. to be worthy of
   c. to acclaim
   d. to estimate the worth of

2. compromise
   a. to give in
   b. to settle
   c. to give up
   d. to settle by mutual concession

3. conform
a. to adapt oneself to
b. to make rules
c. to regulate
d. to adapt others to

4. controversy
a. a confusing argument
b. a dispute
c. a discussion with no opposition
d. something unable to be settled

5. crass
a. tired
b. abrupt
c. sensitive
d. insensitive

6. curt
a. mean
b. marked by abruptness
c. loud
d. marked by insensitivity

7. emulate
a. to regulate
b. to prepare for
c. to imitate
d. to try

8. plaintiff
a. a complaining person
b. the defendant
c. a person in a dispute
d. the complaining person in a lawsuit

9. pretense
a. a false claim
b. a secret claim
c. one who hides
d. an unusual claim

10. traditional
a. reactionary
b. customary
c. ancient
d. contemporary

Exercise 11

11. assumption
a. the act of taking for granted with facts
b. the act of proving
c. the act of taking
d. the act of taking for granted without proof

12. assurance
a. insecurity
b. a policy
c. certainty
d. an insurance claim

13. awry
a. clever humor
b. away from the expected direction
c. turning
d. the hoped for direction

14. expend
a. to quit
b. to tire
c. to spend a lot of money
d. to use up

15. extricate
a. to free from difficulties
b. to cut out
c. to escape
d. to endure difficulties

16. gullible
a. not very interesting
b. able to be frightened
c. easily cheated
d. able to be made to laugh

17. inevitable
a. able to try
b. certain
c. not too certain
d. not able to happen

18. infidelity
a. a divorce
b. a problem
c. a battle between husband and wife
d. unfaithfulness

19. remorse
a. hope
b. regret for past misdeeds
c. wrongdoing
d. atoning for sins

20. spouse
a. relative
b. a brother or sister
c. a parent
d. a husband or wife

Exercise 12

21. anticipate
a. to pray for
b. to be able to see in advance
c. to expect
d. to look at

22. astute
a. stout
b. clever
c. always correct
d. showy

23. charisma
a. a strange power
b. a use of charm for evil
c. a special gift
d. a special charm

24. cope
a. to try
b. to struggle
c. to deal with
d. to avoid problems

25. duration
a. a brief period of time
b. persistence
c. everlasting time
d. continuance in time

26. idealist
a. perfection
b. never unrealistic
c. one who conforms to excellence
d. one who is never impractical

27. motivate
a. to be active
b. to give power to
c. to make angry
d. to stimulate to action

28. reality
a. the state of doing
b. what actually exists
c. what is practical
d. what is impossible

29. skeptical
a. confused
b. unquestioning
c. not believing easily
d. concerned about truth

30. tedious
a. being tired
b. hard work
c. boring
d. continuing

TRUE/FALSE TEST 4

Directions: This is a true/false test on Exercises 10–12. Read each sentence carefully. Decide whether it is true or false. Put a *T* for *true* or an *F* for *false* in the blank. The number after the sentence tells you if the word is from Exercise 10, 11 or 12.

_______ 1. A skeptic is one who believes that everything will turn out all right. 12

_______ 2. An astute person is considered shrewd. 12

_______ 3. An idealist is usually not a realist. 12

_______ 4. When someone waives his or her rights, he or she gives them up. 10

_______ 5. A spouse can be a male or female. 11

_______ 6. When you improvise something, you are well-prepared. 11

_______ 7. Most Catholic priests practice celibacy. 11

_______ 8. Assumptions are based on facts and are usually true. 11

_______ 9. Persons without morale would probably be low in spirits. 12

_______ 10. Tedious work is fun to do. 12

_______ 11. Something that lasts for a duration must always last for a long period of time. 12

_______ 12. A gullible person is not able to be easily deceived. 11

_______ 13. Someone austere can be a lenient and kind person. 12

_______ 14. *Esoteric* and *famous* are synonyms. 11

_______ 15. The prosecutor and the plaintiff are on the same side. 10

_______ 16. When you emulate someone, you make fun of the person. 10

_______ 17. A person who has remorse does not feel guilty or sorry about anything. 11

_______ 18. "John, an unhappy young man, is not happy," is a redundant statement. 10

_______ 19. *Awe* and *love* are synonyms. 10

_______ 20. *Insurance* and *assurance* are synonyms. 11

STOP. Check answers for both tests at the end of Chapter Five (pp. 155–156).

SCORING OF TESTS

Multiple-Choice Vocabulary Test

Number Wrong	*Score*
0–2	Excellent
3–5	Good
6–8	Weak
Above 8	Poor
Score ________	

True/False Test

Number Wrong	*Score*
0–1	Excellent
2–3	Good
4–5	Weak
Above 5	Poor
Score ________	

1. If you scored in the excellent or good range on *both tests,* you are doing well. Go on to Chapter Six.
2. If you scored in the weak or poor range on either test, look below and follow directions for Additional Practice. Note that the words on the tests are arranged so that you can tell in which exercise to find them. This will help you if you need additional practice.

ADDITIONAL PRACTICE SETS

A. Directions: Write the words you missed on the tests from the three exercises in the space provided. Note that the tests are presented so that you can tell to which exercises the words belong.

Exercise 10 Words Missed

1. ________ 6. ________
2. ________ 7. ________
3. ________ 8. ________
4. ________ 9. ________
5. ________ 10. ________

Exercise 11 Words Missed

1. ________ 6. ________
2. ________ 7. ________
3. ________ 8. ________
4. ________ 9. ________
5. ________ 10. ________

Exercise 12 Words Missed

1. ____________________ 6. ____________________
2. ____________________ 7. ____________________
3. ____________________ 8. ____________________
4. ____________________ 9. ____________________
5. ____________________ 10. ____________________

B. Directions: Restudy the words that you have written down on p. 148 and this page. Do Step I and Step II for those you missed. Note that Step I and Step II are on the following pages.

Exercise 10—pp. 121–123.

Exercise 11—pp. 128–130.

Exercise 12—pp. 135–136.

C. Directions: Do Additional Practice 1 on this page and p. 150 if you missed words from Exercise 10. Do Additional Practice 2 on p. 150 if you missed words from Exercise 11. Do Additional Practice 3 on p. 151 if you missed words from Exercise 12. Now go on to Chapter Six.

Additional Practice 1 for Exercise 10

Directions: Ten sentences with missing words follow. Underline the word that *best* fits the sentence. Two choices are given for each sentence.

1. Since he is such a (curt, crass) fellow, I'm sure that he will not be very sensitive to Mrs. Brown's feelings.
2. After trying to be an individualist all my life, I find it hard to (emulate, conform).
3. The students decided to (compromise, appraise) the merit of their position before they went any further with their plan.
4. No one could believe that the (pretense, controversy) would get so out of hand that it would split the school right in half.
5. It was hard to get the factions to (conform, compromise) on any issue.
6. When my (curt, crass) friend introduced Jim to our group, he said about five words, and he said them in such a way that you thought the room was on fire.

7. I made no (compromise, pretense) about the fact that I was very disappointed that I did not get the position.
8. All my life I have tried to (appraise, emulate) people that I look up to, because I want to be just like them.
9. I come from a (crass, traditional) family, so everything I do has to meet with conventional standards.
10. The (controversy, plaintiff) in the lawsuit was suing for a million dollars.

STOP. Check answers at the end of Chapter Five (p. 156).

Additional Practice 2 for Exercise 11

Directions: Ten sentences follow. Define the underlined word.

1. What assurance do you have that they will stand behind what they say? __________________
2. I decided not to go to the party because my spouse was not invited. __________________
3. Larry is so gullible that when he went to New York someone sold him stock in the Brooklyn Bridge. __________________
4. Mr. Brown doesn't think that he will ever be able to extricate himself from the financial difficulties that he has gotten himself into. __________________
5. Have you ever had one of those awful days in which everything goes awry? __________________
6. Ed felt great remorse when he heard that his friend had gotten hurt in an automobile accident after he and his friend had quarreled. __________________
7. It seems inevitable that you and Frank will win the disco contest. __________________
8. The employees said that they would not expend another ounce of energy on the project because they didn't like it. __________________
9. When we saw Mr. Brown with a beautiful young girl, we all made the assumption that she was his girlfriend, but she turned out to be his daughter. __________________
10. In our society infidelity seems to be a way of life for some people, but this does not mean that everyone is not trustworthy. __________________

STOP. Check answers at the end of Chapter Five (p. 156).

Additional Practice 3 for Exercise 12

Directions: Ten sentences containing the meanings of vocabulary presented in Exercise 12 follow. Choose the word that *best* fits the meaning of the word or phrase underlined in the sentence.

Word List

anticipate, idealist, motivate, skeptical, duration, astute, cope, charisma, reality, tedious.

1. Persons claim that I am an unrealistic individual because I expect people to be sensitive, caring, and ethical. ____________________
2. My friend may not be too knowledgeable when it comes to book learning, but he is very shrewd when it comes to street survival. ____________________
3. Philosophers have been discussing what the state of being actual is for many centuries. ____________________
4. After my parents became divorced, I had to learn to deal with many problems that I had that stemmed from my inability to adjust to their divorce. ____________________
5. For the time during which I stay here I will abide by your rules. ____________________
6. In the experiments the psychologists used different techniques to try to stimulate their subjects. ____________________
7. Many people said that they voted for the politician because of his magnetic charm. ____________________
8. If I had been able to foresee the consequences, this tragedy might have been prevented. ____________________
9. Even though this job pays well, many people quit because it is a very tiresome job. ____________________
10. I'm inclined to doubt anyone who says that he has a quick cure for whatever ails you. ____________________

STOP. Check answers at the end of Chapter Five (p. 156).

ANSWERS: Chapter Five

Exercise 10 (pp. 121-128)

Practice A

(1) traditional, (2) controversy, (3) appraise, (4) crass, (5) plaintiff, (6) emulate, (7) compromise, (8) pretense, (9) curt, (10) conform.

Practice B

(1) appraise, (2) none–conform, (3) compromise, (4) emulate, (5) none–precedent, (6) pretense, (7) none–segregate, (8) none–plaintiff, (9) crass, (10) none–traditional, (11) adept, (12) trite, (13) none–turmoil, (14) discreet, (15) docile, (16) curt, (17) none–famished.

WORD SQUARE

N	A	P	R	E	T	E	N	S	E
O	P	R	E	A	D	E	P	T	D
T	P	E	T	R	I	T	E	V	O
C	R	A	S	S	S	T	U	I	C
E	A	S	R	S	C	U	R	T	I
L	I	U	T	U	R	M	O	I	L
M	S	I	P	R	E	Q	L	M	E
A	E	L	M	O	E	P	M	E	O
E	M	U	L	A	T	E	O	A	P
C	O	M	P	R	O	M	I	S	E

Practice C

(1) pretense, (2) traditional, (3) emulate, (4) crass, (5) compromise, (6) controversy, (7) conformed, (8) appraise.

Additional Words (p. 127)

1. **awe.** Respect tinged with fear; an overwhelming feeling of respect, fear, admiration, and so on produced by someone or something powerful or the like.
2. **apt.** Exactly suitable; appropriate; inclined to.
3. **redundant.** Extra; not needed; wordy; needlessly repetitive; superfluous; using more words than is necessary.

4. **waive.** To voluntarily give up a right, claim, or privilege.
5. **amend.** To better; to improve; to correct; to change, rephrase, or add to or subtract from something such as a motion, bill, or constitution.

Practice for Additional Words (pp. 127–128)

A. (1) c, (2) d, (3) e, (4) b, (5) a.
B. (1) amend, (2) diligent, (3) affront, (4) apt, (5) redundant, (6) waive, (7) awe, (8) delete.

Exercise 11 (pp. 128–135)

Practice A

(1) awry, (2) expend, (3) spouse, (4) extricate, (5) assurance, (6) infidelity, (7) remorse, (8) assumption, (9) inevitable, (10) gullible.

Practice B

(1) husbands or wives, (2) guarantee, (3) use up, (4) regret, (5) free, (6) supposition, (7) unfaithfulness, (8) wrong, (9) certain, (10) easily deceived.

Practice C

(1) extricate—to free from difficulties, (2) remorse—deep regret for wrongdoing, (3) expend—to use up, (4) awry—wrong, (5) spouse—husband or wife, (6) inevitable—certain, (7) assumption—the act of taking for granted without proof.

WORD SQUARE

L	O	T	A	M	E	I	U	I	A
A	E	O	W	A	O	N	N	N	S
E	X	T	R	I	C	A	T	E	S
P	P	E	Y	N	O	C	I	V	U
R	E	M	O	R	S	E	E	I	M
O	N	O	U	T	P	L	L	T	P
S	D	T	R	U	O	E	M	A	T
E	R	H	E	O	U	V	O	B	I
D	A	A	L	V	S	E	R	L	O
R	O	V	E	L	E	N	E	E	N

Additional Words (p. 133)

1. **abortion.** The induced termination of a pregnancy; arrest of development.
2. **celibacy.** The state of not being married; the act of not engaging in sexual intercourse.
3. **esoteric.** Understood by a select few; secret; confidential.
4. **query.** A question; an inquiry; to ask questions about.
5. **improvise.** To make up something on the spur of the moment; to make up out of what is on hand.

Practice for Additional Words (pp. 134–135)

A. (1) d, (2) c, (3) e, (4) b, (5) a.
B. (1) affluent, (2) query, (3) celibacy, (4) overt, (5) apt, (6) improvise, (7) lethal, (8) esoteric, (9) abortion, (10) redundant.

Exercise 12 (pp. 135–141)

Practice A

(1) motivate, (2) skeptical, (3) idealist, (4) duration, (5) astute, (6) tedious, (7) anticipate, (8) charisma, (9) reality, (10) cope.

Practice B

(1) tedious, (2) cope, (3) anticipate, (4) charisma, (5) idealist, (6) astute, (7) duration, (8) skeptical, (9) reality, (10) motivate.

Practice C

(1) skeptical, (2) inevitable, (3) spouse, (4) infidelity, (5) astute, (6) charisma, (7) motivated, (8) idealist, (9) coping, (10) anticipated.

Additional Words (pp. 139–140)

1. **morale.** The mental or emotional condition of a person or a group; a sense of common purpose with respect to a group.
2. **compensate.** To be equivalent to; to make an appropriate counterbalancing payment to; to offset an error, undesired effect, or defect.
3. **delve.** To search deeply; to make a careful or detailed search for information.
4. **deprecate.** To express disapproval of.
5. **austere.** Stern and forbidding in manner and appearance; somber; grave; unadorned; simple.

Practice for Additional Words (pp. 140–141)

A. (1) b, (2) a, (3) d, (4) e, (5) c.
B. (1) morale, (2) improvised, (3) austere, (4) esoteric, (5) deprecated, (6) compensate, (7) delved, (8) query, (9) redundant, (10) apt.

Crossword Puzzle 4 (pp. 141–142)

Word Scramble 4 (pp. 142–143)

(1) appraise, (2) conform, (3) anticipate, (4) crass, (5) tedious, (6) pretense, (7) skeptical, (8) idealist, (9) cope, (10) emulate, (11) gullible, (12) extricate, (13) expend, (14) spouse, (15) awry, (16) astute, (17) remorse, (18) charisma, (19) curt, (20) motivate.

Analogies 4 (pp. 143–144)

(1) spouse, (2) curt, (3) remorseful, (4) plaintiff, (5) gloomy, (6) traditional, (7) crass, (8) controversy, (9) assurance, (10) evaluate, (11) yielding, (12) awe, (13) supposition, (14) infidelity, (15) extra, (16) austere, (17) emulate, (18) actuality, (19) impractical, (20) charisma.

Multiple-Choice Vocabulary Test 4 (pp. 144–146)

Exercise 10

(1) d, (2) d, (3) a, (4) b, (5) d, (6) b, (7) c, (8) d, (9) a, (10) b.

Exercise 11

(11) d, (12) c, (13) b, (14) d, (15) a, (16) c, (17) b, (18) d, (19) b, (20) d.

Exercise 12

(21) c, (22) b, (23) d, (24) c, (25) d, (26) c, (27) d, (28) b, (29) c, (30) c.

True/False Test 4 (p. 147)

(1) F, (2) T, (3) T, (4) T, (5) T, (6) F, (7) T, (8) F, (9) T, (10) F, (11) F, (12) F, (13) F, (14) F, (15) T, (16) F, (17) F, (18) T, (19) F, (20) F.

STOP. Turn to page 148 for the scoring of the tests.

Additional Practice Sets (pp. 148–151)

Additional Practice 1

(1) crass, (2) conform, (3) appraise, (4) controversy, (5) compromise, (6) curt, (7) pretense, (8) emulate, (9) traditional, (10) plaintiff.

Additional Practice 2

(1) guarantee, (2) husband or wife, (3) easily deceived, (4) free, (5) wrong, (6) regret, (7) certain, (8) spend, (9) supposition, (10) unfaithfulness.

Additional Practice 3

(1) idealist, (2) astute, (3) reality, (4) cope, (5) duration, (6) motivate, (7) charisma, (8) anticipate, (9) tedious, (10) skeptical.

CHAPTER SIX

Exercises 13–15

Crossword Puzzle 5

Word Scramble 5

Analogies 5

Multiple-Choice Vocabulary Test 5

True/False Test 5

Scoring of Tests

Additional Practice Sets

Answers

EXERCISE 13

Step I. Vocabulary Words in Sentences

Directions: Sentences using the ten vocabulary words from Exercise 13 follow. See whether you can figure out the meanings of the underlined words from the clues in the sentences. Blanks are provided for your estimates of the definitions. Check your meanings with those in Step 11.

1. True/false exams are more comprehensive than essay exams because you can cover a much larger area on a true/false exam. ____________________
2. Our instructor usually gives us an exam with both objective and subjective questions on it. ____________________; ____________________
3. All our instructor's questions require cognitive ability. ____________________
4. Sometimes our instructor asks us to give a synopsis of something. ____________________
5. When we write papers, we are warned about plagiarism. Our instructor makes a big point about giving proper citations. ____________________; ____________________

6. Our instructor told us that we need to give citations for material, even though we are not using the exact words but are paraphrasing it.

   ____

7. Many of the questions our instructor asks concern the protagonist of a story, novel, or play. We usually have to analyze the main character and explain his or her motives for acting the way he or she does.

   ____

8. When we go over exams, I try to clear up any concepts that I didn't understand or that had previously confused me. ____________________

Step II. Vocabulary Words

1. **citation** (ci · ta · tion) (sī · tā′ shun) *n.* The quoting of a passage, author, book, and so on; a quotation or a reference given as an authority for facts, opinions, and so on; an official summons to appear before a court. *To back up my theory about something, I use a number of* ***citations*** *from well-known authorities in the field.*
2. **cognitive** (cog · ni · tive) (kog′ ni · tiv¢) *adj.* Having to do with thinking, knowing, perception. *Reading is a* ***cognitive*** *act, and, unless thinking is taking place, there is no reading.*
3. **comprehensive** (com · pre · hen · sive) (kom · pre · hen′ siv¢) *adj.* Of large scope; including much; in insurance, covering or providing broad protection against loss; broad. *Our instructor said that our final exam would be a* ***comprehensive*** *one that would include the whole term's work.*
4. **concept** (con · cept) (kon′ sept) *n.* Idea; a thought or notion. *A* ***concept*** *is something that is formed in the mind, and as such it is an abstraction; it is not something that is concrete and can be touched.*
5. **objective** (ob · jec · tive) (ob · jek′ tiv¢) *n.* Purpose, goal, aim; something that one is attempting to achieve. *adj.* Unbiased; not affected by personal feelings or prejudice; based on facts; having to do with a material object rather than with something mental such as an idea or concept. *It is very difficult for anyone to try to be totally* ***objective*** *because not one of us is totally free from some kind of bias.*
6. **paraphrase** (par · a · phrase) (par′ a · frāz¢) *n.* A restatement of a text or passage giving the meaning in another form or in other words usually to make the meaning more clear; a rewording. *v.* To reword or restate some-

thing usually for clarity. *Our instructor told us that we need to give citations even when we* ***paraphrase*** *someone's work.*

7. **plagiarism** (pla · gia · rism) (plā′ ja · riz · um) *n.* The act of taking the thoughts, writings, inventions, and so on of another and presenting them as one's own. *When you are writing a report, you should give proper citations so that you will not be suspected of* ***plagiarism.***

8. **protagonist** (prō · tag′ o · nist) *n.* The main character in a novel, story, or play; the leader of or spokesperson for a movement, cause, and so on. *In the play the* ***protagonist*** *was a strong character who seemed to control the destiny of all who came in contact with him.*

9. **subjective** (sub · jec · tive) (sub · jek′ tiv¢) *adj.* Existing in the mind; belonging to the thinking subject rather than to the object thought of; personal; individual thought; influenced by an individual's state of mind. *A* ***subjective*** *test is difficult to grade because different persons grading the same exam will usually grade the exam differently, based on the individual person's bias.*

10. **synopsis** (syn · op · sis) (si · nop′ sis) *n.* (*pl.* **ses**) A brief statement giving a general view of a passage, story, play, and so on; a summary. *My English literature instructor requires that we write a* ***synopsis*** *of ten plays that we have read during the semester.*

Special Notes

The terms *subjective* and *objective* are opposites. Things that can be directly observed are objective; opinions and ideas that obviously cannot be directly observed are subjective. Objective examinations such as true/false and multiple-choice tests have only one correct answer, whereas subjective tests such as essay exams have more than one correct answer and are consequently more difficult to grade.

In grammar, the term *objective* is used to refer to the objective case. Something is in the objective case if it receives the action. Example: He loves *her. Her* is in the objective case. *Her* is the object of *love. Her* is receiving the action.

In grammar, the term subjective is used to refer to the subjective case. In the sentence "He loves her," *He* is in the subjective case. It is about *He* that something is said. *He* is the subject doing the action.

Concept is also defined as "a group of stimuli with common characteristics." According to this definition *John* or *Mary* is not a concept, but *men* or *women* is a concept.

Step III. Practice

A. Directions: The words from Exercise 13 follow. Match the words with their meanings.

________	1. comprehensive	a. the main character in a story
________	2. citation	b. the act of taking the writings of another and presenting them as one's own
________	3. plagiarism	c. existing in the mind
________	4. objective	d. a summary
________	5. subjective	e. a restatement of a passage
________	6. cognitive	f. based on facts
________	7. concept	g. of large scope
________	8. synopsis	h. having to do with thinking
________	9. paraphrase	i. idea
________	10. protagonist	j. the quoting of a passage

STOP. Check answers at the end of Chapter Six (p. 186).

B. Directions: Ten sentences follow. Define the underlined word.

1. It's very difficult to be <u>objective</u> about things that directly affect you or your family. ____________________
2. In the television movie, when the reporter was found guilty of <u>plagiarism</u> and was fired from his job, he tried to prove that he had not passed off someone else's work as his own. ____________________
3. The <u>protagonist</u> in the story was a self-made man who didn't allow anyone or anything to stand in his way. ____________________
4. The question that you ask is a very <u>subjective</u> one that I find difficult to answer because my answer would be influenced by how I feel at the moment. ____________________
5. Our instructor told us that it's better to <u>paraphrase</u> other people's writings rather than to give the exact words. ____________________
6. Of course, when other people's ideas are used or if <u>citations</u> are given, their sources should be presented. ____________________
7. Whenever I write a <u>synopsis</u> of something, it helps me to remember the material better. ____________________

8. Concepts such as truth, goodness, and beauty are difficult to explain because they are abstractions. ____________________

9. Cognitive ability is required for reading comprehension. ____________________

10. I feel that your plan is too comprehensive and that you should try to streamline it a bit. ____________________

STOP. Check answers at the end of Chapter Six (p. 186).

C. Directions: Each sentence has a missing word. Choose the word that *best* completes the sentence. There are more words in the list than you need.

Word List

paraphrase, concept, citation, synopsis, subjective, objective, comprehensive, plagiarism, cognitive, protagonist, tedious, gullible, assumption, expend, awry, idealist, reality.

1. A person who has had brain damage might have difficulty working in areas that require ____________________ ability.
2. That is one of the most ____________________ reports that I have ever seen because it seems to cover everything.
3. I don't think it is fair to ask ____________________ questions that deal with feelings or opinions on an exam.
4. I prefer ____________________ questions that require one correct answer.
5. Persons are always taking advantage of Fred because he is so ____________________.
6. The ____________________ in the novel was a young man who had difficulty relating to his father; however, after his father died, the young man gained a better understanding of him.
7. When you write a short ____________________ of a story, you should give the main idea of the story and the most important details that help to develop the main idea.
8. Although this is ____________________ work, I can't afford to quit.
9. Things always seem to go ____________________ when you least expect them to.
10. I will not ____________________ any more energy in that direction.

STOP. Check answers at the end of Chapter Six (p. 186).

EXTRA WORD POWER

en. To cause to be; make; made of. *En* is placed at the end of an adjective to form verbs. When *en* is used to form verbs from adjectives, it is used to indicate *being, becoming,* or *causing to be.* Examples: *cheap, cheapen*—to make cheap; *red, redden*—to make red; *hard, harden*; *sweet, sweeten*; *bright, brighten*; *ripe, ripen. En* is also placed at the end of nouns to form adjectives. When *en* is used to form adjectives from nouns, it is used to indicate "made of or resembling." Examples: *ash, ashen*—resembling ashes, or made from the wood of the ash tree; *gold, golden*—made of or containing gold; *wool, woolen*; *earth, earthen*; *wood, wooden.*

ite. A native or inhabitant of; a person associated with; a mineral or a rock substance. *Ite* is found at the end of words. Examples: *New Jerseyite*—a native of New Jersey; *laborite*—a person associated with labor; *graphite*—carbon used in lead pencils; *meteorite*—a rocklike substance that comes from the sky.

Additional Words

From your ability to use context clues, can you figure out the meanings of the following words?

1. **libel** (li · bel) (lī′ bul) *n., v. A number of actors and actresses have sued magazines for* ***libel*** *because the magazines have printed false statements about them.*

 ____

2. **feasible** (fea · si · ble) (fē′ zi · bul) *adj. The students said that they would choose a plan that was the most* ***feasible*** *for the amount of time in which they had to carry it out.*

 ____

3. **ominous** (om′ i · nǿus) *adj. In the film, we knew that something dreadful would happen soon because everyone spoke in such* ***ominous*** *tones; the music was ominous; and even the weather had black ominous clouds.*

 ____

4. **intrinsic** (in · trin · sic) (in · trin′ sik) *adj. Freedom of speech is an* ***intrinsic*** *part of a democracy.*

 ____

5. **extrinsic** (ex • trin • sic) (ek • strin′ sik) *adj. We didn't accomplish very much at the meeting because we spent most of the time discussing* ***extrinsic*** *matters rather than those that were relevant to the meeting.*

____

STOP. Check answers at the end of Chapter Six (p. 186).

Practice for Additional Words

A. Directions: Match each word with the *best* definition.

________ 1. libel	a. practical
________ 2. extrinsic	b. any false or damaging statement about a person
________ 3. intrinsic	c. threatening
________ 4. feasible	d. not belonging to the essential nature of something
________ 5. ominous	e. essential

STOP. Check answers at the end of Chapter Six (p. 186).

B. Directions: Ten sentences containing the meanings of vocabulary words that you have met in this and other exercises follow. Write the word in the blank that *best* fits the meaning of the word or phrase underlined in the sentence.

1. We decided to call off the picnic because of the strong winds and the threatening clouds. ____________________
2. That does not seem to be a very suitable plan for our purposes.
   ____
3. The reporter's question took us by surprise. ____________________
4. When the actor forgot his lines, he had to make up some on the spur of the moment. ____________________
5. I am highly stimulated to achieve and to succeed. ____________________
6. John expects great things to happen in his life. ____________________
7. The fighter said that he had not been under drugs during the fight and that he would sue the person who had made the damaging statement about him.
   ____
8. I don't know what the essential value of that is. ____________________
9. The chairperson said that all discussion should be limited to the matter at hand rather than include unessential matters. ____________________

10. The shrewd lawyer was able to help his client win his case by finding a loophole in the law. ____________

STOP. Check answers at the end of Chapter Six (p. 186).

EXERCISE 14

Step I. Vocabulary Words in Sentences

Directions: Sentences using the ten vocabulary words from Exercise 14 follow. See whether you can figure out the meanings of the underlined words from the clues in the sentences. Blanks are provided for your estimates of the definitions. Check your meanings with those in Step II.

1. My girlfriend and I are just not compatible. We always seem to be in a state of discord rather than harmony. ____________; ____________; ____________
2. We literally cannot agree on anything, and I mean anything. ____________
3. It's probably because we are both such dominant persons. Each one of us seems to want to be in control and to determine what the other should do. ____________
4. Unfortunately for our relationship, we are also very dogmatic persons. We usually state our views as if they were facts rather than opinions. ____________
5. It's amazing that our relationship has been as durable as it has. It really shouldn't have lasted this long. ____________
6. I am not interested in status symbols, but my girlfriend is. I really don't care about my position in relation to others. ____________
7. My girlfriend, on the other hand, is exceedingly interested in prestige and how we stand in the eyes of others. ____________; ____________

Step II. Vocabulary Words

1. **compatible** (com • pat • i • ble) (kom • pat′ i • bul) *adj.* Capable of living in an agreeable manner with another; able to exist together; able to get on well together; capable of orderly operation and integration with other

elements in a system; consistent. *Next semester I am going to room with someone else because my roommate and I are just not* ***compatible.***

2. **discord** (dis · cord) (dis′ kord) *n.* Lack of agreement among persons, groups, or things; difference of opinion; dispute; dissension; disagreement; a confused or harsh mingling of sounds; a din. *If there is a great amount of* ***discord*** *between spouses, the marriage usually ends in divorce.*

3. **dogmatic** (dog · mat · ic) (dog · mat′ ik) *adj.* Asserting opinions as if they were facts; excessively positive in stating opinions; opinionated. *It's difficult to have a discussion with Kevin because he is so* ***dogmatic*** *and overbearing.*

4. **dominant** (dom′ i · nant) *adj.* Ruling; most influential; controlling; exerting authority or influence; occupying a commanding position. *Jim is the most* ***dominant*** *person in our group, and once he makes up his mind about something, you know that everyone will follow him and help him accomplish it.*

5. **durable** (du · ra · ble) (dur′ a · bul) *adj.* Lasting; highly resistant to wear; capable of existing a long time; not easily worn out. *My jeans are so* ***durable*** *that they usually last for about five years.*

6. **exceedingly** (ex · ceed · ing · ly) (ek · sē′ ding · lē) *adv.* Extremely. *John is an* ***exceedingly*** *happy young man because he just won a scholarship to the college of his choice.*

7. **harmony** (har · mo · ny) (har′ mo · nē) *n.* Agreement; getting along well together; accord; agreement of feelings, ideas, or actions; in music, the sounding together of two or more tones. *In our community there is so much disagreement among the elected officials that it seems impossible to achieve* ***harmony*** *among them.*

8. **literally** (lit · er · al · ly) (lit′ er · al · lē) *adv.* Word for word; in a strict sense; actually. *After what happened, he* ***literally*** *went out of his mind; that is, he had a nervous breakdown.*

9. **prestige** (pres · tige) (pres · tēzh′) *n.* High reputation or influence gained from success; the power to command respect, admiration, and so on from a group; status. *We couldn't believe that a man with such* ***prestige*** *would lend his name to such a disreputable firm.*

10. **status** (stā′ tus) *n.* The position of an individual in relation to another or others; the condition of; the state of; social standing; high standing; prestige. *The protagonist in the play was always trying to improve his* ***status,*** *but for every step forward that he made, he went three steps backward.*

Step III. Practice

A. Directions: The words from Exercise 14 follow. Match the words with their meanings.

________	1. compatible	a. extremely
________	2. literally	b. agreement
________	3. dogmatic	c. disagreement
________	4. harmony	d. the power to command respect
________	5. durable	e. the position of an individual in relation to others
________	6. exceedingly	f. ruling
________	7. discord	g. asserting opinions as if they were facts
________	8. prestige	h. lasting
________	9. dominant	i. able to exist together
________	10. status	j. word for word

STOP. Check answers at the end of Chapter Six (p. 186).

B. Directions: Ten sentences containing the meanings of vocabulary words presented in this exercise follow. Choose a word from this exercise that *best* fits the meaning. Put your answer in the blank.

1. I feel that an instructor should present information to students and that he or she should attempt to give both sides of an issue rather than be opinionated. ________________

2. This semester there is so much disagreement among the students in my dormitory that I intend to live off campus next semester.

   ____

3. An environment in which there is accord rather than continuous disagreement will not be found in my home. ________________

4. This has actually been the worst situation I have ever encountered.

   ____

5. My roommate is an extremely nice guy, but he has insomnia, so he never sleeps. ________________

6. We are not able to get on well together because he keeps me up all night, and he burdens me with all his personal problems. ________________

7. My roommate is very concerned about his position in relation to others.

____

8. He likes to be with persons who have the power to command respect.

____

9. I'm an easy fellow to get along with, and I'm not interested in exerting power over anyone; my friend, however, is a controlling person.

____

10. It's easy to see why our friendship was not a lasting one.

____

STOP. Check answers at the end of Chapter Six (p. 187).

C. Directions: There are fifteen scrambled words from this exercise and Exercise 13 in the word list. There are ten definitions. Choose the scrambled word that matches the definition. Unscramble the word, and put it in the blank.

Word List

inantmod, aeudrlb, aromnyh, drcoids, tapmocielb, ssttau, teeirpgs, laaiismpgr, tccnoep, vetieocjb, ysnssiop, godtamci, iealllytr, yleeecxdgni, itonatic.

1. idea ______________
2. actually ______________
3. extremely ______________
4. a quotation given as an authority for facts ______________
5. lasting ______________
6. asserting opinions as if they were facts ______________
7. the power to command respect ______________
8. able to exist together ______________
9. exerting authority or influence ______________
10. disagreement ______________

STOP. Check answers at the end of Chapter Six (p. 187).

EXTRA WORD POWER

demi. Half. *Demi* is found at the beginning of words. Examples: *demitasse*—a small cup of strong black coffee; *demigod*—a mythological being that is partly a god and partly a man.

semi. Half; not fully; partly; occurring twice in a period. *Semi* is found at the beginning of a number of words. Examples: *semicircle*—a half circle; *semimonthly*—occurring twice a month; *semiweekly*—occurring twice a week; *semirigid*—not fully rigid; *semiprivate*—not fully private; *semiyearly*—twice a year; *semiprecious*—having value but not as much as a precious gem; *semiprofessional*—partly professional; *semiskilled*—partly skilled. Can you think of some more words that begin with *semi*?

Additional Words

From your ability to use context clues, can you figure out the meanings of the following words?

1. **placid** (plac • id) (plas′ id) *adj. He has always been such a **placid** fellow that it is hard for me to believe that he was the person responsible for the riot in which three people were hospitalized.*

   ____

2. **ornate** (or • nāte′) *adj. I like modern furniture because it has simple lines and it is functional, but my friend likes French Provincial furniture because it is so **ornate.***

   ____

3. **dire** (dīer) *adj. If we had followed her advice, we would be in **dire** circumstances now.*

   ____

4. **pretentious** (pre • ten • tious) (pre • ten′ shus) *adj. There was one person at the costume ball who wore an exceedingly ornate costume and who behaved in such a **pretentious** manner that you would think she was the Queen of Sheba.*

   ____

5. **poignant** (poign • ant) (poin′ yant) *adj. The movie was filled with many emotional scenes, but the most **poignant** scene concerned the five orphans who refused to be separated.*

   ____

STOP. Check answers at the end of Chapter Six (p. 187).

Practice for Additional Words

A. Directions: Match each word with the *best* definition.

________ 1. placid	a. extreme
________ 2. ornate	b. piercing
________ 3. dire	c. much adorned
________ 4. pretentious	d. calm
________ 5. poignant	e. making claims to importance

STOP. Check answers at the end of Chapter Six (p. 187).

B. Directions: Ten sentences containing the meanings of vocabulary words that you have met in this and other exercises follow. Write the word in the blank that *best* fits the meaning of the word or phrase underlined in the sentence.

1. When the dam broke, the whole town was in terrible danger of being destroyed. ________________
2. It's amazing how Mike, who is usually a very calm fellow, becomes violent when he has had more than two drinks. ________________
3. We feel that this is an essential part of the plan, and we do not want it to be taken out. ________________
4. The reporters had many questions to ask about the unsuccessful mission to free the hostages. ________________
5. Her showy dress was fine for a ball, but it was certainly out of place at the party. ________________
6. Some of the women wore elaborate costumes and behaved in a haughty manner and were making claims to importance. ________________
7. The scene in which the lovers had to say "good-bye" was a piercing one. ________________
8. The rescue attempt was not practical, and it failed. ________________
9. Although my professor is a very severe man, he is fair. ________________
10. The deeper we searched into the mystery, the more confusing and frightening it became. ________________

STOP. Check answers at the end of Chapter Six (p. 187).

EXERCISE 15

Step I. Vocabulary Words in Sentences

Directions: Sentences using the ten vocabulary words from Exercise 15 follow. See whether you can figure out the meanings of the underlined words from the clues in the sentences. Blanks are provided for your estimates of the definitions. Check your meanings with those in Step II.

1. At school I room with a fellow who is the most meticulous person in the world. I'm the extreme opposite, a person who can't be concerned with details. ____________________
2. He can't stand anything being in disarray, so he is constantly picking up after me. I can't stand this. ____________________
3. I have implored him to please leave my things alone, but it is to no avail. ____________________; ____________________
4. He has gone to great extents to try to get me to be less sloppy. ____________________
5. One day he finally became totally fed up and reached his saturation point. ____________________
6. I had been in the room all weekend studying for exams while Jim, my roommate, was away. When Jim came back, the room was piled high with books, papers, clothes, and food. A fetid smell emanated from the room from the rancid butter and other spoiled food. Interestingly, I wasn't aware of this stinking smell until Jim entered the room. ____________________; ____________________; ____________________
7. Jim slowly surveyed the room, shook his head, let out a long, soft whistle, and left. I have never seen him again. ____________________

Step II. Vocabulary Words

1. **avail** (a · vāil′) *v.* To be of use or of value; to be of profit or advantage to; to help; to make use of. *n.* Use; help; benefit. *The firefighters tried to put out the fire before it spread to the neighboring buildings, but their efforts were to no **avail**.*
2. **disarray** (dis · ar · rāy′) *n.* Disorder; confusion; disordered or insufficient dress. *v.* To throw into disorder; to put into confusion. *The robbers left our room in such **disarray** that it took my roommate and me all day to straighten it out.*

3. **emanate** (em′ a • nāte̸) *v.* To come forth; to come out or proceed from a source; to give out. *The leak seemed to* ***emanate*** *from an underground pipe, but the men could not determine which pipe it was.*

4. **extent** (ex • tent) (ek • stent′) *n.* The degree to which something extends; length, area, volume, or scope; magnitude; range. *She went to great* ***extents*** *to try to convince us that she was telling the truth, but the evidence was so strong that nothing she did could convince us of her innocence.*

5. **fetid** (fet′ id) *adj.* Having a heavy offensive smell; stinking; smelling very bad; rancid. *The* ***fetid*** *smell that emanated from the house was so strong that not one of us was able to enter it to get our things.*

6. **implore** (im • plore̸′) *v.* To beg or plead for earnestly or urgently. *The patient* ***implored*** *the nurse to give him something for the pain, but the nurse ignored the man's pleadings because it wasn't time for his medication.*

7. **meticulous** (me • tic • u • lous) (me • tik′ yu • lo̸us) *adj.* Extremely careful and precise; extremely careful about details. *We knew that something was amiss when we saw how Susan looked, because normally she is such a* ***meticulous*** *dresser that not one hair is ever out of place.*

8. **rancid** (ran • cid) (ran′ sid) *adj.* Stale; spoiled; having an unpleasant, stale smell or taste; fetid. *When we were served* ***rancid*** *food in the restaurant after having waited for it for an hour, we were all in a terrible state.*

9. **saturated** (sat • u • rat • ed) (sach′ a • rā • tid) *adj.* Full; soaked thoroughly; wet. *I was so* ***saturated*** *from the rain that I thought I would never dry out.*

10. **survey** (sur • vey) (sur • vā′) *v.* To take a general, broad, or comprehensive view of; to look at, consider, or view as a whole; to determine the area, boundaries, or elevations of land by means of measuring angles and distances. *n.* A general or comprehensive view; a sampling or partial collection of opinions, facts, or figures taken and used to make an approximation of what a complete collection would be; a formal or official inspection or examination of the particulars of something in order to determine conditions, values, and so on. *Our political science instructor asked us if we would help him do a* ***survey*** *of people's opinions on the effectiveness of sex education in the schools.*

Step III. Practice

A. Directions: Each sentence has a missing word. Choose the word that *best* completes the sentence.

Word List

avail, disarray, extent, fetid, emanated, meticulous, rancid, saturated, survey implored.

1. We were asked to what ________________ we would be willing to risk our lives to try to save the others.
2. It's not good to eat food that is ________________ with fat.
3. To save our friend's reputation, we had to find out where the rumor ________________ from, and then we had to find some way to stop it.
4. Opposites must attract if Marsha, who is the most ________________ person I know, is going with George, who is the most disorganized person I know.
5. The parents of the missing child went on national television and ________________ the kidnappers to safely return their child.
6. If butter is left outside too long, it will become ________________.
7. The chemicals gave off an exceedingly ________________ odor.
8. The hostages felt that no efforts would ________________ them now.
9. Before reading a chapter, it's a good idea to ________________ it first.
10. Everything was in such a state of ________________ after the hurricane struck our community that it took us months to clean up, repair the damage, and get back to normal.

STOP. Check answers at the end of Chapter Six (p. 187).

B. Directions: Choose the word from the word list that *best* fits the definition. A word may be used only once.

Word List

avail, disarray, emanate, extent, meticulous, rancid, survey, saturated, fetid, implore.

1. soaked thoroughly ________________
2. spoiled ________________
3. stinking ________________
4. extremely careful and precise ________________
5. length ________________
6. disorder ________________

7. to be of use ____________

8. to view as a whole ____________

9. to come out from a source ____________

10. to beg for ____________

STOP. Check answers at the end of Chapter Six (p. 187).

C. Directions: There are ten words in the Word Square from this exercise and from Exercise 14. Find the ten words and then define each one.

WORD SQUARE

H	A	R	M	O	N	Y	O	L
D	I	S	A	R	R	A	Y	I
E	M	A	N	A	T	E	S	T
D	P	V	N	N	E	T	E	E
I	L	A	F	C	R	O	A	R
R	O	I	O	I	M	P	T	A
E	R	L	G	D	N	R	U	L
S	E	X	T	E	N	T	S	L
D	O	G	M	A	T	I	C	Y

Words *Meanings*

1. ____________
2. ____________
3. ____________
4. ____________
5. ____________
6. ____________
7. ____________
8. ____________
9. ____________
10. ____________

STOP. Check answers at the end of Chapter Six (pp. 187–188).

EXTRA WORD POWER

hemi. Half. *Hemi* is found at the beginning of words. Examples: *hemisphere*—a half sphere or globe; *hemicycle*—a half circle; *hemicerebrum*—the right or left half of the cerebrum (brain).

per. Throughout; through. *Per* is found at the beginning of many words. Examples: *percolate*—to filter through; *persuade*—to win over; *perplex*—to bewilder; *permit*—to allow through; *peruse*—to read through thoroughly; *perfume*—to fill with sweet odor.

Additional Words

From your ability to use context clues, can you figure out the meanings of the following words?

1. **stipulate** (stip · u · late) (stip′ yu · lāt~~e~~) *v.* *The lawyer **stipulated** the terms of the contract and said that his client would not sign it unless all the terms were met.*

   ____

2. **specious** (spe · cious) (spē′ shus) *adj.* *I do not like to debate against Martha because her **specious** arguments always sound logical even though they are not.*

   ____

3. **didactic** (di · dac · tic) (dī · dak′ tik) *adj.* ***Didactic** folktales are supposed to help children learn a moral lesson.*

   ____

4. **entice** (en · tice) (en · tīs~~e~~′) *v.* *In the fairy tale the witch was able to **entice** the children into her house by promising them delicious things to eat.*

   ____

5. **converge** (con · verge) (kon · verj′) *v.* *When the two roads **converged** into one at the crossroad, we met another car and almost had an accident.*

   ____

STOP. Check answers at the end of Chapter Six (p. 188).

Practice for Additional Words

A. Directions: Match each word with the *best* definition.

________ 1. stipulate	a. to tend to meet in a point
________ 2. specious	b. morally instructive
________ 3. didactic	c. deceptive
________ 4. entice	d. to state exactly the conditions
________ 5. converge	e. to attract by offering some reward

STOP. Check answers at the end of Chapter Six (p. 188).

B. Directions: Each sentence has a missing word. Choose the word from the word list that *best* completes the sentence. Some words are from previous exercises.

Word List

esoteric, inevitable, tactful, obfuscate, tenet, didactic, specious, stipulate, entice, converge.

1. We decided to ____________________ all our efforts toward the big celebration.
2. Freedom of speech is a basic ____________________ of our Bill of Rights.
3. Bill always tries to ____________________ the issue by using double talk.
4. There did not seem to be any ____________________ way in which to tell Jim that he didn't make the team.
5. Television commercials try to ____________________ us to buy things.
6. The fable is usually a(n) ____________________ tale.
7. His ____________________ arguments sound so convincing that I am always taken in by them.
8. Some of my professors use such ____________________ terms that I have a lot of difficulty following the lectures.
9. The engineer said that she would ____________________ the exact dimensions that we needed to complete the job.
10. If you continue to neglect yourself as you are now doing, it is ____________________ that you will become ill.

STOP. Check answers at the end of Chapter Six (p. 188).

CROSSWORD PUZZLE 5

Directions: The meanings of a number of the words from Exercises 13–15 follow. Your knowledge of these words will help you solve this crossword puzzle. Note that *combining form* is abbreviated as *comb. f.*

Across

1. Exactly suitable
3. The power to command respect
11. Same as #8 Down
12. ___ Rico
13. Abbreviation for *before noon*
14. To remove from office
16. A way of saying *mother*
17. A small island
18. Past tense ending for regular verbs
19. A boy's name
22. A small word used to make a comparison
23. Same as #1 Down
24. Same as #18 Across
25. A grant of the temporary use of something
26. Same as #1 Down
27. The act of thinking

Down

1. An indefinite article
2. Baked foods with fillings
3. This comes from an infection
4. The straight stalk of tall grass
5. A suffix used to form the comparative
6. Abbreviation for *Saint*
7. A small word indicating direction
8. A personal pronoun
9. Vasco da ___
10. Proceeded from
12. Edgar Allan ___
14. Lack of agreement
15. The act of taking the writings of another
19. A sound made to frighten someone

31. A small word used to indicate a place
32. Abbreviation for *box office*
33. Same as #8 Down
34. Means "to kid"
35. To quote a passage as an authority
37. Elaborately adorned
40. To leave
42. Same as #18 Across
43. To regard with love
44. Moves smoothly as a bird
46. The twentieth letter of the alphabet
47. A place to eat
49. Comb. f. for *to cause to be*
51. Abbreviation for *population*
52. Makes words plural
53. To be of use or of value
55. Agreement

20. Spoiled
21. A small word used to indicate inclusion
22. Same as #1 Down
24. Extreme
25. To print something damaging about someone
28. An interjection
29. Used to form the past participle of many verbs
30. A musical syllable
31. Same as #31 Across
32. This is used for transporting people on water
36. Comb. f. for *a native of*
38. To lower and raise the head as if in agreement
39. A decade is this amount of years
41. Roman numeral *eleven*
44. A color
45. Abbreviation for *Southeast*
48. Abbreviation for *East*
50. Same as #29 Down
51. A way of saying *father*
54. Roman numeral *five*

STOP. Check answers at the end of Chapter Six (p. 188).

WORD SCRAMBLE 5

Directions: Word Scramble 5 is based on words from Exercises 13–15. The meanings are your clues to arranging the letters in correct order.

		Meanings
1. ptcceon	______________	idea
2. sssyoinp	______________	a summary
3. aaiipgrsml	______________	taking the writings of another as one's own
4. iitvengoc	______________	having to do with thinking
5. ioscddr	______________	disagreement
6. ymnohar	______________	agreement

7. bleardu ____________________ lasting
8. citdgoma ____________________ asserting opinions as if facts
9. inamdont ____________________ ruling
10. patbliemco ____________________ able to exist together
11. geitrpse ____________________ the power to command respect
12. ssttau ____________________ the position of an individual in relation to another
13. laaiv ____________________ to be of value
14. ietfd ____________________ smelling very bad
15. ioemplr ____________________ to beg or plead for
16. cidnar ____________________ spoiled
17. tteenx ____________________ length
18. ratsatedu ____________________ soaked thoroughly
19. urvesy ____________________ to take a general view of
20. eiuuomtcsl ____________________ extremely careful and precise

STOP. Check answers at the end of Chapter Six (p. 189).

ANALOGIES 5

Directions: Find the word from the following word list that *best* completes each analogy. There are more words in the list than you need. A word may be used only once.

Word List

length, tight, dry, saturated, discord, internal, objective, subjective, skim, place, mental, bitter, concept, taste, smell, plead, meticulous, please, pleasure, synopsis, reword, terrible, hard, tired, extremely, pleasant, reward, fetid, durable, strange, external, protagonist, dominant, reword, synopsis, reorder, calm, prestige.

1. Arrogant : haughty :: extrinsic : ____________________.
2. Affront : compliment :: objective : ____________________.
3. Optimist : pessimist :: extrinsic : ____________________.
4. Integrate : segregate :: harmony : ____________________.
5. Astute : clever :: paraphrase : ____________________.

6. Crass : sensitive :: saturated : ____________________.

7. Peruse : study :: survey : ____________________.

8. Paradox : contradiction :: idea : ____________________.

9. Changeable : variable :: lasting : ____________________.

10. Initiate : begin :: implore : ____________________.

11. Query : question :: dire : ____________________.

12. Frank : candid :: exceedingly : ____________________.

13. Appraise : estimate :: placid : ____________________.

14. Post : position :: status : ____________________.

15. Curt : rude :: summary : ____________________.

16. Fetid : stinking :: goal : ____________________.

17. Thrifty : economical :: ruling : ____________________.

18. Sedate : calm :: extent : ____________________.

19. Ancient : young :: dry : ____________________.

20. Asset : liability :: sloppy : ____________________.

STOP. Check answers at the end of Chapter Six (p. 189).

MULTIPLE-CHOICE VOCABULARY TEST 5

Directions: This is a test on words in Exercises 13–15. Words are presented according to exercises. *Do all exercises before checking answers.* Underline the meaning that *best* fits the word.

Exercise 13

1. citation
   a. a saying
   b. a quotation
   c. a wise saying
   d. important writings

2. concept
   a. writing
   b. thinking
   c. quotation
   d. idea

3. comprehensive
   a. referring to an exam
   b. referring to insurance
   c. of large scope
   d. understanding

4. cognitive
   a. of large scope
   b. having to do with working
   c. referring to an idea
   d. having to do with thinking

5. objective
a. biased
b. goal
c. belonging to the mind
d. having to do with mental things

6. paraphrase
a. taking the writings of another as one's own
b. a rewording of the writings of another
c. repeating the writings of another
d. using someone's work

7. subjective
a. existing in the mind
b. referring to a person
c. unbiased
d. a brief statement

8. synopsis
a. a restatement
b. a quotation
c. a brief statement
d. a summary of a passage

9. protagonist
a. a fighter
b. a novelist
c. the main character
d. a person of worth

10. plagiarism
a. a leader for a cause
b. the rewriting of something
c. a liar
d. the act of taking the writings of another as one's own

Exercise 14

11. discord
a. agreement
b. opinions
c. disagreement
d. lasting

12. dogmatic
a. positive
b. asserting opinions as if fact
c. negative
d. differing of opinions

13. durable
a. opinionated
b. agreement
c. lasting
d. disagreement

14. dominant
a. opinionated
b. ruling
c. agreement
d. saying a lot

15. harmony
a. disagreement
b. agreement
c. having to do with art
d. opinionated

16. exceedingly
a. hardly
b. possibly
c. extremely
d. trying

17. literally
a. having to do with writing
b. word for word
c. able to read
d. able to write

18. compatible
a. capable
b. able to live together
c. able to survive
d. living together

19. prestige
a. the occupation of a person
b. power to command respect
c. powerful
d. a successful person

20. status
a. success
b. a powerful person
c. the state of
d. leadership

Exercise 15

21. avail
a. to plead for
b. to confuse
c. to be of use
d. to use up

22. extent
a. length
b. space
c. position
d. purpose

23. fetid
a. an odor
b. smelling
c. stinking
d. offensive

24. emanate
a. to bring up
b. to proceed from
c. to plead
d. to supply

25. saturated
a. full of fat
b. able to hold
c. wet
d. smelling

26. meticulous
a. not in order
b. extremely
c. full of moisture
d. careful

27. rancid
a. full of moisture
b. full of fat
c. spoiled
d. running over

28. disarray
a. helplessness
b. a wrong arrangement
c. an arrangement
d. disorder

29. survey
a. to hold
b. a general view of
c. to compose
d. general

30. implore
a. to view
b. to hold
c. to leave
d. to beg

TRUE/FALSE TEST 5

Directions: This is a true/false test on Exercises 13–15. Read each sentence carefully. Decide whether it is true or false. Put a *T* for *true* or an *F* for *false* in the blank. The number after the sentence tells you if the word is from Exercise 13, 14, or 15.

________ 1. *Concept* and *cognitive* are synonyms. 13

________ 2. Something comprehensive is usually narrow. 13

_________ 3. Plays do not have protagonists. 13

_________ 4. Something fragile is durable. 14

_________ 5. If something is feasible, you probably would not be able to accomplish it. 13

_________ 6. The president of a company would have status. 14

_________ 7. Rancid food tastes good. 15

_________ 8. Persons would enjoy living next to a fetid stream. 15

_________ 9. When you survey something, you study it in depth. 15

_________ 10. Something in a state of discord would be confusing. 14

_________ 11. If you are saturated with something, you have probably had enough of it. 15

_________ 12. A dominant person would try to control the situation. 14

_________ 13. If you have prestige, you will be respected. 14

_________ 14. Someone who is meticulous would probably be careless. 15

_________ 15. A dogmatic person is usually open-minded. 14

_________ 16. Writers use citations to lend authority to their works. 13

_________ 17. a didactic story is usually intended to teach a lesson. 15

_________ 18. Someone who is in dire trouble does not have too much to worry about. 14

_________ 19. Compatible persons are always in a state of discord. 14

_________ 20. A placid person is usually violent. 14

STOP. Check answers for both tests at the end of Chapter Six (p. 189).

SCORING OF TESTS

Multiple-Choice Vocabulary Test		True/False Test	
Number Wrong	*Score*	*Number Wrong*	*Score*
0–2	Excellent	0–1	Excellent
3–5	Good	2–3	Good
6–8	Weak	4–5	Weak
Above 8	Poor	Above 5	Poor
Score _________		Score _________	

1. If you scored in the excellent or good range on *both tests,* you are doing well. Go on to Chapter Seven.

2. If you scored in the weak or poor range on either test, look below and follow directions for Additional Practice. Note that the words on the tests are arranged so that you can tell in which exercise to find them. This will help you if you need additional practice.

ADDITIONAL PRACTICE SETS

A. Directions: Write the words you missed on the tests from the three exercises in the space provided. Note that the tests are presented so that you can tell to which exercises the words belong.

Exercise 13 Words Missed

1. ____________________ 6. ____________________
2. ____________________ 7. ____________________
3. ____________________ 8. ____________________
4. ____________________ 9. ____________________
5. ____________________ 10. ____________________

Exercise 14 Words Missed

1. ____________________ 6. ____________________
2. ____________________ 7. ____________________
3. ____________________ 8. ____________________
4. ____________________ 9. ____________________
5. ____________________ 10. ____________________

Exercise 15 Words Missed

1. ____________________ 6. ____________________
2. ____________________ 7. ____________________
3. ____________________ 8. ____________________
4. ____________________ 9. ____________________
5. ____________________ 10. ____________________

B. Directions: Restudy the words that you have written down on this page. Do Step I and Step II for those you missed. Note that Step I and Step II are on the following pages:

Exercise 13—pp. 157–159.

Exercise 14—pp. 164–165.

Exercise 15—pp. 170–171.

C. Directions: Do Additional Practice 1 on this page if you missed words from Exercise 13. Do Additional Practice 2 on this page and p. 185 if you missed words from Exercise 14. Do Additional Practice 3 on p. 185 if you missed words from Exercise 15. Now go on to Chapter Seven.

Additional Practice 1 for Exercise 13

Directions: Eight sentences follow. Define the underlined word.

1. Since reading is a thinking act, it requires cognitive ability.

   ____

2. Our final exam is a comprehensive one that goes back to the beginning of the term. ____________________
3. Our instructor asked us to paraphrase a history passage.

   ____

4. On our exam we had to give a synopsis of the story. ____________________
5. We feel that your opinions should be less subjective and more objective.

   ____________________; ____________________

6. The protagonist in the play is in practically every scene in the play.

   ____

7. That is a difficult concept for young children to grasp. ____________________
8. I try to give proper and adequate citations for my papers so that no one will accuse me of plagiarism. ____________________; ____________________

STOP. Check answers at the end of Chapter Six (p. 189).

Additional Practice 2 for Exercise 14

Directions: Ten sentences follow. Define the underlined word.

1. Mrs. Brown is the dominant spouse in the marriage. ____________________
2. Mrs. Brown is a dogmatic person, but her husband is more prone to put off making a judgment until he has facts. ____________________
3. Mr. and Mrs. Brown always seem to be in a state of discord because they can't agree on anything. ____________________

4. I couldn't live like Mr. and Mrs. Brown because I need harmony in my life. ____________

5. Their life seems to be an exceedingly difficult one. ____________

6. My brother has the prestige of a well-known firm behind him. ____________

7. He has gained status by belonging to that club. ____________

8. Married persons should be compatible. ____________

9. That is literally the worst film that I have ever seen. ____________

10. My jeans are so durable that they will last for another ten years. ____________

STOP. Check answers at the end of Chapter Six (pp. 189–190).

Additional Practice 3 for Exercise 15

Directions: Ten sentences follow. Define the underlined word.

1. I will not be able to avail myself of your services. ____________

2. In the film the man implored his jailer for mercy. ____________

3. His office is in such disarray that you can't find anything there. ____________

4. The rancid butter ruined my sandwich. ____________

5. It is probably not good to eat food that is saturated with lots of fat. ____________

6. Although she is very meticulous about her work, she is quite careless about her dress. ____________

7. The fetid pond is being drained. ____________

8. To what extent will you pursue the matter? ____________

9. Our instructor asked us to survey the chapter before we read it. ____________

10. A person is probably not able to emanate happiness unless he or she is happy. ____________

STOP. Check answers at the end of Chapter Six (p. 190).

ANSWERS: Chapter Six

Exercise 13 (pp. 157-164)

Practice A

(1) g, (2) j, (3) b, (4) f, (5) c, (6) h, (7) i, (8) d, (9) e, (10) a.

Practice B

(1) unbiased, (2) the act of taking the writings of another as one's own, (3) main character, (4) personal, (5) reword, (6) quotations, (7) summary, (8) Ideas, (9) Thinking, (10) broad.

Practice C

(1) cognitive, (2) comprehensive, (3) subjective, (4) objective, (5) gullible, (6) protagonist, (7) synopsis, (8) tedious, (9) awry, (10) expend.

Additional Words (pp. 162-163)

1. **libel.** A written or printed statement or picture that tends to damage a person's reputation or hold him or her up to public ridicule; any false or damaging statement about a person; to write or print something damaging about someone; to write or say something false or damaging about a person.
2. **feasible.** Capable of being accomplished or brought about; practical; suitable.
3. **ominous.** Threatening; of a bad or evil omen; unfavorable.
4. **intrinsic.** Belonging to the essential nature of a thing; essential; belonging to or lying within a given part; inherent; innate.
5. **extrinsic.** Not forming part of or belonging to a thing; originating from or on the outside; external; not an essential part of something.

Practice for Additional Words (pp. 163-164)

A. (1) b, (2) d, (3) e, (4) a, (5) c.
B. (1) ominous, (2) feasible, (3) query, (4) improvise, (5) motivated, (6) anticipates, (7) libeled, (8) intrinsic, (9) extrinsic, (10) astute.

Exercise 14 (pp. 164-169)

Practice A

(1) i, (2) j, (3) g, (4) b, (5) h, (6) a, (7) c, (8) d, (9) f, (10) e.

Practice B

(1) dogmatic, (2) discord, (3) harmony, (4) literally, (5) exceedingly, (6) compatible, (7) status, (8) prestige, (9) dominant, (10) durable.

Practice C

(1) (tccnoep) concept, (2) (iealllytr) literally, (3) (yleeecxdgni) exceedingly, (4) (itonatic) citation, (5) (aeudrlb) durable, (6) (godtamci) dogmatic, (7) (teeirpgs) prestige, (8) (tapmocielb) compatible, (9) (inantmod) dominant, (10) (drcoids) discord.

Additional Words (p. 168)

1. **placid.** Calm; quiet; peaceful.
2. **ornate.** Overly decorated; elaborately decorated; flashy; showy.
3. **dire.** Extreme; terrible; having terrible or dreadful consequences; dreadful.
4. **pretentious.** Making claims to importance; making usually unjustified or excessive claims to importance.
5. **poignant.** Appealing to the emotions; piercing; painfully affecting the feeling; deeply affecting.

Practice for Additional Words (p. 169)

A. (1) d, (2) c, (3) a, (4) e, (5) b.
B. (1) dire, (2) placid, (3) intrinsic, (4) queries, (5) ornate, (6) pretentious, (7) poignant, (8) feasible, (9) austere, (10) delved.

Exercise 15 (pp. 170–175)

Practice A

(1) extent, (2) saturated, (3) emanated, (4) meticulous, (5) implored, (6) rancid, (7) fetid, (8) avail, (9) survey, (10) disarray.

Practice B

(1) saturated, (2) rancid, (3) fetid, (4) meticulous, (5) extent, (6) disarray, (7) avail, (8) survey, (9) emanate, (10) implore.

Practice C

(1) harmony—agreement, (2) disarray—disorder, (3) emanate—to come forth, (4) extent—length, (5) dogmatic—opinionated, (6) dire—terrible, (7) implore—to beg, (8) avail—to be of use, (9) rancid—spoiled, (10) literally—actually.

WORD SQUARE

H	A	R	M	O	N	Y	O	L
D	I	S	A	R	R	A	Y	I
E	M	A	N	A	T	E	S	T
D	P	V	N	N	E	T	E	E
I	L	A	F	C	R	O	A	R
R	O	I	O	I	M	P	T	A
E	R	L	G	D	N	R	U	L
S	E	X	T	E	N	T	S	L
D	O	G	M	A	T	I	C	Y

Additional Words (p. 174)

1. **stipulate.** To state exactly the agreement; to require as an essential condition in making an agreement.
2. **specious.** Deceptive; not genuine; having a false look of truth.
3. **didactic.** Morally instructive; intended to teach.
4. **entice.** To attract by offering some reward; to tempt; to lure.
5. **converge.** To tend to meet in a point; to tend to a common result; to come together in a common interest.

Practice for Additional Words (p. 175)

A. (1) d, (2) c, (3) b, (4) e, (5) a.

B. (1) converge, (2) tenet, (3) obfuscate, (4) tactful, (5) entice, (6) didactic, (7) specious, (8) esoteric, (9) stipulate, (10) inevitable.

Crossword Puzzle 5 (pp. 176–177)

	1 A	2 P	T	■	3 P	4 R	5 E	6 S	7 T	8 I	9 G	10 E
	■	11 I	■	12 P	U	E	R	T	O	■	13 A	M
	14 D	E	15 P	O	S	E	■	■	■	■	16 M	A
	17 I	S	L	E	■	18 D	■	19 B	20 R	21 I	A	N
22 A	S	■	23 A	■	24 D	■	25 L	O	A	N	■	26 A
■	27 C	28 O	G	29 N	I	30 T	I	O	N	■	31 A	T
32 B	O	■	33 I	■	34 R	I	B	■	35 C	36 I	T	E
37 O	R	38 N	A	39 T	E	■	40 E	41 X	I	T	■	42 D
43 A	D	O	R	E	■	44 G	L	I	D	E	45 S	■
46 T	■	47 D	I	N	48 E	R	■	■	■	■	49 E	50 N
■	51 P	■	52 S	■	■	53 A	54 V	A	I	L		
55 H	A	R	M	O	N	Y						

Word Scramble 5 (pp. 177–178)

(1) concept, (2) synopsis, (3) plagiarism, (4) cognitive, (5) discord, (6) harmony, (7) durable, (8) dogmatic, (9) dominant, (10) compatible, (11) prestige, (12) status, (13) avail, (14) fetid, (15) implore, (16) rancid, (17) extent, (18) saturated, (19) survey, (20) meticulous.

Analogies (pp. 178–179)

(1) external, (2) subjective, (3) internal, (4) discord, (5) reword, (6) dry, (7) skim, (8) concept, (9) durable, (10) plead, (11) terrible, (12) extremely, (13) calm, (14) prestige, (15) synopsis, (16) objective, (17) dominant, (18) length, (19) saturated, (20) meticulous.

Multiple-Choice Vocabulary Test 5 (pp. 179–181)

Exercise 13

(1) b, (2) d, (3) c, (4) d, (5) b, (6) b, (7) a, (8) d, (9) c, (10) d.

Exercise 14

(11) c, (12) b, (13) c, (14) b, (15) b, (16) c, (17) b, (18) b, (19) b, (20) c.

Exercise 15

(21) c, (22) a, (23) c, (24) b, (25) c, (26) d, (27) c, (28) d, (29) b, (30) d.

True/False Test 5 (pp. 181–182)

(1) F, (2) F, (3) F, (4) F, (5) F, (6) T, (7) F, (8) F, (9) F, (10) T, (11) T, (12) T, (13) T, (14) F, (15) F, (16) T, (17) T, (18) F, (19) F, (20) F.

STOP. Turn to page 182 for the scoring of the tests.

Additional Practice Sets (pp. 183–185)

Additional Practice 1

A. (1) thinking, (2) broad, (3) reword, (4) summary, (5) personal, unbiased, (6) main character, (7) idea, (8) quotations, the act of using someone's writings as one's own.

Additional Practice 2

(1) ruling, (2) opinionated, (3) disagreement, (4) accord, (5) extremely,

(6) reputation, (7) social standing, (8) able to get along together, (9) actually, (10) highly resistant to wear.

Additional Practice 3

(1) benefit, (2) begged, (3) confusion, (4) spoiled, (5) thoroughly soaked, (6) careful, (7) stinking, (8) length, (9) view as a whole, (10) to give out.

CHAPTER SEVEN

Exercises 16–18

Crossword Puzzle 6

Word Scramble 6

Analogies 6

Multiple-Choice Vocabulary Test 6

True/False Test 6

Scoring of Tests 6

Additional Practice Sets

Answers

EXERCISE 16

Step I. Vocabulary Words in Sentences

Directions: Sentences using the ten vocabulary words from Exercise 16 follow. See whether you can figure out the meanings of the underlined words from the clues in the sentences. Blanks are provided for your estimates of the definitions. Check your meanings with those in Step II.

1. The politician's popularity began to <u>wane</u> when he started to <u>deviate</u> from what his <u>constituents</u> wanted to hear. The voters in the politician's district only wanted to hear about things that would directly benefit them.
______________; ______________; ______________

2. The politician <u>espoused</u> views that sounded like <u>heresy</u> in the district. He told the people the truth about the economy and what would have to be done to conquer the <u>rampant</u> inflation that was overtaking the country.
______________; ______________; ______________

3. He was <u>adamant</u> about the fact that everyone was <u>vulnerable</u> in a state of runaway inflation. He was very firm in his belief that eventually everyone would be hurt by inflation. ______________; ______________

4. He condemned those persons who acted as though they were in a state of lethargy or indifference. ____________________

5. He called on all his voters to assess their situations carefully and then to try to figure out what they could do to try to control inflation.

____

Step II. Vocabulary

1. **adamant** (ad′ a • mant) *adj.* Unyielding; firm; immovable; stubborn. *Joe said that he was* ***adamant*** *about not attending the dinner and that nothing anyone said could change his mind.*

2. **assess** (as̸ • ses̸′) *v.* To estimate the value of property, income, and so on for tax purposes; to fix or determine the amount of a tax, damages, a fine, and so on; to impose a tax on; to estimate the value or merit of something; to evaluate. *At school each student is* ***assessed*** *a certain amount of money that goes to the student government.*

3. **constituent** (con • stit • u • ent) (kon • stich′ ū • ent) *adj.* Forming a necessary part; serving as part of a whole; component. *n.* Someone represented by another; client; one who elects or assists in electing another as his or her representative; a voter. *The congressman said that he had to vote against the bill because he had promised his* ***constituents*** *that he would.*

4. **deviate** (de • vi • ate) (dē′ vē • āte̸) *v.* To turn aside or wander from the right or common path; to turn aside from a course, truth, line, way, and so on; to differ from the norm. *n.* (dē′ vē • it) A person whose moral and social standards differ from the norm or from the accepted moral and social standards; a sexual pervert. *We decided to* ***deviate*** *from our usual way of doing things for a change, so we went dancing instead of bowling.*

5. **espouse** (es • pouse) (e • spouze̸′) *v.* To adopt or support some cause, view, and so on; to make one's own; to give one's loyalty and support to; to advocate. *The cause that he* ***espoused*** *was not a very popular one, but that did not stop this courageous man from supporting it.*

6. **heresy** (her • e • sy) (her′ e • sē) *n.* An opinion or doctrine not in agreement with accepted doctrine; any belief or theory that varies strongly from accepted or established beliefs, customs, and so on. *In the Middle Ages many persons were tried for* ***heresy*** *because their religious views deviated from those of the Church.*

7. **lethargy** (leth • ar • gy) (leth′ ar • jē) *n.* The state and quality of being drowsy and dull; sluggish inactivity; apathy. *No one believed that he was the same fellow who had climbed the highest mountain range in the world*

because he now was merely a shadow of his former self, and each day he was sinking into a deeper state of ***lethargy.***

8. **rampant** (ram′ pant) *adj.* Growing without any check; widespreading; violent in action or spirit; raging; angry; excited. *In the monster film, the trees and animals grew to incredible sizes, and, unless their* ***rampant*** *growth was stopped, they would conquer the world.*

9. **vulnerable** (vul • ner • a • ble) (vul′ ner • a • bul) *adj.* Unprotected from danger; capable of being hurt; open to attack, criticism, temptation, and so on. *Everyone is* ***vulnerable*** *in one way or another, so an opponent tries to find what the person's weak spot is and then uses that to attack the person.*

10. **wane** (wānɇ) *v.* To decrease gradually in size, amount, intensity, or degree; to decline; to show a decrease, such as from full moon to new moon. *n.* A gradual declining; in or on the wane, growing less. *Although many diseases such as polio and smallpox are on the* ***wane,*** *others such as heart disease and cancer are on the increase.*

Step III. Practice

A. Directions: Each sentence has a nonsense word. Choose a word from the word list that *best* replaces the nonsense word.

Word List

wane, espouse, rampant, adamant, vulnerable, heresy, deviate, constituent, assess, lethargy.

1. Before our parents' divorce, they had to planken everything that they jointly owned. ____________________
2. It's one thing to dreidle such beautiful principles, but it's another thing to carry them out. ____________________
3. I try very hard not to mandle from my routine. ____________________
4. The strikers were onert about the fact that they would not return to work until they had received the package that they were asking for.

   ____
5. A proin wrote a letter of complaint to his congressman.

   ____
6. It was considered breim for anyone to question the board's decision.

   ____
7. Fear is loment in our neighborhood because of the number of muggings, murders, and rapes. ____________________

8. At the beginning of spring, my friends and I can barely drag ourselves to class because we are in a state of hertomy. ____________________

9. The value of the dollar is on the ftot, but the value of gold is on the rise. ____________________

10. The boxer's manager told his boxer to keep his guard up so that he wouldn't be blont to the opponent's jab. ____________________

STOP. Check answers at the end of Chapter Seven (p. 220).

B. Directions: The words from Exercise 16 follow. Match the words with their meanings.

1. lethargy	____________________	a. voter
2. wane	____________________	b. an opinion not in agreement with accepted doctrine
3. adamant	____________________	c. unprotected from danger
4. constituent	____________________	d. sluggish inactivity
5. espouse	____________________	e. widespreading
6. assess	____________________	f. to decline
7. heresy	____________________	g. unyielding
8. deviate	____________________	h. evaluate
9. rampant	____________________	i. to differ from the norm
10. vulnerable	____________________	j. to adopt or support some cause

STOP. Check answers at the end of Chapter Seven (p. 221).

C. Directions: Define the underlined word(s) in each of the following sentences.

1. Pat said that she would change her plans as Susan was adamant about not changing hers. ____________________

2. Before an election politicians usually court their constituents. ____________________

3. Once I make up my mind to follow a certain course, it is difficult for me to deviate from it. ____________________

4. Galileo was tried for heresy because he espoused the view that the sun and not the earth was the center of the universe. ____________________ ; ____________________

5. After I flunked three exams in one week, I decided to assess my study habits. ____________________

6. There is sure to be conflict in a relationship in which one person's desire for the other is on the increase, whereas the other person's desire is on the wane. ____________________

7. The rampant growth of the plants in our backyard has dwarfed our house and made it appear as though we live in a jungle. ____________________

8. Each of us has an Achilles' heel in that each of us is vulnerable in one way or another. ____________________

9. When my friend went on a crash diet and lost twenty pounds in a short period of time, she found it difficult to engage in any activities, and she went into such a state of lethargy that we insisted she see a doctor.

____

STOP. Check answers at the end of Chapter Seven (p. 221).

EXTRA WORD POWER

ana. Denoting a collection of materials on a certain subject; the sayings of and writings on a specific subject. When *ana* is found at the end of a noun, it tells us that it has to do with a collection of materials on that topic. For example, *Americana* has to do with historical materials relating to America.

ana. Upward; according to; back; again; thoroughly. *Ana* has different meanings when it appears at the beginning of words. Examples: *analogy*—according to a logical inference; **anachronism**—backward or reversed in time or anything out of its proper time frame; *anatomy*; *analysis.*

Additional Words

From your ability to use context clues, can you figure out the meanings of the following words?

1. **impediment** (im • ped′ i • ment) *n. A well-known entertainer's fear of flying is an* ***impediment*** *that she will have to overcome because she has to commute from California to New York twice a month.*

____

2. **eclectic** (ec • lec • tic) (e • klek′ tik) *adj. I use an* ***eclectic*** *approach in teaching because I feel that it is better to use the best from a variety of approaches rather than just one approach.*

____

3. **intrepid** (in • trep′ id) *adj. The **intrepid** men volunteered to rescue the hostages, even though they knew that the rescue mission was very dangerous and that they themselves might lose their lives.*

____

4. **itinerant** (ī • tin′ er • ant) *adj. The children of **itinerant** workers usually have a difficult life, and they usually do not do very well in school because they do not stay very long in one place.*

____

5. **propriety** (pro • pri • e • ty) (pro • prī′ e • tē) *n. Years ago, children were looked upon as miniature adults, and **propriety** demanded that they not speak unless they were spoken to.*

____

STOP. Check answers at the end of Chapter Seven (p. 221).

Practice for Additional Words

A. Directions: Match each word with the *best* definition.

________	1. impediment	a. fearless
________	2. eclectic	b. conforming to existing customs
________	3. intrepid	c. traveling from place to place
________	4. itinerant	d. choosing what appears to be the best from many sources
________	5. propriety	e. a hindrance

STOP. Check answers at the end of Chapter Seven (p. 221).

Practice for Additional Words

B. Directions: Each sentence has a nonsense word. Choose a word from the word list to replace the nonsense word. Some of the words are from previous exercises.

Word List

impediment, itinerant, intrepid, eclectic, propriety, entice, stipulate, placid, dire, compatible.

1. No one had to <u>moim</u> Jennifer into trying out for the play.

   ____

2. Studies have shown that drinking and driving are not <u>jerble</u>.

   ____

3. Graimen demands that we do not attend unless we have a special invitation. ____________________

4. An arible person is one who draws information from many sources rather than from just one. ____________________

5. The child does not speak because she has a speech loinem. ____________________

6. The graimel firefighters rushed into the blazing building to try to rescue the two children who were still in the building. ____________________

7. I think that we can do what you want if you broinen everything for us. ____________________

8. A writer worked for one year as an erton worker so that he could record his experiences in a book. ____________________

9. That child is so letnen that at times I feel like pinching her to see if that will stir her. ____________________

10. Only under hert circumstances will I resort to borrowing money from you. ____________________

STOP. Check answers at the end of Chapter Seven (p. 221).

EXERCISE 17

Step I. Vocabulary Words in Sentences

Directions: Sentences using the ten vocabulary words from Exercise 17 follow. See whether you can figure out the meanings of the underlined words from the clues in the sentences. Blanks are provided for your estimates of the definitions. Check your meanings with those in Step II.

1. She was at the pinnacle of her career in advertising when she suddenly acquired a conscience. It seemed ironic that, now that she had reached the top, she wasn't sure that this was what she wanted. ____________________; ____________________

2. She had always had contempt for those soft-hearted persons who had scruples. ____________________; ____________________

3. She had never worried before about the fact that commercials tend to exploit people. People who make commercials know that we are vulnerable and they take advantage of our vulnerability. ____________________

4. Obese people, thin people, all people seem to be diet conscious, and persons making the commercials know this. ____________________

5. Persons in advertising use propaganda techniques to try to get us to buy products. ____________________

6. The fact that firms spend millions of dollars on commercials each year attests to their effectiveness. ____________________

7. Because commercials run almost incessantly, products become very well known, and persons feel left out if they don't own those products.

____

8. Ms. Swanson may be at the pinnacle of her career, but to stay there she will have to put a leash on her conscience to restrain it. ________________ .

Step II. Vocabulary Words

1. **attest** (at̸ • test′) *v.* To say positively that something is true, correct, or genuine; to certify that something is true by signature or oath; to bear witness to; to testify to. *At the trial the witness **attested** to the fact that she had seen the defendant at the murder scene at nine o'clock.*

2. **contempt** (con • tempt) (kon • tempt′) *n.* The act of despising; the feeling that an act, person, or thing is low or worthless; scorn; disdain. *We had great **contempt** for the person who had beaten and robbed the poor blind man.*

3. **exploit** (ex • ploit) (eks′ ploit) *v.* To turn to economic use; to take advantage of; to make use of unjustly for one's own advantage. *n.* Deed; act (especially a daring deed or act); feat. *It took me a long time to find out that Beth was **exploiting** our friendship by using my name to get to meet certain people.*

4. **incessantly** (in • ces • sant • ly) (in • ses′ s̸ant • lē) *adv.* Continuing without interruption; continually. *When the bells continued to ring **incessantly**, everyone ran to the center of town to find out what had happened.*

5. **ironic** (i • ron • ic) (ī • ron′ ik) *adj.* Characterized by the use of words to mean the opposite of their literal meaning; characterized by an event that is opposite to what would be expected or what usually occurs. *It was certainly **ironic** that the firehouse should catch on fire while the firefighters were busy putting out a fire two miles away.*

6. **obese** (ō • bēse̸′) *adj.* Extremely fat; corpulent. *It used to be difficult for **obese** persons to get employment, but more employers are hiring very fat people today because it is illegal to discriminate against them.*

7. **pinnacle** (pin • na • cle) (pin′ n̸a • kul) *n.* The highest point; any tall, pointed formation, such as a mountain peak. *Does anyone know when he or she has reached the **pinnacle** of success or fame?*

8. **propaganda** (prop • a • gan′ da) *n.* Information or ideas systematically spread to promote or injure a cause, group, or nation; the deliberate

spreading of opinions, ideas, or information. *Schools today are helping children to be better discerners of information by teaching them how to spot the use of* ***propaganda*** *in commercials.*

9. **restrain** (re • strāin′) *v.* To hold back from action; to keep in check or under control; to deprive of freedom or liberty. *The police were unable to* ***restrain*** *the crowd from attacking the killer of three small children.*

10. **scruple** (scru • ple) (skrū′ pul) *n.* A moral or ethical consideration that keeps one from doing something. *A person without* ***scruples*** *is dangerous because he or she acts out of need or desire and does not worry about the ethics or morality of the situation.*

Step III. Practice

A. Directions: The words from Exercise 17 follow. Match the words with their meanings.

1. contempt	a. the highest point
2. exploit	b. continuing without interruption
3. propaganda	c. extremely fat
4. pinnacle	d. to say positively that something is true
5. obese	e. to hold back from action
6. ironic	f. to take advantage of
7. restrain	g. the deliberate spreading of ideas
8. scruple	h. scorn
9. incessantly	i. a moral consideration that keeps someone from doing something
10. attest	j. characterized by the use of words to mean the opposite of their literal meaning

STOP. Check answers at the end of Chapter Seven (p. 221).

B. Directions: Each sentence has a missing word. Choose the word that *best* completes the sentence. There are more words in the list than you need.

Word List

contempt, ironic, attest, heresy, rampant, adamant, assess, restrain, scruples, exploit, propaganda, incessantly, obese, wane, heresy, pinnacle.

1. The police were unable to ____________________ the crowd when the famous rock group arrived at the theater.

2. Throughout the ages leaders of nations have used ____________________ to stir people to their point of view.

3. People who are power-hungry usually ____________________ others for their own gain.

4. Not one of us was able to ____________________ the truth of the statement because not one of us was present when the statement was made.

5. At the circus I felt sorry for the ____________________ lady and did not feel that she should be part of the circus.

6. It is ____________________ that the sugar king is unable to eat anything with sugar in it.

7. I have a sister who speaks ____________________, and when she is around no one can get in one word.

8. All the students in the class had ____________________ for the student who violated the honor code.

9. In an interview the star said that, as far as she was concerned, she had reached the ____________________ of her career.

10. Anyone with any ____________________ would not work for such an unethical firm.

STOP. Check answers at the end of Chapter Seven (p. 221).

C. Directions: Ten sentences follow. Define the underlined word.

1. It was obvious from her behavior that she didn't have one scruple and that she would do anything to get her way. ____________________

2. It's ironic that the doctor got a heart attack on his way to see a patient who had just suffered a heart attack. ____________________

3. "I do not feel that I have reached the pinnacle of my career," said the executive to the reporter. ____________________

4. After I fell and hit my head, my ears rang incessantly for three days, and the doctors did not know how to stop the ringing. ____________________

5. A witness was offered a bribe to attest to the fact that the defendant was with him at the time of the robbery. ____________________

6. A television show recently explored the feelings of the obese person, and some of the findings were quite surprising. ____________________

7. Many times reporters exploit a tragedy in order to get a human interest story. ____________________

8. During World War II, Hitler used propaganda to get the German people to follow him. ____________________

9. It was difficult for me to restrain myself from crying when I saw the condition of the three children and how their parents had abused them.

____

10. I had contempt for the parents of the children who had been so badly mistreated. ______________________

STOP. Check answers at the end of Chapter Seven (p. 221).

EXTRA WORD POWER

ate. To become; to cause to become; to form or produce; to make; to arrange for. *Ate* is usually found at the end of verbs or nouns. Examples of verbs: *evaporate*—to become vapor; *maturate*—to become mature; *validate*—to make valid; *abbreviate*—to make brief; *activate*—to cause to become active; *ulcerate*; *pollinate*; *salivate*; *exaggerate*; *enervate*; *educate.* Examples of nouns: *potentate, deviate* (both a noun and a verb), *mandate* (both a noun and a verb), *electorate, magistrate.*

ly. Like; characteristic of; every; in the manner of. When *ly* is used to form adjectives from nouns, it usually means "like, characteristic of, or every." Examples: *hourly*—every hour; *daily*—every day; *quarterly*—every quarter; *monthly*—every month; *yearly*—every year; *manly*—like a man; *womanly*—like a woman; *saintly*—like a saint; *queenly*—like a queen; *fatherly*—like a father. When *ly* is added to the end of adjectives to form adverbs, it usually means "in the manner of or characteristic of." Examples: *gladly, happily, merrily, cheerfully, justly, friendly, nicely, sadly, literally.*

Additional Words

From your ability to use context clues, can you figure out the meanings of the following words?

1. **enervate** (en′ er • vāt~~e~~) *v. I was so* ***enervated*** *after taking all my finals that I literally collapsed.*

____

2. **placate** (pla • cate) (plā′ kāt~~e~~) *v. It was difficult to* ***placate*** *the victims' families because complaints had been made about the gas leak weeks ago, but nothing had been done to take care of the condition.*

____

3. **latent** (lā′ tent) *adj. In the film, the protagonist has **latent** powers that no one knows about, and it is only when the protagonist is in danger that these powers reveal themselves.*

____

4. **glib** (glib) *adj. The woman who was arrested was so **glib** that not only had she talked many people out of their money, but she almost talked the police out of arresting her.*

____

5. **empirical** (em • pir • i • cal) (em • pir′ i • kal) *adj. A good scientist usually relies on both **empirical** and theoretical knowledge.*

____

STOP. Check answers at the end of Chapter Seven (p. 222).

Practice for Additional Words

A. Directions: Match each word with the *best* definition.

________	1. enervate	a. relying upon observation
________	2. empirical	b. speaking too smoothly to be sincere
________	3. glib	c. to soothe the anger of
________	4. latent	d. to deprive of strength
________	5. placate	e. present, but not active

STOP. Check answers at the end of Chapter Seven (p. 222).

B. Directions: Each sentence has a missing word. Choose the word that *best* completes the sentence. There are more words in the list than you need.

Word List

enervate, constraints, arrogant, vestige, thrifty, replenish, improvise, esoteric, deprecate, morale, austere, glib, latent, empirical, placate.

1. The spokesperson for the neighborhood organization said that the only way that the city could ________________ the people in the neighborhood was by reinstalling a police officer on the beat.
2. Jim is such a(n) ________________ talker that he could probably talk you out of the shirt on your back.
3. The police said that they needed ________________ evidence to prove that a crime had taken place.

4. If no _________________ were put on me, I said that I would take the job.

5. My friend and I are not compatible when it comes to money because he's a spendthrift, whereas I'm a very _________________ person.

6. Even though they have gone through a great deal, their _________________ has remained high.

7. I wonder if criminals have special _________________ characteristics that are sparked or ignited when they are in certain situations.

8. Running ten miles will certainly _________________ even a hearty person.

9. Unless they _________________ our supplies soon, we will run out of everything.

10. The marchers held signs to _________________ the building of the waste disposal plant in their community.

STOP. Check answers at the end of Chapter Seven (p. 222).

EXERCISE 18

Step I. Vocabulary Words in Sentences

Directions: Sentences using the ten vocabulary words from Exercise 18 follow. See whether you can figure out the meanings of the underlined words from the clues in the sentences. Blanks are provided for your estimates of the definitions. Check your meanings with those in Step II.

1. When I learned that my <u>prospective</u> boss had been a former classmate of mine, I was a little upset. _________________

2. Actually, I was more than a little upset. I was green with envy and <u>livid</u>. _________________

3. The reason for my anger was that this former classmate of mine was a <u>conniver</u> and one of the most unscrupulous individuals that I had ever met. He was always involved in some form of <u>intrigue</u>, and he was always taking credit for other people's work. _________________; _________________

4. He used to <u>feign</u> illness in order to get out of doing something that he didn't want to do. At first we all used to feel sorry for him because we thought that he was really ill, but we soon caught on. _________________

5. The thing that was so incredible was that he was able to <u>beguile</u> so many

of us. He just seemed to be able to deceive us, one after the other, by using his charm. __________

6. After the personnel manager told me who my prospective boss would be if I took the job, I tried to maintain my equanimity. I certainly did not want to lose my composure. __________

7. I'm usually not a very taciturn person, and I'm noted for being a great conversationalist, but the mention of my former classmate's name made me speechless. __________

8. The personnel director asked me whether I felt all right. I must have looked as though I was in a stupor. __________

9. I realized that, in the state I was in, I would make some very caustic remarks soon, which would under the circumstances be highly unprofessional. Rather than lowering myself by making bitter remarks about my former classmate, I told the personnel director that I had to leave and that I would probably take employment elsewhere. __________

Step II. Vocabulary Words

1. **beguile** (be · gu̸īle̸′) *v.* To deceive; to influence by deceit; to cheat; to charm or wile away pleasantly. *At the amusement park, we were **beguiled** by all the people selling their wares, the rides, and other attractions.*

2. **caustic** (caus · tic) (ko′ stik) *adj.* Able to burn, eat away, or dissolve by chemical action; cutting; stinging; biting; sarcastic. *Her **caustic** remarks made everyone realize that she was still very angry and that she had not been placated.*

3. **conniver** (con · niv · er) (kon̸ · nīv′ er) *n.* A person who closes his or her eyes to wrongdoing; a person who gives aid to wrongdoing by helping the wrongdoing secretly or by not telling of the wrongdoing. *I wouldn't trust him because he is a known **conniver** who has been involved in a number of secret schemes.*

4. **equanimity** (e · qua · nim · i · ty) (ek · wa · nim′ i · tē) *n.* The quality of being calm or even-tempered; composure; evenness of mind; balance. *Even under the greatest stress, our teacher, Mrs. Brown, always maintained her **equanimity**.*

5. **feign** (fān) *v.* To pretend; to make believe; to put on a false appearance of; to represent falsely; to invent. *He always **feigned** ignorance whenever I asked him questions about his friend's background because he thought that I was working for the police, and he wanted to protect his friend.*

6. **intrigue** (in · trigue) (in · trēgu̸e̸′) *n.* A secret or underhanded scheme; a

secret love affair. *There was always intrigue going on at the palace, and it seemed as if the king was the last one to know about it.*

7. **livid** (liv′ id) *adj.* Discolored by bruising; ashen; pale; extremely angry; furious. *When she heard how the conniver had tricked her, she was* ***livid*** *with rage.*
8. **prospective** (pro • spec • tive) (pro • spek′ tive̸) *adj.* Likely to come about; probable; expected; likely to be or become. *The doctor told the* ***prospective*** *mother that she would probably have twins.*
9. **stupor** (stū′ por) *n.* A dazed condition; the lessening or loss of the power to feel; a state of extreme sluggishness or lack of feeling resulting often from stress or shock. *After Jane's last final, she appeared to be in a* ***stupor.***
10. **taciturn** (tac • i • turn) (tas′ i • turn) *adj.* Untalkative; uncommunicative; inclined to silence. *Everyone was very surprised when my usually* ***taciturn*** *friend offered to make a speech in honor of the occasion.*

Step III. Practice

A. Directions: Ten sentences containing the meanings of vocabulary presented in Exercise 18 follow. Choose the word that *best* fits the meaning of the word or phrase underlined in the sentence. There are more words in the list than you need.

Word List

contempt, obese, propaganda, scruples, prospective, equanimity, stupor, conniver, livid, intrigue, beguile, taciturn, feign, caustic, exploit, wane, deviate, rampant.

1. Even though a sickout is not technically a strike, it has the force of a strike, so on a specified day, the workers agreed to pretend illness and stay home from work. ____________________
2. She tried to deceive him into thinking that she was in love with him.

   ____
3. Even the most poised chairperson's composure was broken when the waiter dropped the whole tray of food on her honored guest.

   ____
4. Most persons try to stay out of Sandra's way because she has a sharp tongue, and her biting remarks remain with you for a long time.

   ____
5. Jane was furious when she heard that she had been tricked by an amateur.

   ____

6. When we learned about the underhanded scheme in which our company was involved because they wanted to get the government contract, we were shocked. ______________

7. My boss is a person who closes his eyes to wrongdoing, and it doesn't seem to bother him one bit, but I am not that kind of person.

____

8. When we saw the man lying on the ground in a dazed condition, we called for an ambulance. ______________

9. My friend Jim is extremely talkative, and my friend Fred is completely untalkative; however, they get along very well together. ______________

10. I was exceedingly embarrassed and upset when I learned that someone had been poking fun at my probable boss. ______________

STOP. Check answers at the end of Chapter Seven (p. 222).

B. Directions: In the Word Rectangle there are twelve words from Exercises 16, 17, and 18. Find the words and match them with their correct meanings. Note that there are *more* meanings than words. If there is no word in the rectangle for a meaning, write *none,* and give the word.

WORD RECTANGLE

C	A	U	S	T	I	C	O	P
A	E	S	T	U	P	O	R	R
E	Q	U	A	L	A	N	A	O
B	U	F	E	I	G	N	M	S
E	A	O	W	O	I	I	P	P
G	N	M	A	E	R	V	A	E
U	I	N	N	I	O	E	N	C
I	M	A	E	A	N	R	T	T
L	I	V	I	D	I	O	M	I
E	T	A	O	U	C	I	E	V
A	Y	S	C	R	U	P	L	E

Meanings *Words*

1. very fat ______________
2. underhanded scheme ______________

3. characterized by an event that is opposite to what would be expected ____________
4. the highest point ____________
5. a moral consideration that keeps someone from doing something ____________
6. probable ____________
7. to pretend ____________
8. composure ____________
9. furious ____________
10. a dazed condition ____________
11. to deceive ____________
12. biting ____________
13. untalkative ____________
14. someone who closes his or her eyes to wrongdoing ____________
15. to decline ____________
16. to say positively that something is true ____________
17. scorn ____________
18. continually ____________
19. to keep in check ____________
20. growing without any check ____________

STOP. Check answers at the end of Chapter Seven (p. 222).

C. Directions: Each sentence has a missing word. Choose the word that *best* completes the sentence.

Word List

beguile, conniver, intrigue, feign, equanimity, livid, caustic, prospective, stupor, taciturn.

1. The James Bond films involve foreign ____________.
2. No one can upset Mrs. Green's ____________ except her husband.
3. To survive, the agent had to ____________ death.
4. She was ____________ when she heard that someone else had been chosen to go in her place after she had worked so hard to get the invitation.

5. The consumer agency accused the company of using ________________ compounds in their cleaning fluids.

6. Every company usually has at least one ________________ who is always willing to do anything for money.

7. Everyone was shocked when sweet, shy Mrs. Brown was arrested for spying at our company, because she was in line to be our ________________ boss.

8. Mrs. Brown was a(n) ________________ person who spoke to hardly anyone, but she was very competent.

9. It's amazing that she was able to ________________ us for so long.

10. When we found out about Mrs. Brown, some of us looked as though we were in a(n) ________________ .

STOP. Check answers at the end of Chapter Seven (p. 223).

EXTRA WORD POWER

be. Thoroughly; all around; to make. *Be* is usually found at the beginning of verbs and makes them more intense or stronger. Examples: *begrudge*—to thoroughly envy; *belittle*—to make or cause a person to seem small; *bewilder*; *bewitch*; *bemoan*; *belabor*; *befriend*; *betray*; *becloud*; *bewail*; *beguile*.

ob. Against; toward; to; on; over. *Ob* is found at the beginning of a number of words. Examples: *obstacle*—something that stands in the way of; *obscure*—to darken; *obscene*—against decency; *oblige*—to bind to.

Additional Words

From your ability to use context clues, can you figure out the meanings of the following words?

1. **obtrusive** (ob • trū′ siv~~e~~) *adj.* *I was very embarrassed when one of the people sitting at my table behaved in such an* ***obtrusive*** *manner that other people in the restaurant turned to stare at us.*

____

2. **bizarre** (bi • zar~~re~~′) *adj.* *The child's* ***bizarre*** *behavior frightened the parents, for their child had always been a very normal child who had never behaved in an odd or strange manner.*

____

3. **expedient** (ex • pe • di • ent) (ek • spē′ dē • ent) *adj. What she did was **expedient**, but in the long run it will prove to have been the wrong thing to have done.*

___

4. **predatory** (pred • a • to • ry) (pred′ a • tor • ē) *adj. Mark, like **predatory** animals, preys on others for his own gain.*

___

5. **pragmatist** (prag′ ma • tist) *n. I have always been a **pragmatist**, and as such I believe strongly that, if something works, it's good.*

___

STOP. Check answers at the end of Chapter Seven (p. 223).

Practice for Additional Words

A. Directions: Match each word with the *best* definition.

________	1. obtrusive	a. odd
________	2. bizarre	b. a person who believes in the practical consequences of things
________	3. expedient	c. undesirably noticeable or showy
________	4. predatory	d. characterized by a tendency to injure others for one's own gain
________	5. pragmatist	e. characterized by what is suitable or convenient for a particular occurrence

STOP. Check answers at the end of Chapter Seven (p. 223).

B. Directions: In the following sentences, give the meaning that *best* fits the underlined word.

1. The most expedient thing at the moment is to clip this together, but tomorrow I'll have it properly mended. ________________

2. I have seen some strange things in my life, but his behavior is by far the most bizarre. ________________

3. I feel that I have some latent ability, but when will it come out? ________________

4. Jane's obtrusive behavior embarrassed everyone in her midst. ________________

5. Carol said that, as a pragmatist, she had no intention of working on anything that did not have some practical application. ________________

6. The plan is <u>feasible</u>, and it should be accomplished in the time that we have allotted. ____________________

7. The hawk is a <u>predatory</u> bird. ____________________

8. The father said that he would not <u>waive</u> his rights to see the children. ____________________

9. He is as <u>variable</u> as the weather in the Northeast. ____________________

10. We told our supplier that, unless he could <u>expedite</u> the delivery of the goods to us, we would have to go to another supplier. ____________________

STOP. Check answers at the end of Chapter Seven (p. 223).

Lack of word meanings can be painful.

CROSSWORD PUZZLE 6

Directions: The meanings of a number of the words from Exercises 16–18 follow. Your knowledge of these words will help you solve this crossword puzzle. Note that *combining form* is abbreviated as *comb. f.*

Across

1. Story
5. At that time
9. Within easy reach
14. Same as #2 Down
15. Same as #4 Down
17. Strangely beautiful
19. A grain
21. To quote
23. Opponent
24. Same as #2 Down
25. Crazy
27. Same as #5 Down
28. Abbreviation for *harbor*
29. Abbreviation for *detail*
30. Abbreviation for *class*
31. Abbreviation for *right side*
33. Abbreviation for *company*
34. Evaluate
37. Same as #22 Down
38. Region around the North Pole
40. Frighten
42. A dazed condition
44. An Asiatic tree
45. A waste piece of cloth
46. Same as #16 Down
47. To make the natural noise of an insect in motion
48. A weapon
50. Abbreviation for *Latin*
51. Same as #22 Down
52. You do this when you're sleepy
55. A conjunction
56. Appropriate
57. Same as #16 Down
58. Homonym of *two*
60. Stubborn
64. Abbreviation for *National League*
65. Elevated railroad
66. Antonym of *off*
67. To go to ruin
68. Antonym of *exit*
71. Past tense ending for regular verbs
72. To pretend

Down

1. The act of being considerate
2. An indefinite article
3. Sluggish inactivity
4. A female sheep
5. Abbreviation for *tablespoon*
6. A belief that varies from established beliefs
7. All buildings have these
8. Abbreviation for *November*
9. Natural elevation of earth
10. Abbreviation for *alternating current*
11. Used to form the part participle of many verbs
12. Perform
13. Orange-fleshed sweet potato
16. Comb. f. for *out of*
18. Untalkative
20. Unspoken
22. A personal pronoun
24. Haughty
26. Easily taught
29. To protect
32. Moral considerations that keeps one from doing something
35. Abbreviation for *Senior*
36. "Yes" in Spanish
38. Abbreviation for *Associated Press*
39. Same as #5 Down
40. Lacking freshness or originality
41. Abbreviation for *each*
42. A young hog
43. A sound that indicates a hesitation
49. Abbreviation for *New Testament*
53. Same as #2 Down
54. To decrease gradually in size
59. Ancient
61. People who are not compatible usually do this
62. A man who lives in a monastery

74. Homonym of *know*
75. Used to form plurals
76. Same as #11 Down
77. The third Gospel in the New Testament
79. Abbreviation for *and so on*
81. Useless
82. To turn aside or prevent from acting

63. Dogma
66. A small word
69. A short informal letter
70. Abbreviation for *recipe*
73. Sick
76. Abbreviation for *name unknown*
78. Past tense ending for regular verbs
80. Abbreviation for *credit*

STOP. Check answers at the end of Chapter Seven (p. 223).

WORD SCRAMBLE 6

Directions: Word Scramble 6 is based on the words from Exercises 16–18. The meanings are your clues to arranging the letters in correct order.

		Meanings
1. tanmarp	________________	growing without any check
2. enwa	________________	to decrease gradually in size
3. tanmaad	________________	unyielding
4. ssssae	________________	evaluate
5. eehrsy	________________	any belief that varies from established beliefs
6. seseoup	________________	to adopt or support some cause
7. tttsae	________________	to say positively that something is true
8. iicron	________________	use of words to mean the opposite of their literal meaning
9. eeosb	________________	extremely fat
10. toilpex	________________	to take advantage of
11. riastern	________________	to hold back from action
12. eupscrl	________________	a moral consideration that keeps someone from doing something
13. ttmncpoe	________________	the act of despising
14. lecannip	________________	the highest point

15. eignf ______________________ to pretend

16. iivld ______________________ ashen

17. sortup ______________________ a dazed condition

18. turnitac ______________________ untalkative

19. icaustc ______________________ biting

20. lebeiug ______________________ to deceive

STOP. Check answers at the end of Chapter Seven (p. 224).

ANALOGIES 6

Directions: Find the word from the following word list that *best* completes each analogy. There are more words in the list than you need. A word may be used only once.

Word List

affluent, equanimity, disagreement, happy, wordy, placid, livid, biting, help, impediment, lethargy, feeling, power, husband, help, feign, prospective, proper, brother, contempt, save, pervert, spouse, adamant, obese, wane, exploit, evaluate, rampant, taciturn, espouse, attest, constituent.

1. Drizzle : downpour :: plump : ______________________.
2. Ornate : showy :: voter : ______________________.
3. Sister : sibling :: wife : ______________________.
4. Jeopardy : danger :: pretend : ______________________.
5. Plain : ornate :: yielding : ______________________.
6. Apt : suitable :: assess : ______________________.
7. Beguile : deceive :: caustic : ______________________.
8. Concise : verbose :: talkative : ______________________.
9. Fat : obese :: angry : ______________________.
10. Sedate : calm :: deed : ______________________.
11. Infidelity : faithfulness :: poor : ______________________.
12. Intrepid : fearless :: scorn : ______________________.
13. Rancid : spoiled :: widespreading : ______________________.
14. Optimist : pessimist :: deny : ______________________.

15. Entice : lure :: apathy : ______________________.

16. Diligent : hardworking :: probable : ______________________.

17. Astute : clever :: composure : ______________________.

18. Inclination : leaning :: hindrance : ______________________.

19. Futile : useless :: deviate : ______________________.

20. Subjective : objective :: wax : ______________________.

STOP. Check answers at the end of Chapter Seven (p. 224).

MULTIPLE-CHOICE VOCABULARY TEST 6

Directions: This is a test on words in Exercises 16–18. Words are presented according to exercises. *Do all exercises before checking answers.* Underline the meaning that *best* fits the word.

Exercise 16

1. adamant
   a. yielding
   b. friendly
   c. stubborn
   d. angry

2. assess
   a. praise
   b. add
   c. figure out
   d. evaluate

3. constituent
   a. someone represented by another
   b. a person running for office
   c. a leader
   d. a member of Congress

4. deviate
   a. at the norm
   b. to roam
   c. to change
   d. to wander from what is right

5. espouse
   a. to advocate
   b. to be married
   c. a husband or wife
   d. to adopt

6. heresy
   a. an opinion
   b. an opinion not in agreement with established ones
   c. a favorable opinion
   d. an opinion in agreement with established ones

7. lethargy
   a. without sleep
   b. sluggish inactivity
   c. fearful
   d. restless state

8. rampant
   a. a long path
   b. able to be checked
   c. widespreading
   d. useless

9. vulnerable
   a. protected from danger
   b. capable of being hurt
   c. difficult to get to
   d. ready to hurt

10. wane
   a. to decline
   b. referring to the moon
   c. to increase
   d. illuminating

Exercise 17

11. attest
   a. to test
   b. to try to help
   c. to speak at a trial
   d. to testify

12. contempt
   a. disagreement
   b. refusal to speak to
   c. scorn
   d. yelling at

13. exploit
   a. to help
   b. to encourage
   c. to take advantage of
   d. referring to economics

14. incessantly
   a. sudden interruptions
   b. continually
   c. intermission
   d. not continual

15. ironic
   a. referring to opposites
   b. funny opposites
   c. words that mean the opposite of their literal meaning
   d. words that confuse

16. obese
   a. growing a lot
   b. very fat
   c. plump
   d. pleasingly plump

17. pinnacle
   a. a tall building
   b. referring to height
   c. the highest point
   d. anything pointed

18. propaganda
   a. incidental spreading of ideas
   b. ideas in conflict
   c. ideas
   d. deliberate spreading of ideas

19. restrain
   a. to give liberty to
   b. to strain
   c. to work against
   d. to keep in check

20. scruple
   a. an unethical consideration
   b. an immoral consideration
   c. any consideration
   d. a moral consideration that keeps one from doing something

Exercise 18

21. beguile
   a. to cheat
   b. to confuse
   c. to tease
   d. to play with

22. caustic
   a. the result
   b. sarcastic
   c. bitter tasting
   d. mean

23. conniver
a. a helpful person
b. a criminal
c. a person who aids wrongdoing
d. a businessman

24. equanimity
a. unbalanced
b. able to judge
c. equal
d. composure

25. feign
a. a believer
b. to pretend
c. to play games
d. to worry

26. intrigue
a. a battle
b. a social affair
c. a problem
d. a secret scheme

27. livid
a. referring to the liver
b. ashen
c. referring to color
d. alive

28. prospective
a. future husband
b. unlikely
b. referring to a prospect
d. probable

29. stupor
a. a dazed condition
b. not intelligent
c. not well
d. in a coma

30. taciturn
a. communicative
b. untalkative
c. friendly
d. unfriendly

TRUE/FALSE TEST 6

Directions: This is a true/false test on Exercises 16–18. Read each sentence carefully. Decide whether it is true or false. Put a *T* for *true* or an *F* for *false* in the blank. The number after the sentence tells you if the word is from Exercise 16, 17, or 18.

________ 1. A person who is adamant usually gives in easily. 16

________ 2. Politicians try to court their constituents. 16

________ 3. Criminals deviate from the norm. 16

________ 4. A glib person can easily talk himself or herself out of almost anything. 17

________ 5. When someone attests to something, he or she usually doesn't believe it is true. 17

________ 6. It would be considered ironic if the firehouse caught on fire while the firefighters were busy putting out another fire. 17

________ 7. A person in a stupor would probably have difficulty recalling things. 18

_________ 8. Your prospective partner is the one you will probably not get. 18

_________ 9. An obese person is not corpulent. 17

_________ 10. A secret love affair would involve intrigue. 18

_________ 11. When you are at the pinnacle of your career, you are at the bottom. 17

_________ 12. When the bells rang incessantly, they stopped ringing every few minutes. 17

_________ 13. When you are livid, you are probably very calm. 18

_________ 14. If the growth of plants is rampant, you would probably want to fertilize the plants to stimulate growth. 16

_________ 15. A person would not feel very active if he or she were in a state of lethargy. 16

_________ 16. A vulnerable person usually gets hurt. 16

_________ 17. A person with scruples is usually highly unethical. 17

_________ 18. A taciturn person is gregarious. 18

_________ 19. When the moon wanes, it shows an increasing illuminated area. 16

_________ 20. Propaganda is only used to injure a cause. 17

STOP. Check answers for both tests at the end of Chapter Seven (p. 224).

SCORING OF TESTS

Multiple-Choice Vocabulary Test

Number Wrong	*Score*
0–2	Excellent
3–5	Good
6–8	Weak
Above 8	Poor
Score _________	

True/False Test

Number Wrong	*Score*
0–1	Excellent
2–3	Good
4–5	Weak
Above 5	Poor
Score _________	

1. If you scored in the excellent or good range on *both tests,* you are doing well. *You have now completed the work in this text.*

2. If you scored in the weak or poor range on either test, turn to the next page and follow directions for Additional Practice. Note that the words on the tests are arranged so that you can tell in which exercise to find them. This will help you if you need additional practice.

ADDITIONAL PRACTICE SETS

A. Directions: Write the words you missed on the tests from the three exercises in the space provided. Note that the tests are presented so that you can tell to which exercises the words belong.

Exercise 16 Words Missed

1. ________________	6. ________________
2. ________________	7. ________________
3. ________________	8. ________________
4. ________________	9. ________________
5. ________________	10. ________________

Exercise 17 Words Missed

1. ________________	6. ________________
2. ________________	7. ________________
3. ________________	8. ________________
4. ________________	9. ________________
5. ________________	10. ________________

Exercise 18 Words Missed

1. ________________	6. ________________
2. ________________	7. ________________
3. ________________	8. ________________
4. ________________	9. ________________
5. ________________	10. ________________

B. Directions: Restudy the words that you have written down on this page. Do Step I and Step II for those you missed. Note that Step I and Step II are on the following pages:

Exercise 16—pp. 191–193.

Exercise 17—pp. 197–199.

Exercise 18—pp. 203–205.

C. Directions: Do Additional Practice 1 on p. 219 if you missed words from Exercise 16. Do Additional Practice 2 on pp. 219–220 if you missed words from Exercise 17. Do Additional Practice 3 on p. 220 if you missed words from Exercise 18.

Additional Practice 1 for Exercise 16

Directions: Ten sentences containing the meanings of vocabulary presented in Exercise 16 follow. See if you can figure out what the word is.

1. Since we are going to sell our house, we need to have it evaluated.
   ____
2. I can't belong to that club because they advocate views that I do not like.
   ____
3. The workers were unyielding in their demands. ____________________
4. The voters in the congressman's district said that they would not vote for him. ____________________
5. She always puts herself in a position where she is capable of being hurt.
   ____
6. There are some persons who never wander from the right path.
   ____
7. Every spring I seem to go into a state of sluggish inactivity.
   ____
8. Any opinion that strongly varies from established beliefs is frowned upon by my colleagues. ____________________
9. Unless the widespreading growth of the weeds is checked, they will overtake my lawn. ____________________
10. His interest in her decreased gradually as she became more and more difficult to live with. ____________________

STOP. Check answers at the end of Chapter Seven (p. 224).

Additional Practice 2 for Exercise 17

Directions: Ten sentences follow. Define the underlined word.

1. The noise continued incessantly with no relief in sight. ____________________
2. He reached the pinnacle of his career in record time. ____________________
3. The witness refused to attest to an important statement.
   ____
4. It's ironic that the shoemaker's child has torn shoes. ____________________

5. In the film, the manager was exploiting all his clients. ______________

6. It's probably a myth that obese people are cheerful and jolly.

____

7. I have contempt for anyone who behaves in such a distasteful manner.

____

8. Many leaders use propaganda to get the people to follow them.

____

9. In the film, the boxer's manager had no scruples about what he was doing.

____

10. At the end of the film, it was difficult for the clients to restrain themselves from murdering their manager. ______________

STOP. Check answers at the end of Chapter Seven (p. 225).

Additional Practice 3 for Exercise 18

Directions: The words from Exercise 18 follow. Match the words with their meanings.

________	1. beguile	a. composure
________	2. livid	b. untalkative
________	3. feign	c. a secret love affair
________	4. conniver	d. in a dazed state
________	5. caustic	e. to pretend
________	6. taciturn	f. probable
________	7. prospective	g. to deceive
________	8. equanimity	h. a person who closes his or her eyes to wrongdoing
________	9. stupor	i. furious
________	10. intrigue	j. biting

STOP. Check answers at the end of Chapter Seven (p. 225).

ANSWERS: Chapter Seven

Exercise 16 (pp. 191–197)

Practice A

(1) assess, (2) espouse, (3) deviate, (4) adamant, (5) constituent, (6) heresy, (7) rampant, (8) lethargy, (9) wane, (10) vulnerable.

Practice B

(1) d, (2) f, (3) g, (4) a, (5) j, (6) h, (7) b, (8) i, (9) e, (10) c.

Practice C

(1) unyielding, (2) voters, (3) wander, (4) any belief that is not in accord with established beliefs; advocated, (5) evaluate, (6) decline, (7) widespreading, (8) capable of being hurt, (9) apathy.

Additional Words (pp. 195-196)

1. **impediment.** A hindrance; an obstruction; some physical defect that retards speech; a speech disorder.
2. **eclectic.** Choosing what appears to be the best from many sources; choosing from various sources; not following any one system.
3. **intrepid.** Fearless; brave; courageous; bold.
4. **itinerant.** Traveling from place to place; a person who travels from place to place.
5. **propriety.** Conforming to existing customs; the quality or state of being proper; the standard of what is socially correct; correctness.

Practice for Additional Words (pp. 196-197)

A. (1) e, (2) d, (3) a, (4) c, (5) b.
B. (1) entice, (2) compatible, (3) Propriety, (4) eclectic, (5) impediment, (6) intrepid, (7) stipulate, (8) itinerant, (9) placid, (10) dire.

Exercise 17 (pp. 197-203)

Practice A

(1) h, (2) f, (3) g, (4) a, (5) c, (6) j, (7) e, (8) i, (9) b, (10) d.

Practice B

(1) restrain, (2) propaganda, (3) exploit, (4) assess, (5) obese, (6) ironic, (7) incessantly, (8) contempt, (9) pinnacle, (10) scruples.

Practice C

(1) moral consideration, (2) characteristic of irony, that is, an event that is opposite to what would be expected, (3) highest point, (4) continually, (5) testify, (6) very fat, (7) take advantage of, (8) deliberate spreading of ideas, (9) control, (10) scorn.

Additional Words (pp. 201-202)

1. **enervate.** To deprive of strength; to weaken; to destroy the vigor of.
2. **placate.** To soothe the anger of; to pacify.
3. **latent.** Present, but not active or visible; dormant.
4. **glib.** Speaking too smoothly to be sincere; marked by ease and informality; easy and fluent of speech and writing.
5. **empirical.** Relying on observation or experience; capable of being verified or disproved by observation or experiment.

Practice for Additional Words (pp. 202-203)

A. (1) d, (2) a, (3) b, (4) e, (5) c.
B. (1) placate, (2) glib, (3) empirical, (4) constraints, (5) thrifty, (6) morale, (7) latent, (8) enervate, (9) replenish, (10) deprecate.

Exercise 18 (pp. 203-210)

Practice A

(1) feign, (2) beguile, (3) equanimity, (4) caustic, (5) livid, (6) intrigue, (7) conniver, (8) stupor, (9) taciturn, (10) prospective.

Practice B

(1) none–obese, (2) none–intrigue, (3) ironic, (4) none–pinnacle, (5) scruple, (6) prospective, (7) feign, (8) equanimity, (9) livid, (10) stupor, (11) beguile, (12) caustic, (13) none–taciturn, (14) conniver, (15) wane, (16) none–attest, (17) none–contempt, (18) none–incessantly, (19) none–restrain, (20) rampant.

WORD RECTANGLE

C	A	U	S	T	I	C	O	P
A	E	S	T	U	P	O	R	R
E	Q	U	A	L	A	N	A	O
B	U	F	E	I	G	N	M	S
E	A	O	W	O	I	I	P	P
G	N	M	A	E	R	V	A	E
U	I	N	N	I	O	E	N	C
I	M	A	E	A	N	R	T	T
L	I	V	I	D	I	O	M	I
E	T	A	O	U	C	I	E	V
A	Y	S	C	R	U	P	L	E

Practice C

(1) intrigue, (2) equanimity, (3) feign, (4) livid, (5) caustic, (6) conniver, (7) prospective, (8) taciturn, (9) beguile, (10) stupor.

Additional Words (pp. 208-209)

1. **obtrusive.** Undesirably noticeable or showy; protruding.
2. **bizarre.** Odd; markedly unusual or strange.
3. **expedient.** Characterized by what is suitable or convenient for a particular occurrence; appropriate to the purpose at hand; a means to an end.
4. **predatory.** Characterized by a tendency to injure others for one's own gain; preying upon other animals; characterized by plunder (robbery, devastation).
5. **pragmatist.** A person who believes in the practical consequences of things.

Practice for Additional Words (pp. 209-210)

A. (1) c, (2) a, (3) e, (4) d, (5) b.
B. (1) suitable, (2) strange, (3) dormant, (4) showy, (5) person who believes in the practical consequences of things, (6) practical, (7) preying, (8) give up, (9) changeable, (10) hasten.

Crossword Puzzle 6 (pp. 210-212)

1 T	2 A	3 L	4 E	■	5 T	6 H	7 E	8 N	■	9 H	10 A	11 N	12 D	13 Y	■	
14 A	■	15 E	W	16 E	■	17 E	X	O	18 T	I	C	■	19 O	A	20 T	
21 C	22 I	T	E	■	■	23 R	I	V	A	L	■	24 A	■	25 M	A	26 D
27 T	■	28 H	■	■	29 D	E	T	■	30 C	L	■	31 R	32 S	■	33 C	O
■	■	34 A	35 S	36 S	E	S	S	■	37 I	■	38 A	R	C	39 T	I	C
40 T	41 E	R	R	I	F	Y	■	42 S	T	43 U	P	O	R	■	44 T	I
45 R	A	G	■	■	46 E	■	■	47 H	U	M	■	48 G	U	49 N	■	50 L
51 I	■	52 Y	53 A	54 W	N	■	■	55 O	R	■	■	56 A	P	T	■	57 E
58 T	59 O	■	■	60 A	D	61 A	62 M	A	N	63 T	■	64 N	L	■		
65 E	L	■	66 O	N	■	67 R	O	T	■	68 E	69 N	T	E	70 R		
	71 D	■	72 F	E	73 I	G	N	■	■	74 N	O	■	75 S			
	■	76 N	■	■	77 L	U	K	78 E	■	79 E	T	80 C	■			
	81 F	U	T	I	L	E	■	82 D	E	T	E	R	■			

Word Scramble 6 (pp. 212–213)

(1) rampant, (2) wane, (3) adamant, (4) assess, (5) heresy, (6) espouse, (7) attest, (8) ironic, (9) obese, (10) exploit, (11) restrain, (12) scruple, (13) contempt, (14) pinnacle, (15) feign, (16) livid, (17) stupor, (18) taciturn, (19) caustic, (20) beguile.

Analogies 6 (pp. 213–214)

(1) obese, (2) constituent, (3) spouse, (4) feign, (5) adamant, (6) evaluate, (7) biting, (8) taciturn, (9) livid, (10) exploit, (11) affluent, (12) contempt, (13) rampant, (14) attest, (15) lethargy, (16) prospective, (17) equanimity, (18) impediment, (19) pervert, (20) wane.

Multiple-Choice Vocabulary Test 6 (pp. 214–216)

Exercise 16

(1) c, (2) d, (3) a, (4) d, (5) a, (6) b, (7) b, (8) c, (9) b, (10) a.

Exercise 17

(11) d, (12) c, (13) c, (14) b, (15) c, (16) b, (17) c, (18) d, (19) d, (20) d.

Exercise 18

(21) a, (22) b, (23) c, (24) d, (25) b, (26) d, (27) b, (28) d, (29) a, (30) b.

True/False Test 6 (pp. 216–217)

(1) F, (2) T, (3) T, (4) T, (5) F, (6) T, (7) T, (8) F, (9) F, (10) T, (11) F, (12) F, (13) F, (14) F, (15) T, (16) T, (17) F, (18) F, (19) F, (20) F.[1]

STOP. Turn to page 217 for the scoring of the tests.

Additional Practice Sets (pp. 218–220)

Additional Practice 1

(1) assessed, (2) espouse, (3) adamant, (4) constituents, (5) vulnerable, (6) deviate, (7) lethargy, (8) Heresy, (9) rampant, (10) waned.

[1] It can also be used to further a cause.

Additional Practice 2

(1) continually, (2) top, (3) testify, (4) characterized by a state of irony in which an event opposite to what is expected occurs, (5) using for one's own gain, (6) very fat, (7) scorn, (8) the deliberate spreading of ideas, (9) ethical considerations, (10) control.

Additional Practice 3

(1) g, (2) i, (3) e, (4) h, (5) j, (6) b, (7) f, (8) a, (9) d, (10) c.

APPENDIXES

APPENDIX A: THE DICTIONARY

The dictionary, which is an important reference book for all persons, is filled with information about individual words, as well as other useful information. Even though the dictionary is a necessary tool, with which all students should be familiar, it should not be used as a crutch; that is, every time you meet a word whose meaning is unknown to you, you should first try to use your knowledge of combining forms and context clues to unlock the meaning. If these techniques do not help, and the word is essential for understanding the passage, then you should look up the meaning.

To use the dictionary effectively, you should know that the purpose of dictionaries is not to prescribe or make rules about word meanings and pronunciations, but only to describe. Lexicographers use various methods to compile the words in the dictionary. One important method is based on citations of usage and research consulting older dictionaries. Another method involves choosing a group of people and recording the ways in which these subjects pronounce and use words. These then are recorded as the accepted standard spellings, definitions, and word usage.

Difficulties exist concerning pronunciation because persons in different parts of the country often pronounce words differently. Pronunciation in the East is often different from that in the South or Midwest. As a result, pronunciation of a word as given in the dictionary may not be in accord with your region's pronunciation of it.

Also, to compound this problem, different dictionaries may use different pronunciation keys. The pronunciation key is composed of words with diacritical marks. To know how to pronounce a word in a particular dictionary, you must familiarize yourself with the pronunciation key in that dictionary. For example, look at the way that five different dictionaries present a few similar words.

Word	Webster's New Twentieth Century Dictionary	Webster's Third New International Dictionary	Random House Dictionary of the English Language	The American Heritage Dictionary of the English Language	Funk & Wagnalls Standard College Dictionary
1. coupon	c̱ou′pon	′k(y)ü, pän	ko͞o′pon	ko͞o′pŏn	ko͞o′pon
2. courage	c̱our′age	′kər • ij	kûr′ij	kûr′ĭj	kûr′ij
3. covet	c̱ov′ ėt	′kəvə̇t	kuv′it	kŭv′ĭt	kuv′it

If you had no knowledge of the pronunciation key of the specific dictionary, you would have difficulty in pronouncing the word. (See p. 231 for the Guide to Pronunciation in *Webster's New Twentieth Century Dictionary,* 2nd ed.) Pronunciation guides are generally found at the beginning of dictionaries. Many dictionaries also have a simplified pronunciation key at the bottom of every page. (See pp. 232–233 for two pages from *Webster's New Twentieth Century Dictionary.*)

Because this text will be used in various parts of the country, this book uses a simplified pronunciation key, which is presented in Chapter One.

Before reading any further, list in the following space all the uses that you can think of for the dictionary.

USES OF THE DICTIONARY

____

____

____

____

____

Now compare your list with the following:

I. *Uses of the Dictionary*

A. *Information Concerning a Word*

1. Spelling.
2. Definitions.
3. Correct usage.
4. Pronunciation.
5. Syllabication.
6. Antonyms.
7. Synonyms.
8. Parts of speech.
9. Idiomatic phrases.
10. Etymology—the history of the word.
11. Semantics—the analysis of the word's meanings.

B. *Other Useful Information*

1. Biographical entries.
2. Lists of foreign countries, provinces, and cities with their population figures.
3. Charts of other geographical data.
4. Air distances between principal cities.
5. Listing of foreign words and phrases.
6. Complete listing of abbreviations in common use.
7. Tables of weights and measures.
8. Signs and symbols.
9. Forms of address.

Most persons do not realize what an abundance of information can be gained from the dictionary. (The kind of information presented varies according to the dictionary.)

Using your dictionary, answer the following questions:

1. In what countries do centaurs live? ____________________
2. Where is Mount Everest? ____________________
3. Was Prometheus the goddess of fire? ____________________
4. Is a songstress a man who writes songs? ____________________
5. Is *Miss.* an abbreviation for *Missus*? ____________________
6. Is haiku a Hawaiian mountain? ____________________
7. Did Andrew Jackson fight in the Civil War? ____________________
8. Is a statute a work of art? ____________________
9. Is a quadruped an extinct animal? ____________________
10. Is a centipede a unit of measurement in the metric system? ______________

Using the given dictionary page (see p. 232), see how well you can answer the following questions. Answers are on the next page.

1. Would the word *Porphyrio* be found on this page? ____________________
2. Between what two words would you find *porose*? ____________________
3. How many definitions are given for *pore*? ____________________
4. What parts of speech can *pore* be? ____________________
5. In what seas do you find porcupine fish? ____________________

6. What was *pork* originally? ____________________
7. What is the slang meaning of *pork barrel*? ____________________
8. Is there such a thing as porcupine grass? ____________________
9. What is the Latin for *pore*? ____________________
10. What is *populus alba*? ____________________
11. How many syllables does the word *poriferous* have? ____________________
12. Which syllable is accented in *porism*? ____________________
13. Which syllable is accented in *porismatic*? ____________________
14. According to the pronunciation key at the bottom of the page, *ā* sounds like *a* in what word? ____________________
15. The *c* in the word *porotic* sounds like ____________________ in the word ____________________ in the pronunciation key at the bottom of the page.
16. The *c* in the word *porcelain* sounds like ____________________ in the word ____________________ in the pronunciation key.

ANSWERS

1. no, *porphyrine* is the last word–*rio* would be after *rine*
2. *Porosa* and *porosity*
3. six
4. noun and verb
5. tropical
6. pig or hog
7. government appropriations for political patronage
8. yes
9. *porus*
10. the European white poplar
11. four
12. first
13. third
14. fate
15. c̲; cat or chord
16. *c*; ace

GUIDE TO PRONUNCIATION

PRONUNCIATION in this dictionary is indicated directly on the entry word by a system of symbols, or diacritical marks. Thus, the symbol ç is used to indicate the sound of the hard **c** in **cat**, and the word is entered in the vocabulary as **çat**. The Key to Pronunciation printed below gives a complete description of the symbols used and the sounds they represent. The modified sounds are unmarked, as the **e** in **cent**, the **a** in **apply**, the **i** in **pin**, the **u** in **tub**, the **o** in **on**, and the **y** in **myth**.

When two vowels stand together, only the one which indicates the sound of the word is marked, as in **strēak, brāin, mōat**. The clusters **ae** and **oe** ending a syllable are pronounced as **ē**; when followed by a consonant in the same syllable they are pronounced as **e** in **met**.

In a few instances it is impossible to indicate the pronunciation on the word itself; in such cases the word, or part of it, is respelled in parentheses immediately following the entry. The word is respelled phonetically, that is, according to its sound, regardless of the letters that compose it. Examples of respelling are **ẹight** (āt); **guīde** (gīd); **heir** (âr); and **här'le-quin** (-kin *or* -kwin).

The accents are indicated thus: primary ', secondary ''. The secondary accent or subordinate stress is normally indicated only when it falls at an irregular interval from the primary or main stress, that is, at an interval other than two syllables.

Although full vowel quality is indicated in all syllables, it should be understood that in totally unstressed syllables the vowel quality is variously reduced, or weakened, in colloquial speech to a more or less neutral sound. To avoid the confusion of excessive diacritical marks, sounds in non-English words are indicated by the English sounds most nearly approximating these.

KEY TO PRONUNCIATION

ā as in fāte, āle, ā'corn, be-rāte', nat''u-ral-i-zā'tion.
ä " " fär, fä'ther, ärch, mär'shal, cär-toon'; also as in whät, wänt.
ȧ " " fȧst, glȧss, a-lȧs'; also as in so'dȧ, ȧ-dapt'ȧ-ble.
a̤ " " fa̤ll, pa̤w, a̤w'ful, ap-pla̤ud'.
ă " " fi'năl, sea'măn, tol'er-ănt, men'ăce.
â " " câre, âir, mil'i-târ-y, de-clâre'.
a " " at, ac-cord', com-par'i-son, car'ry.

ē " " ēve, mēte, hē, Ē'den, in-ter-vēne'; also as in hēre, drēar'y.
ẹ " " prẹy, ẹight, o-bẹy'.
ẽ " " hẽr, vẽrse, sẽr'vice, in-tẽr'.
e " " met, ebb, en-dorse', mon'e-tar-y, dis-tend'.
ee " " feed, pro-ceed', lee'way.

ī " " pīne, ī-de'a, īce'berg, de-cīde', al-lī'ance.
ï " " clïque, ma-rïne'; also as in Mar-tï'ni.
ĩ " " bĩrd, stĩr, ex'tĩr-pate, fĩrm'a-ment.
i " " it, hit, re-mit', cit'y; also as in pos'si-ble, grav'i-ty, pu'pil.

ō " " nōte, ōat, sō, ō'pen, hel-lō'; also as in ren'ō-vate, prō-pel'.
ö " " möve, pröve, tömb.
ǫ " " lǫng, crǫss, ǫff, ǫrb, fǫr-bid', dǫr'mer.
ŏ " " at'ŏm, plŏv'er; also as in ac'tŏr, wŏrd, wŏrk.
o " " not, for'est, non'sense; also as in dog, broth, cost; also as in con-fess', con-cur'.
ọọ " " mọọn, cọọ, fọọd, brọọd'er.
oo " " book, hood, foot, look, cook'y.

ū " " ūse, fūse, ū-til'i-ty, fū'tile, im-mūne'.
ụ " " bụll, pụt, fụl-fil', boun'ti-fụl.
ü " " brüte, jü'ry; also used for the German ü.
ũ " " tũrn, fũr, bũr-lesque', de-mũr'.
u " " up, rub, sun'set, in-sult'.

ȳ " " crȳ, eȳe.
y " " myth, cit'y.

ç " " çat, to-baç'ço.
ç " " ma-çhine'.
c " " ace, ce'dar.
ch " " church.
çh " " çhord.

ġ as in ġem.
ñ " " añ'ger, sphiñx.
ṅ " " French boṅ.
ng " " ring.
ş " " mi'şer, aş.

th " " this.
th " " thin.
z̧ " " az̧ure.

au " " umlaut.
aw " " straw.

ou " " out.
oi " " oil.
oy " " boy.

ew " " new, few.

ow " " now.

-tūre as -chẽr (in picture).
-tion, **-sion** } as -shun (in nation, tension).

-ciăn, **-tiăn**, **-siăn** } as -shun (in Martian, Melanesian, mortician).

-şiăn, **-şion** } as -zhun (in Persian, fusion).

-liŏn as -lyun *or* -yun (in million).

-ceous, **-(s)cious** } as -shus (in cretaceous, delicious, conscious).

qu as kw (in queen).
-ous as -us (in porous).

ph- as f- (in phone, etc.).

-le as -l (at end of syllable, as in able, cycle, etc.).

-iȧ as -yȧ (in pharmacopoeia).

wh- as hw- in whale, etc.

kh as in German doch (dokh).

xii

---

pop'ū·lāte, *v.t.*; populated, *pt.*, *pp.*; populating, *ppr.* [from ML. *populatus*, pp. of *populare*, to populate, from L. *populus*, the people.]
1. to be or become the inhabitants of; to inhabit.
2. to people; to furnish with people or inhabitants, either by natural increase or by immigration or colonization.

pop'ū·lāte, *v.i.* to propagate; to increase. [Obs.]

pop·ū·lā'tion, *n.* [LL. *populatio.*]
1. all the people in a country, region, etc.
2. the number of these.
3. a (specified) part of the people in a given area; as, the Japanese *population* of Hawaii.
4. a populating or being populated.
5. in biology, all the organisms living in a given area.
6. in statistics, a group of items or individuals.
population explosion; the very great and continuing increase in human population in modern times.

pop'ū·lā·tŏr, *n.* one who populates or peoples.

pop'ū·lin, *n.* [L. *populus*, poplar, and *-in.*] a crystallizable substance found in the bark, root, and leaves of the *Populus tremula*, or aspen, along with salicin.

Pop'ū·lism, *n.* [from L. *populus*, the people; and *-ism.*]
1. the theory and policies of Populists.
2. the Populistic movement.

Pop'ū·list, *n.* one belonging to the People's party.

Pop'ū·list, *a.* same as *Populistic.*

Pop·ū·list'iç, *a.* 1. of Populists or their views.
2. having to do with the People's party.

pop'ū·lous, *a.* [L. *populosus.*] full of people; thickly populated.

pop'ū·lous·ly, *adv.* with many inhabitants in proportion to the extent of country.

pop'ū·lous·ness, *n.* the state of being populous.

Pop'ū·lus, *n.* [L., poplar.] a genus of trees which includes the common poplar. *Populus alba* is the European white poplar.

pọr'bēa″gle, *n.* [from Corn. dial.] any shark of the genus *Lamna*, especially *Lamna cornubica*, found in northern seas: it is large and fierce and brings forth living young rather than eggs.

por'çāte, por'çā·ted, *a.* [L. *porca*, a ridge.] ridged; formed in ridges.

pōr'ce·lain (-lin), *n.* [so called from its resemblance to the Venus shell, which is, in It., *porcellana*, from *porcella*, a little pig, the upper surface of the shell resembling the curve of a pig's back.]
1. a fine, white, translucent, hard earthenware with a transparent glaze; china.
2. porcelain dishes or ornaments, collectively.

pōr'ce·lain, *a.* made of porcelain.

pōr'ce·lain çrab, a crab having a very smooth, polished shell, as *Porcellana platycheles*, the broad-clawed species.

pōr'ce·lain·īzed, *a.* altered by heating so as to resemble porcelain; in geology, metamorphosed so as to resemble white earthenware, as clays, shales, etc.

pōr'ce·lain jas'pēr, porcelanite.

pōr·ce·lā'nē·ous, pōr·cel·lā'nē·ous, *a.* of or resembling porcelain.

pọr'ce·lȧ·nīte, pọr'cel·lȧ·nīte, *n.* a semi-vitrified clay or shale, somewhat resembling jasper.

pọr'ce·lȧ·nous, por'cel·lȧ·nous, *a.* same as *porcelaneous.*

pōrch, *n.* [ME. and OFr. *porche*, from L. *porticus*, from *porta*, a gate, entrance, or passage.]
1. a covered entrance to a building, usually projecting from the wall and having a separate roof.
2. an open or enclosed gallery or room on the outside of a building; a veranda.
3. a portico; a covered walk. [Obs.]
the Porch; a portico in Athens where the Stoic philosopher Zeno taught his disciples.

pōrch çlīmb'ēr (klīm'), a burglar who gains entrance to a house by climbing the porch. [Slang.]

pọr'çīne, *a.* [L. *porcinus*, from *porcus*, hog.] of or like pigs or hogs.

pọr'çū·pīne, *n.*; *pl.* **pọr'çū·pīneṣ** or **pọr'çū·pīne,** [ME. *porkepyn*, *pork despyne*; OFr. *porc espin*, the spinous hog, or spine hog; L. *porcus*, and *spina*, a spine or thorn.] any of a number of related gnawing animals; specifically, (a) the old-world porcupine, *Hystrix cristata*, of the family *Hystricidæ*, bearing long, stiff, erectile spines sometimes a foot in length; (b) the North American porcupine, of the family *Erethizontidae*, which is armed with short, sharp quills or spines that may be easily detached from the body. The two species of this porcupine are *Erethizon dorsatus* of the eastern part of the United States and Canada, and *Erethizon epixanthus* of the West.

PORCUPINE

pọr'çū·pīne ant'ēat·ēr, an echidna, an ant-eating mammal resembling a porcupine.

pọr'çū·pīne çrab, a Japanese crab having long spines on its carapace and limbs; the *Lithodes hystrix.*

pọr'çū·pīne fish, a fish of the tropical seas, *Diodon hystrix*, which is covered with spines or prickles capable of being erected by its inflating the body; also, any fish with similarly erectile spines.

pọr'çū·pīne grȧss, the common prairie grass, *Stipa spartea*, of the United States.

pọr'çū·pīne wood, the outer wood of the cocoanut palm, which, when cut horizontally, presents markings resembling porcupine quills.

pōre, *n.* [ME. *pore*, *poor*; L. *porus*; Gr. *poros*, a passage, a pore, from *perān*, to pierce.]
1. originally, a passage; a channel.
2. a tiny opening, usually microscopic, as in plant leaves, skin, etc., through which fluids may be absorbed or discharged.
3. a similar opening in rock or other substances.

pōre, *v.i.*; pored, *pt.*, *pp.*; poring, *ppr.* [ME. *poren*, *pouren.*]
1. to gaze intently or steadily.
2. to look searchingly; to read carefully; to study minutely (with *over*); as, he *pored over* the book.
3. to think deeply and thoroughly; to ponder; meditate (with *on*, *upon*, or *over*); as, he *pored on* the wonders of science.

pōr'ēr, *n.* one who pores.

pọr'gee, *n.* same as *porgy.*

pọr'gy (*or* -ji), *n.*; *pl.* **pọr'gieṣ** or **pọr'gy,** [prob. var. of *pogy.*] any of a large number of salt-water food fishes having spiny fins and a wide body covered with large scales.

Pō·rif'e·rȧ, *n.pl.* [*pore*, and L. *ferre*, to bear.] in zoology, a phylum of invertebrates which includes sponges.

pō·rif'ēr·ăn, *n.* any of the *Porifera.*

pō·rif'ēr·ous, *a.* 1. having pores.
2. in zoology, of or related to the *Porifera.*

pō'ri·fọrm, *a.* [L. *porus*, pore, and *form.*] resembling a pore.

pōr'i·ness, *n.* the state of being porous, or having numerous pores.

pō'riṣm, *n.* [ME. *porysme*; ML. *porisma*; Gr. *porisma*, lit., a thing brought, from *porizein*, to bring.] in ancient mathematics, a geometrical proposition variously defined; specifically, (a) a proposition deduced from some other demonstrated proposition; a corollary; (b) a proposition that uncovers the possibility of finding such conditions as to make a specific problem capable of innumerable solutions.

pō·riṣ·mat'iç, *a.* pertaining to a porism; seeking to determine by what means and in how many ways a problem may be solved.

pō·riṣ·mat'iç·ăl, *a.* porismatic.

pō'rīte, *n.* a coral of the family *Poritidæ*, or of the genus *Porites.*

Pō·rī'tēṣ, *n.* [LL., from L. *porus*, pore.]
1. in zoology, a genus of perforate madreporarian corals, having small twelve-rayed calicles and a very porous structure.
2. a genus of millepores.

Pō·rit'i·dae, *n.pl.* a family of corals of which *Porites* is the type genus.

pōrk, *n.* [ME. and OFr. *porc*; L. *porcus*, a pig.]
1. originally, a pig or hog.
2. the flesh of a pig or hog, used, fresh or cured, as food.

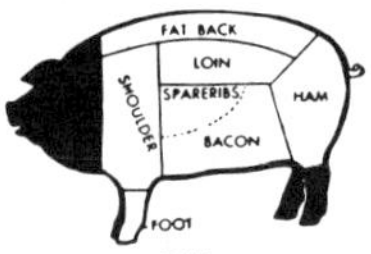

PORK

3. money, position, etc. received from the government through political patronage. [Slang.]

pōrk bar'rel, government appropriations for political patronage, as for local improvements to please legislators' constituents. [Slang.]

pōrk'ēr, *n.* a hog, especially a young one, fattened for use as food.

pōrk'et, *n.* a young hog. [Rare.]

pōrk'fish, *n.*; *pl.* **pōrk'fish·eṣ** or **pōrk'fish,** a black grunt, *Anisotremus virginicus*, with yellow stripes, of the West Indies.

pōrk'i·ness, *n.* the state or quality of being porky.

pōrk'ling, *n.* a young pig.

pōrk pīe, 1. a meat pie made of chopped pork, usually eaten cold.
2. a soft hat with a round, flat crown, worn by men: now often *porkpie.*

pōrk'pīe, *n.* same as *pork pie*, sense 2.

pōrk'y, *a.*; *comp.* porkier; *superl.* porkiest,
1. of or like pork.
2. fat, as though overfed.
3. saucy, cocky, presumptuous, impertinent, or the like. [Slang.]

pọr'nō, *n.* pornography. [Slang.]

pọr'nō, *a.* pornographic. [Slang.]

pọr·noç'rȧ·cy, *n.* [Gr. *pornē*, prostitute, and *kratein*, to rule.] government by prostitutes; domination, sway, or influence of profligate women; specifically, the government of Rome in the early part of the tenth century.

pọr·nō·graph'iç, *a.* of, or having the nature of, pornography; obscene.

pọr·nog'rȧ·phy, *n.* [Gr. *pornē*, prostitute, and *graphein*, to write.]
1. originally, a description of prostitutes and their trade.
2. writings, pictures, etc. intended to arouse sexual desire.
3. the production of such writings, pictures, etc.

pọr·o·mēr'iç, *n.* [arbitrary coinage, prob. from *porous*, and poly*meric.*] a synthetic, leather-like, porous material, often coated or impregnated with a polymer.

pō·rō·phyl'lous, *a.* [Gr. *poros*, pore, and *phyllon*, leaf.] in botany, having leaves covered with transparent points or dots.

Pō·rō'sȧ, *n.pl.* same as *Perforata.*

pō·rōse', *a.* [LL. *porosus*, full of pores.]
1. porous.
2. of or pertaining to the *Porosa.*

pō·ros'i·ty, *n.*; *pl.* **pō·ros'i·tieṣ,** [ME. *porositee*; ML. *porositas*, from *porosus*, from L. *porus*, a pore.]
1. the quality or state of being porous.
2. the ratio of the volume of a material's pores to that of its solid content.
3. anything porous.
4. a pore.

pō·rot'iç, *n.* [Gr. *pōros*, a callus.] any medicine which assists in the formation of callus.

pō'rous, *a.* [from *pore.*] full of pores, or tiny holes through which fluids, air, or light may pass; as, a *porous* skin; *porous* wood; *porous* earth.

pō'rous·ly, *adv.* in a porous manner.

pō'rous·ness, *n.* the quality or state of having pores; porosity; as, the *porousness* of the skin of an animal, or of wood.

pọr'pen·tīne, *n.* porcupine. [Obs.]

pọr·phy·rā'ceous, *a.* same as *porphyritic.*

pọr'phȳre, *n.* porphyry. [Obs.]

pọr'phy·rin, *n.* [from *hematoporphyrin*, from *hemato-*, and Gr. *porphyra*, purple, purple product of hemoglobin decomposition.] any of a group of pyrrole derivatives of hemoglobin and chlorophyll, containing no iron or magnesium.

pọr'phy·rīne (-rēn), *n.* a chemical substance, colorless and uncrystallized, obtained from the bark of an Australian tree, *Alstonia constricta.*

Por·phyr′i·ō, *n.* [Gr. *porphyriōn,* the purple gallinule, from *porphyra,* purple.]
1. a genus of birds of the rail family, including *Porphyrio hyacinthinus,* the purple or hyacinthine gallinule, a bird found in Europe, Asia, and Africa, having a strong beak and long legs.
2. [p-] a bird of this genus.

PORPHYRIO

por′phy·rīte, *n.* any rock of a porphyritic nature.

por·phy·rit′iç, *a.* [ME. *porphiritike;* ML. *porphyriticus;* L. *porphyrites;* Gr. *porphyritēs,* porphyry.]
1. composed of or pertaining to porphyry.
2. resembling porphyry; containing distinct crystals embedded in a fine-grained mass.

por″phy·ri·zā′tion, *n.* the act or process of porphyrizing, or the condition or quality of being porphyrized.

por′phy·rīze, *v.t.* to cause to resemble porphyry.

por′phy·rō·ġēne″, *a.* [Gr. *porphyra,* purple, and *gennān,* to beget.] born to the purple or of royal descent.

por″phy·rō·ġē·net′iç, *a.* [Gr. *porphyritēs,* porphyry, and *gennān,* to beget.] of or relating to porphyrogenitism.

por″phy·rō·ġen′i·tism, *n.* the mode of succession in some royal families, notably the Byzantine, whereby a younger son, if born in the purple, that is, after the accession of his parents to the throne, was preferred to an older son, who was born before the parents' accession.

por″phy·rō·ġen′i·tus, *n.* [Gr. *porphyra,* purple, and *gennētos,* from *gennān,* to beget.] a son born to a sovereign, especially in the Byzantine Empire.

por′phy·roid, *n.* a rock that resembles, or has the structure of, porphyry.

por′phy·ry, *n.; pl.* **por′phy·ries,** [ME. *purfire, porfirie;* OFr. *porfire;* ML. *porphyreus,* from Gr. *porphyros,* purple.]
1. originally, a hard Egyptian rock having red and white feldspar crystals embedded in a fine-grained, dark-red or purplish groundmass.
2. any igneous rock of similar texture.

por′phy·ry shell, a univalve shell of the genus *Murex;* also, a seashell, *Oliva porphyria,* that is spotted like porphyry.

Por′pi·tȧ, *n.* [Gr. *porpē,* brooch.] a genus of bright-colored, disk-shaped marine siphonophores.

por′poise (-pus), *n.; pl.* **por′pois·es** or **por′poise,** [ME. *porcpisce, porpesse, porpese, porpus,* lit., swine fish, from L. *porcus,* a pig or swine, and *piscis,* a fish.]
1. any of a number of small, related cetaceans of the genus *Phocæna,* dark above and white below, with a triangle-shaped fin on the back, a blunt snout, and many teeth.

PORPOISE

2. a dolphin or any of several other small cetaceans.

por′pō·rāte, *a.* arrayed in purple or royal raiment.

por′pus, *n.* a porpoise. [Dial.]

por·rā′ceous, *a.* [L. *porraceus,* from *porrum,* a leek or onion.] greenish; resembling the leek in color.

por·rect′, *a.* in zoology, denoting a part which extends forth horizontally.

por′rect′, *v.t.* [L. *porrectus,* pp. of *porrigere,* to extend.] to extend horizontally.

por·rec′tion, *n.* [L. *porrectio,* from *porrigere; por,* for *pro,* forward, and *regere,* to direct.] the act of stretching forth.

por′ret, *n.* [It. *porretta;* L. *porrum,* a leek.] a scallion; a leek or small onion. [Now Dial.]

por′ridġe, *n.* [altered from *pottage* by confusion with ME. *porrey;* OFr. *poree;* LL. *porrata,* leek broth, from L. *porrum,* leek.]
1. originally, pottage.
2. a soft food made of cereal or meal boiled in water or milk until thick. [Chiefly Brit.]

por′rin·ġēr, *n.* [earlier *pottanger, pottager,* from Fr. *potager,* soup dish: altered by association with *porridge.*]
1. a small metal vessel for porridge, etc., especially one from which children are fed.
2. a headdress in the shape of a porringer. [Rare.]

pōrt, *n.* [ME. *porte, port;* OFr. *porte;* L. *porta,* a door.]
1. a gateway; a portal. [Obs. except Scot.]
2. (a) a porthole; (b) the covering for this.
3. an opening, as in a cylinder face or valve face, for the passage of steam, gas, water, etc.
4. a mouthpiece of curved metal used in some bridle bits.

pōrt, *v.t.* [ME. *porten;* OFr. *porter;* L. *portare* to carry.]
1. originally, to carry.
2. to carry, hold, or place (a rifle or sword) diagonally in front of one, crossing the left shoulder, as for inspection.

pōrt, *n.* [ME. *porte;* OFr., from the v.]
1. the manner in which one carries oneself; carriage; deportment; demeanor.
2. the position of porting a weapon.
3. purport; meaning.
4. state; splendid or stately manner of living. [Obs.]
5. a piece of iron, somewhat in the shape of a horseshoe, fixed to the saddle or stirrup, and used to carry the lance when held upright. [Obs.]

pōrt, *n.* [ME., from OFr. and AS. *port,* port, haven, harbor, from L. *portus,* a haven; akin to L. *porta,* gate; Gr. *poros,* a passage.]
1. a harbor; a haven; any bay, cove, inlet, or recess of the sea or of a lake, or the mouth of a river, which ships or vessels can enter, and where they can lie safe from injury by storms.
2. a city or town with a harbor where ships arrive and depart, and load or unload cargoes.
3. a port of entry.

pōrt, *n.* [from *port* (harbor), with reference to the side opposite the steering oar.] the left-hand side of a ship or airplane as one faces forward, toward the bow; larboard: opposed to *starboard.*

pōrt, *a.* of or on the port, or left-hand side.

pōrt, *v.t.* and *v.i.* to move or turn (the helm) to the left.

pōrt, *n.* [from *Oporto,* Portugal.] a fortified sweet wine, usually dark-red, originally from Portugal.

pōr′tȧ, *n.; pl.* **pōr′tae,** [L.] the entrance for nerves and ducts into an organ.

pōrt·ȧ·bil′i·ty, *n.* the condition or quality of being portable.

pōrt′ȧ·ble, *a.* [L. *portabilis.*]
1. that can be carried.
2. easily carried.
3. bearable; endurable. [Obs.]

pōrt′ȧ·ble, *n.* anything portable.

pōrt′ȧ·ble·ness, *n.* the quality or state of being portable.

pōr′tăġe, *n.* [ME.; OFr.; ML. *portaticum,* from *portare,* to carry.]
1. the act of transporting or carrying.
2. the cost or price of transporting or carrying.
3. capacity for carriage; tonnage; burden. [Obs.]
4. a carrying or transporting of boats and supplies overland between navigable rivers, lakes, etc., as during a canoe trip.
5. any place or route over which this is done.
6. a sailor's wages.

pōr′tăġe, *v.t.* and *v.i.;* portaged, *pt., pp.;* portaging, *ppr.* to carry or transport (boats, etc.) over a portage.

Pōr′tăġe fọr·mā′tion, a geological subdivision of the Upper Devonian of the United States. It is named after Portage township in New York State.

pōr′tȧ·gūe, *n.* an obsolete Portuguese coin.

pōr′tăl, *n.* [ME.; OFr.; ML. *portale,* orig. neut. of *portalis,* of a door, from L. *porta,* gate.]
1. a doorway or entrance, especially a large and imposing one.
2. in architecture, the lesser gate, where there are two gates of different dimensions.
3. formerly, a little square corner of a room, separated from the rest by a wainscot, and forming a short passage into a room.
4. any entrance: often figurative, as, the *portal* of wisdom. [Poetic.]
5. the portal vein.

pōr′tăl, *a.* [ML. *portalis.*] designating, of, or like the vein carrying blood from the intestines, stomach, etc. to the liver.

pōr′tăl-tō-pōr′tăl pāy, wages for workers based on the total time spent from the moment of entering the mine, factory, etc. until the moment of leaving it.

pōr·tȧ·men′tō, *n.; pl.* **pōr·tȧ·men′tī,** [It., from *portare,* to carry; L. *portare.*] in music, a continuous gliding from one note to another, sounding all intervening tones; a glide.

pōr′tănce, *n.* [Early Mod. Eng., from Fr. *portance,* from *porter,* to bear.] air; mein; carriage; port. [Archaic.]

pōr′tass, *n.* [OFr. *porte-hors; porter,* to carry, and *hors,* out of doors; so called from being easily portable.] a breviary; a prayer book. [Obs.]

pōr′tāte, *a.* [L. *portatus,* pp. of *portare,* to carry.] in heraldry, placed bendwise in an escutcheon; that is, lying as if carried on a person's shoulder, as a cross.

CROSS PORTATE

pōr′tȧ·tive, *a.* [ME. and OFr. *portatif,* lit., that is carried, from L. *portatus,* pp. of *portare,* to carry, and OFr. *-if.*]
1. of or having the power of carrying a load, charge, etc.
2. that can be carried; portable. [Obs.]

pōrt au·thor′i·ty, a governmental commission in charge of the traffic, regulations, etc. of a port.

pọrt çap′tain (-tin), an official of a steamship company who assumes charge of vessels during their stay in port.

pọrt chärġe, in commerce, a fee or duty charged for the privilege of keeping a ship or its cargo in a port.

pōrt′çlūse, *n.* a portcullis. [Obs.]

pōrt″çrāy′ŏn, *n.* [Fr. *porte-crayon; porter,* to carry, and *crayon,* pencil.] a small metallic handle with a clasp for holding a crayon, etc. when used in drawing.

pōrt·çul′lis, *n.* [ME. *portcoles;* OFr. *porte coleïce; porte,* a gate, and *coleïce,* f. of *coleis,* sliding, from L. *colare,* to strain, filter.]
1. in fortification, a heavy grating or latticework of timber or iron with the lower ends pointed like the teeth of a harrow, suspended by chains over the gateway of a castle, fort, etc., to be let down to prevent the entrance of an enemy.
2. a coin used by the East India Company in the reign of Queen Elizabeth I: it had a design of a portcullis on one side. [Obs.]

PORTCULLIS

pōrt·çul′lis, *v.t.* to shut; to bar. [Rare.]

Pōrte, *n.* [the chief office of the Ottoman Empire was styled *Babi Ali,* lit., the High Gate, from the gate (*bāb*) of the palace at which justice was administered. The French translation of this term is *la Sublime Porte:* hence the use of this word.] the Ottoman Turkish government.

pōrte′-çō·chere′ (-shār′), *n.* [Fr. *porte,* gate, and *cochère,* coach.]
1. a large porch outside the entrance of a building, under which vehicles may be driven.
2. a large entrance gateway through which vehicles are driven into a square or courtyard.

pōrt′ed, *a.* having gates. [Obs.]

pōrte′feuille′ (-fē′ye), *n.* [Fr., from *porter,* to carry, and *feuille,* L. *folium,* leaf.] a portfolio.

pōr′tē·gūe, *n.* portague. [Obs.]

pōrte′-lū·miere″ (-myär″), *n.* [Fr., from *porter,* to carry, and *lumière,* light.] a mirror that can be adjusted so as to cast rays of light in any required direction; a simple form of heliostat.

pōrte′mŏn·nāie″ (-nā″), *n.* [Fr., from *porter* to carry, and *monnaie,* money.] a pocketbook for carrying money; a purse.

pọr·tend′, *v.t.;* portended, *pt., pp.;* portending, *ppr.* [L. *portendere, protendere; pro,* forth, and *tendere,* to stretch.]
1. to be an omen or warning of; to fore-

APPENDIX B: GLOSSARY

VOCABULARY WORDS PRESENTED IN *Vocabulary Expansion II*[1]

The number after the meaning refers to the exercise in which the vocabulary word is presented. If there is more than one number, it means that the word has also appeared in Extra Word Power.

Acquisition. The act of obtaining or acquiring; something obtained or gained, as property, knowledge, and so on. 9
Adamant. Unyielding; firm; immovable; stubborn. 16
Adaptation. The act of fitting or suiting one thing to another; an adjusting to fit new conditions; a change for a new use. 5
Adept. Highly skilled; proficient; expert. 9
Aesthetic. Referring to beauty; sensitive to art and beauty; showing good taste; artistic. 7
Affirm. To declare or state positively; to say or maintain that something is true. 4
Affluent. Having an abundance of goods or riches; wealthy; flowing freely. 2
Affront. To insult; an insult; an open and intentional insult. 7
Allot. To divide or distribute by lot; to distribute or parcel out in portions; to appoint. 6
Alternative. A choice between two or more things; a remaining choice; a choice. 3
Amnesty. A pardon from the government; act of letting someone off. 2
Anecdote. A short, entertaining account of some happening, usually personal or biographical. 9
Antagonize. To make unfriendly; to make an enemy of; to oppose; to act against. 7
Antecedent. Going before in time; prior; preceding; previous; the word, phrase, or clause to which a pronoun refers. 4, 5
Anticipate. To expect; to look forward to; to foresee; to act, use, or make in advance. 12
Appraise. To set a value on; to estimate the worth of; to estimate the quantity of; to give an expert judgment of; to evaluate. 10
Apprehensive. Fearful; expecting evil, danger, or harm; anxious. 8
Assess. To estimate the value of property, income, and so on for tax purposes; to fix or determine the amount of a tax, damages, a fine, and so on; to impose a tax on; to estimate the value or merit of something; to evaluate. 16
Asset. Anything owned that has value; any valuable or desirable thing that serves as an advantage. 6

---

[1] Additional words are presented separately, and the words presented in Extra Word Power are presented in the Combining Forms section with the combining forms.

Assumption. The act of taking for granted without proof; a taking to or upon oneself; a supposition. 11

Assurance. The act of making sure or certain; security; certainty; confidence; guarantee. 11

Astute. Shrewd; ingenious; clever; crafty. 12

Attest. To say positively that something is true, correct, or genuine; to certify that something is true by signature or oath; to bear witness to; to testify to. 17

Attitude. A way of acting, thinking, or feeling that shows one's disposition (one's frame of mind) or opinion; the feeling itself; posture. 7

Avail. To be of use or of value; to be of profit or advantage to; to help; to make use of. 15

Awry. With a turn or twist to one side; away from the expected or hoped for direction; wrong. 11

Beguile. To deceive; to influence by deceit; to cheat; to charm or wile away pleasantly. 18

Bland. Mild; soft; gentle; balmy; kindly; soothing. 8

Candid. Honest; outspoken; frank. 1

Caustic. Able to burn, eat away, or dissolve by chemical action; cutting; stinging; biting; sarcastic. 18

Characteristic. Marking the peculiar quality or qualities of a person or thing; distinctive; special; a special trait, feature, or quality; individuality. 7

Charisma. A rare power or personal magic of leadership that an individual possesses that arouses special enthusiasm or loyalty; a special magnetic charm or appeal. 12

Citation. The quoting of a passage, author, book, and so on; a quotation or a reference given as an authority for facts, opinions, and so on; an official summons to appear before a court. 13

Cognitive. Having to do with thinking, knowing, perception. 13

Coincidence. The occurrence of things or events at the same time by chance. 4

Colleague. A fellow worker in the same profession. 5

Compatible. Capable of living in an agreeable manner with one another; able to exist together; capable of orderly operation and integration with other elements in a system; consistent. 14

Comprehensive. Of large scope; including much; in insurance, covering or providing broad protection against loss; broad. 13

Compromise. A settlement of differences in which each side gives up some demands; to settle differences by mutual concessions. 10

Concept. Idea; a thought or notion. 13

Concise. Brief; terse. 3

Conform. To give the same shape, form, or character to; to make like; to be similar or identical; to be in agreement; to adapt oneself to; to act in accordance with rules, customs, and so on. 10

Conniver. A person who closes his or her eyes to wrongdoing; a person who gives aid to wrongdoing by helping it secretly or by not telling of it. 18

Conservative. Tending to maintain established traditions and to resist or oppose any change in these; cautious; moderate; traditional in style or manner; avoiding showiness; one who clings to traditional or long-standing methods, beliefs, and so on. 6

Constituent. Forming a necessary part; serving as part of a whole; component; someone represented by another; client; one who elects or assists in electing another as his or her representative; a voter. 16

Contagious. Spreading by contact; spreading or tending to spread from person to person. 9

Contempt. The act of despising; the feeling that an act, person, or thing is worthless; scorn; disdain. 17

Controversy. A discussion in which there are opposing views; a dispute; a quarrel. 10

Cope. To struggle or fight with on fairly even terms or with some degree of success (usually followed by *with*); to deal with and attempt to overcome problems and difficulties (usually used with *with*). 12

Covert. Secret; concealed; covered over; sheltered. 2

Covet. To desire very much what another has; to crave; to long for. 6

Crass. Insensitive; thick; coarse; lacking delicacy; gross; unfeeling; stupid. 10

Curt. Marked by rude or abrupt shortness of words. 10

Curtail. To shorten; to lessen; to cut off the end or a part. 2

Delete. To take out or remove a letter, word, and so on; to cross out; to erase. 4

Derogatory. Tending to make less well regarded; tending to belittle someone or something; disparaging; belittling. 7, 8

Deviate. To turn aside or wander from the right or common path; to turn aside from a course, truth, line, way, and so on; to differ from the norm; a person whose moral and social standards differ from the norm or from the accepted moral and social standards; a pervert. 16

Dilemma. Any situation that necessitates a choice between equally unfavorable or equally unpleasant alternatives; an argument that presents two equally unfavorable alternatives. 4

Diligent. Applying oneself in whatever is undertaken; working in a constant effort to accomplish something; industrious. 4

Disarray. Disorder; confusion; disordered or insufficient dress; to throw into disorder; to put into confusion. 15

Discord. Lack of agreement among persons, groups, or things; difference of opinion; dispute; dissension; disagreement; a confused or harsh mingling of sounds; a din. 14

Discreet. Careful about what one says or does; prudent; cautious. 8

Disdain. To regard as unworthy; the feeling of scorn; expression of scorn; contempt. 4

Docile. Easy to teach; easy to discipline; obedient. 8

Dogmatic. Asserting opinions as if they were facts; excessively positive in stating opinions; opinionated. 14

Dominant. Ruling; most influential; controlling; exerting authority or influence; occupying a commanding position. 14

Durable. Lasting; highly resistant to wear; capable of existing a long time; not easily worn out. 14

Duration. Persistence or continuance in time; the time during which something exists or lasts. 12

Economize. To use or manage with thrift or prudence; to avoid waste or needless spending; to reduce expenses. 6

Emanate. To come forth; to come out or proceed from a source; to give out. 15

Emulate. To attempt to equal or excel; to imitate. 10

Equanimity. The quality of being calm or even-tempered; composure; evenness of mind; balance. 18

Eradicate. To destroy completely; to pull out by the roots; to wipe out; to exterminate. 4

Espouse. To adopt or support some cause, view, and so on; to make one's own; to give one's loyalty and support to; to advocate. 16

Euphemism. The substitution of a word or phrase that is less direct, milder, or vaguer for one thought to be harsh, offensive, or blunt; a word or phrase considered less distasteful or less offensive than another. 7

Exceedingly. Extremely. 14

Exotic. Foreign; not native; introduced from a foreign country; having the charm of the unfamiliar; strangely beautiful. 9

Expend. To use up; to spend. 11

Exploit. To turn to economic use; to take advantage of; to make use of unjustly for one's own advantage; deed; act (especially a daring deed or act); feat. 17

Extent. The degree to which something extends; length, area, volume, or scope; magnitude; range. 15

Extricate. To free or release from difficulties, entanglements, embarrassing situations, and so on. 11

Famish. To make or be very hungry; starve. 3

Famished. Very hungry. 3

Fatal. Resulting in or capable of causing death; deadly; bringing ruin or disaster; having decisive importance. 2

Fatigue. Physical or mental tiredness; weariness; to tire out. 3

Feign. To pretend; to make believe; to put on a false appearance of; to represent falsely; to invent. 18

Fetid. Having a heavy offensive smell; stinking; smelling very bad; rancid. 15

Fictitious. Imaginary; not real; made up; fabricated. 2

Formidable. Dreaded; causing awe or fear; hard to handle; of discouraging or awesome strength, size, difficulty, and so on. 3

Frugal. Thrifty; not spending freely; avoiding waste. 6

Frustrate. To defeat; to bring to nothing. 1

Frustrated. Filled with a sense of discouragement and dissatisfaction as a result of defeated efforts, inner conflicts, or unresolved problems. 1

Gregarious. Fond of the company of others; sociable; characteristic of a flock, herd, or crowd. 9

Gullible. Easily deceived or cheated. 11

Harmony. Agreement; getting along well together; accord; agreement of feelings, ideas, or actions; in music, the sounding together of two or more tones. 14

Haughty. Having or showing great pride in oneself and disrespect or contempt or scorn for others; overbearing; snobbish; arrogant. 4

Heresy. An opinion or doctrine not in agreement with accepted doctrine; any belief or theory that varies strongly from accepted or established beliefs, customs, and so on. 16

Hostile. Unfriendly; referring to an enemy. 2

Hyperbolic. Relating to a hyperbole or a great exaggeration. 9

Hypocrite. A person who pretends to be what he or she is not; one who pretends to be better than he or she really is. 7

Idealist. A person who acts according to high ideals, that is, one who conforms to ultimate perfection or excellence; one who is unrealistic and impractical; one who believes in something that exists only in the mind. 12

Implore. To beg or plead for earnestly or urgently. 15

Incessantly. Continuing without interruption; continually. 17

Inclination. A personal leaning or bent; a liking; a bending, slanting, or sloping surface; a slope. 7

Inevitable. Not able to be avoided or escaped; sure to happen; certain. 11

Infamous. Having a bad reputation; notorious. 8

Infidelity. Unfaithfulness; a disloyal act; adultery. 11

Initiate. To introduce by doing or using first; to bring into practice or use; to admit as a member into a fraternity, sorority, club, and so on, especially through use of a secret ceremony. 8

Inquisitive. Curious; given to asking many questions; unnecessarily or improperly curious; prying. 1

Integrate. To unite; to make whole or complete by adding together parts. 1

Interrogate. To ask questions of formally; to examine by questioning. 5

Intimidate. To make timid; to cause fear; to scare; to discourage by threats or violence. 7

Intricate. Complicated; difficult to follow or understand; complex. 5

Intrigue. A secret or underhanded scheme; a secret love affair. 18

Ironic. Characterized by the use of words to mean the opposite of their literal meaning; characterized by an event that is opposite to what would be expected or what usually occurs. 17

Isolate. To set apart from others; to place alone; to separate. 4

Lethal. Causing death; deadly. 2

Lethargy The state and quality of being drowsy and dull; sluggish inactivity; apathy. 16

Liability. Something that is owed; a debt; legal obligation to make good any loss or damage that occurs in a transaction (a business deal); something that works to one's disadvantage. 6

Liberal. Giving freely; generous; large or plentiful; tolerant of views differing from one's own; broad-minded; favoring reform or progress. 6

Literally. Word for word; in a strict sense; actually. 14, 17

Livid. Discolored by bruising; ashen; pale; extremely angry; furious. 18

Meticulous. Extremely careful and precise; extremely careful about details. 15

Miscellaneous. Mixed; consisting of several kinds; various. 8

Modify. To change slightly or make minor changes in character, form, and so on; to change or alter; to limit or reduce; in grammar, to limit or restrict a meaning. 6

Motivate. To stimulate to action; to provide with an incentive; to set in motion or arouse. 12

Mundane. Referring to everyday things; referring to that which is routine or ordinary; referring to worldly things rather than more high-minded or spiritual things. 3

Naive. Foolishly simple; childlike; unsophisticated. 1

Nostalgic. Homesick; longing to go back to one's home, hometown, and so on; longing for something far away or long ago. 3

Obese. Extremely fat; corpulent. 17

Objective. Purpose; goal; aim; something that one is attempting to achieve; unbiased; not affected by personal feelings or prejudice; based on facts; having to do with a material object rather than with something mental such as an idea or concept. 13

Omission. Anything left out or not done; failure to include. 8

Opponent. One who opposes another, as in a battle or debate; one who acts against something or another; adversary; antagonist. 9

Optimist. One who is hopeful; a cheerful person; one who tends to take the most hopeful view or expects the best outcome. 3

Overt. Open to view; public; apparent; able to be seen. 2

Paraphrase. A restatement of a text or passage giving the meaning in another form or in other words usually to make the meaning more clear; a rewording. 13

Passive. Not acting; acted upon; unresisting; not opposing; unenthusiastic; inactive. 9

Persevere. To persist; to continue doing something in spite of difficulty. 5

Pertinent. Relevant; relating to or bearing upon the matter in hand; being to the point. 4

Pessimist. One who expects the worst to happen in any situation; one who looks on the dark side of things; a gloomy person. 3

Pinnacle. The highest point; any tall, pointed formation, such as a mountain peak. 17

Plagiarism. The act of taking the thoughts, writings, inventions, and so on of another and presenting them as one's own. 13

Plaintiff. The complaining party in a lawsuit. 10

Precedent. Something done or said that may serve as an example; in law, a legal decision serving as an authoritative rule in future similar cases; preceding; going before; anterior. 5

Prestige. High reputation or influence gained from success; the power to command respect, admiration, and so on from a group; status. 14

Pretense. A false claim; a claim not supported by fact; make-believe; deception by showing what is false and hiding what is real. 10

Propaganda. Information or ideas systematically spread to promote or injure a cause, group, or nation; the deliberate spreading of opinions, ideas, or information. 17

Prospective. Likely to come about; probable; expected; likely to be or become. 18

Protagonist. The main character in a novel, story, or play; the leader of or spokesperson for a movement, cause, and so on. 13

Rampant. Growing without any check; widespreading; violent in action or spirit; raging; angry; excited. 16

Rancid. Stale; spoiled; having an unpleasant, stale smell or taste; fetid. 15

Reality. The state of being real, actual, or true; what actually exists or is. 12, 10

Relevant. Applying to the matter in question; suitable; relating to. 2

Reliable. Dependable; truthworthy. 5

Reluctant. Unwilling; opposed. 5

Remorse. Painful and deep regret for wrongdoing; a strong anguish arising from regret for past misdeeds. 11

Restrain. To hold back from action; to keep in check or under control; to deprive of freedom or liberty. 17

Saturated. Full; soaked thoroughly; wet. 15

Scruple. A moral or ethical consideration that keeps one from doing something. 17

Scrutinize. To observe closely; to examine or inquire into critically; to investigate. 8

Segregate. To set apart from others; to separate. 1

Sentimental. Marked by tendernesss, emotion, feeling, and so on; influenced more by feeling or emotion than by reason; having or showing exaggerated or superficial emotion. 3

Significant. Having or expressing meaning; full of meaning; important. 5

Skeptical. Inclined to doubt; not believing easily; questioning the truth of theories or of facts. 12

Spouse. A husband or wife; either member of a married pair. 11

Stagnant. Lacking motion or current; not flowing or moving; foul from lack of movement; lacking in activity; sluggish; dull. 6

Status. The position of an individual in relation to another or others; the condition of; the state of; social standing; high standing; prestige. 14

Stupor. A dazed condition; the lessening or loss of the power to feel; a state of extreme sluggishness or lack of feeling resulting often from stress or shock. 18

Subjective. Existing in the mind; belonging to the thinking subject rather than to the object thought of; personal; individual thought; influenced by an individual's state of mind. 13

Survey. To take a general, broad, or comprehensive view of; to look at, consider, or view as a whole; to determine the area, boundaries, or elevations of land by means of measuring angles and distances; a general and comprehensive view; a sampling or partial collection of opinions, facts, or figures taken and used to make an approximation of what a complete collection would be. 15

Sustain. To maintain; to keep in existence; to keep going; to uphold; to support. 1

Synopsis. A brief statement giving a general view of a passage, story, play, and so on; a summary. 13

Tacit. Unspoken; not expressed openly but implied. 1

Taciturn. Untalkative; uncommunicative; inclined to silence. 18

Tedious. Tiresome or uninteresting because of extreme length or slowness; boring; monotonous; wearisome. 12

Terse. Brief; concise. 1

Traditional. Handed down by custom or convention; conventional; customary. 10

Trite. Used so often as to be too common; made commonplace by repetition; lacking freshness or originality. 9

Turmoil. Confused motion or state; disturbance; tumult. 9

Unanimous. Agreeing completely; united in opinion; being in complete agreement; being of one mind. 8

Verbose. Wordy. 1

Vulnerable. Unprotected from danger; capable of being hurt; open to attack, criticism, temptation, and so on. 16

Wane. To decrease gradually in size, amount, intensity, or degree; to decline; to show a decrease such as from full moon to new moon; a gradual declining; growing less. 16

ADDITIONAL WORDS PRESENTED IN *Vocabulary Expansion II*

The number after the meaning refers to the exercise in which the vocabulary word is presented.

Abortion. The induced termination of a pregnancy; arrest of development. 11

Abridge. To shorten; to curtail; to give the substance of in fewer words. 9

Amend. To better; to improve; to correct; to change, rephrase, or add to or subtract from something such as a motion, bill, or constitution. 10

Apt. Exactly suitable; appropriate; inclined to. 10

Arrogant. Full of pride and self-importance; overbearing; haughty. 4

Attrition. A gradual wearing down or weakening; a rubbing out or grinding down. 9

Austere. Stern and forbidding in manner and appearance; somber; grave; unadorned; simple. 12

Awe. Respect tinged with fear; an overwhelming feeling of respect, fear, or admiration produced by someone or something powerful or the like. 10

Bizarre. Odd; markedly unusual or strange. 18

Castigate. To correct or subdue by punishing; to criticize with drastic severity; to rebuke. 6

Celibacy. The state of not being married; the condition of not engaging in sexual intercourse. 11

Compensate. To be equivalent to; to make an appropriate counterbalancing payment to; to offset an error, undesired effect, or defect. 12

Constraint. Confinement; the act of restricting; the act of using force; compulsion; coercion; restriction. 3

Converge. To tend to meet in a point; to tend to a common result; to come together in a common interest. 15

Corroborate. To confirm (to strengthen, to make firm, to affirm); to make more certain. 7

Crafty. Sly; skillful in deceiving; cunning. 2

Criterion. A standard of judging; any established law, rule, or principle by which a correct judgment may be formed. 8

Datum. (*Data,* the plural of *datum,* is usually used.) Information given, granted, or admitted; a premise upon which something can be argued; material used as a basis for calculation. 8

Delve. To search deeply; to make a careful or detailed search for information. 12

Deprecate. To express disapproval of. 12

Didactic. Morally instructive; intended to teach. 15

Dire. Extreme; terrible; having terrible or dreadful consequences; dreadful. 14

Eclectic. Choosing what appears to be the best from many sources; choosing from various sources; not following any one system. 16

Ecstasy. Great joy. 1

Empirical. Relying on observation or experience; capable of being verified or disproved by observation or experiment. 17

Enervate. To deprive of strength; to weaken; to destroy the vigor of. 17

Entice. To attract by offering some reward; to tempt, lure. 15

Esoteric. Understood by a select few; secret; confidential. 11

Exonerate. To relieve, as of a charge or blame resting on one; to clear of a charge of guilt; to relieve of a debt or duty. 7

Expedient. Characterized by what is suitable or convenient for a particular occurrence; appropriate to the purpose at hand; a means to an end. 18

Expedite. To hasten; to speed up the progress of; to make easy the progress of. 3

Extrinsic. Not forming part of or belonging to a thing; originating from or on the outside; external; not an essential part of something. 13

Feasible. Capable of being accomplished or brought about; practical; suitable. 13

Futile. Useless; ineffectual; trifling; unimportant. 8

Glib. Speaking too smoothly to be sincere; marked by ease and informality; easy and fluent of speech and writing. 17

Imminent. About to happen; threatening (said especially of danger). 9

Impediment. A hindrance; an obstruction; some physical defect that retards speech; a speech disorder. 16

Improvise. To make up something on the spur of the moment; to make up out of what is on hand. 11

Intrepid. Fearless; brave; courageous; bold. 16

Intrinsic. Belonging to the essential nature of a thing; essential; belonging to or lying within a given part; inherent; innate. 13

Invincible. Impossible to overcome; not able to be conquered. 8

Itinerant. Traveling from place to place; a person who travels from place to place. 16

Jeopardy. Risk; danger; peril. 7

Latent. Present, but not active or visible; dormant. 17

Laudable. Worthy of praise; commendable. 6

Libel. A written or printed statement or picture that tends to damage a person's reputation or hold him or her up to public ridicule; any false or damaging statement about a person; to write or print something damaging about someone; to write or say something false or damaging about a person. 13

Listless. Spiritless; indifferent; inactive; apathetic. 1

Morale. The mental or emotional condition of a person or a group; a sense of common purpose with respect to a group. 12

Obfuscate. To darken; to confuse; to obscure. 3

Obtrusive. Undesirably noticeable or showy; protruding. 18

Ominous. Threatening; of bad or evil omen; unfavorable. 13

Ornate. Overly decorated; elaborately decorated; flashy; showy. 14

Paradox. Contradiction; a self-contradictory statement that is false; a statement that seems absurd, contradictory, or unbelievable but may be true. 9

Peruse. To read carefully; to inspect closely. 1

Phenomenon. Any fact, circumstance, or experience that is apparent to the senses and that can be scientifically described; something extremely unusual. 9

Placate. To soothe the anger of; to pacify. 17

Placid. Calm; quiet; peaceful. 14

Poignant. Appealing to the emotions; piercing; painfully affecting the feeling; deeply affecting. 14

Pragmatist. A person who believes in the practical consequences of things. 18

Predatory. Characterized by a tendency to injure others for one's own gain; preying upon other animals; characterized by plunder (robbery, devastation). 18

Pretentious. Making claims to importance; making usually unjustified or excessive claims to importance. 14

Procrastinate. To put off doing something until a future time; to postpone taking action. 5

Propriety. Conforming to existing customs; the quality or state of being proper; the standard of what is socially correct; correctness. 16

Prudent. Capable of using sound judgment in practical matters; wisely cautious; sensible; not rash. 5

Query. A question; an inquiry; to ask questions about. 11

Redundant. Extra; not needed; wordy; needlessly repetitive; superfluous; using more words than is necessary. 10

Repent. To feel pain, sorrow, or regret for something left undone or done; to feel remorse. 7

Replenish. To supply or fill again. 4

Replete. Well filled or supplied. 4

Satiate. To fill; to satisfy the appetite completely; to supply with anything to excess; to glut (overindulge). 5

Sedate. Calm; composed; quiet; serene; sober; to put under sedation. 6

Specious. Deceptive; not genuine; having a false look of truth. 15

Stipulate. To state exactly the agreement; to require as an essential condition in making an agreement. 15

Tactful. Considerate; conscientiously inoffensive; skillful in dealing with people or difficult situations. 3

Temerity. Rash boldness; foolhardiness. 2

Temperate. Moderate in everything; avoiding extremes or excesses. 7

Tenet. Any opinion, doctrine, principle, dogma, and the like held as true; belief. 2

Tentative. Done on trial or experimentally; not final; uncertain. 1

Tenure. The right to hold or possess something; length of time something is held; status assuring an employee of permanence in his or her position or employment (tenure protects employees such as teachers from being dismissed except for serious misconduct or incompetence). 2

Terminate. To end. 1

Thrifty. Clever at managing one's money; economical; not spending money unnecessarily. 4

Valid. Sound; well grounded on principles or evidence; having legal force. 8

Variable. Changeable; something that may or does vary. 3

Versatile. Changeable; turning with ease from one thing to another; many-sided. 2

Vestige. A trace, mark, or sign of something that once existed but doesn't anymore. 4

Vindicate. To clear from criticism, accusation, or suspicion. 6

Vindictive. Revengeful in spirit; spiteful. 5

Virile. Manly; masculine; forceful; able to procreate (to produce or reproduce). 5

Vital. Necessary to life; essential; energetic. 6

Waive. To give up a right, claim, privilege, and so on voluntarily. 10

COMBINING FORMS AND EXAMPLES OF VOCABULARY DERIVED FROM COMBINING FORMS PRESENTED IN *Vocabulary Expansion II*

The number after the meaning refers to the exercise in which the combining form is presented.

Ab. From; away; away from; off. 11
abduct—to carry off; *abortive*—coming to nothing; *abrupt*—sudden; *absent*—away; *absorb*—to take in or up; *abuse*—to use wrongly.

Abs. (Same as *ab.*) Used before words beginning with *c* and *t.* 11
abscond—to go hurriedly and secretly; *abstain*—to do without something voluntarily.

Age. Condition, state of; action; collection of; place for; 7
haulage—act of hauling; *dosage*—amount to be given; *marriage*—state of being wed; *wastage*—amount wasted; *acreage*—collection of acres; *orphanage*—place for orphans or collection of orphans. Others: *wattage*; *shrinkage*; *spillage*; *courage.*

Al. Of; relating to; belonging to; characterized by; like; the act of. 10
fictional—relating to fiction; *natural*—like nature; *refusal*—the act of refusing; *acquittal*—the act of acquitting or clearing. Others (relating to): *national; directional*; *functional*; *tribal*; (the act of): *rehearsal*; *arrival.*

Ana. Denoting a collection of materials on a certain subject (at the end of nouns). 16
Americana—has to do with material relating to America.

Ana. Upward; according to; back; again; thoroughly (at the beginning of words). 16
analogy—according to a logical inference; *anachronism*—backward or reversed in time or anything out of its proper time. Others: *anatomy*; *analysis.*

Ante. Before. 4
antebellum—before the war; *anteroom*—waiting room; *antedate*—to date before; *antemeridian*—before noon (A.M.); *antecedent*—going before.

Ary. Relating to; connected with. 12
dietary—relating to diet; *military*—relating to soldiers, arms, or war; *voluntary*—relating to one's own choice; *honorary*—relating to honor. Others: *parliamentary*; *reactionary*; *boundary*; *budgetary*; *secondary*; *supplementary.*

Ate. To become; to cause to become; to form or produce; to make; to arrange for. 17

evaporate—to become vapor; *maturate*—to become mature; *validate*—to make valid; *abbreviate*—to make brief; *activate*—to cause to become active. Others: *salivate*; *ulcerate*; *pollinate*; *exaggerate*; *enervate*; *deviate*; *mandate*; *potentate*.

Be. Thoroughly; all around; to make. 18

begrudge—to thoroughly envy; *belittle*—to make or cause a person to seem small. Others: *bewilder*; *bewitch*; *bemoan*; *belabor*; *befriend*; *betray*; *becloud*; *bewail*.

Demi. Half. 14

demitasse—a small cup of strong black coffee; *demigod*—a mythological being that is partly a god and partly a man.

Dom. State or condition of being; rank; total area of. 1

Christendom—the Christian world; *dukedom*—the rank or title of a duke, the area governed by a duke; *freedom*—condition of being free; *stardom*—the status of being a star; *wisdom*—the state of having knowledge.

En. To cause to be; make; made of. 13

cheapen—to make cheap; *redden*—to make red; *ashen*—made from the wood of the ash tree. Others: *harden*; *sweeten*; *brighten*; *ripen*; *golden*; *woolen*; *earthen*; *wooden*.

Ery. Refers to a place of doing, keeping, producing, or selling; refers to practice; refers to a collection or class of things; refers to certain characteristics, behavior, conditions, or status. 12

bakery—a place for baking; *hatchery*—a place for hatching eggs; *trickery*—the practice of underhanded tricks to deceive; *witchery*—the practice of witchcraft; *finery*—a collection of fine clothes; *slavery*—the condition of being a slave. Others: *fishery*; *archery*; *cannery*; *grocery*; *pottery*; *nunnery*.

Ful. Full of. 3

beautiful—full of beauty; *pitiful*—full of pity; *tearful*—full of tears; *shameful*—full of shame.

Hemi. Half. 15

hemisphere—a half sphere or globe; *hemicycle*—a half circle; *hemicerebrum*—the right or left half of the cerebrum (brain).

Ic. Relating to; like. 9

hyperbolic—relating to a hyperbole or a great exaggeration; *heroic*—like a hero; *poetic*—like poetry; *tragic*—like a tragedy, in which something is very sad or there is a disaster; *euphemistic*—relating to euphemism or a milder way of saying something. Others: *enthusiastic*; *majestic*; *realistic*; *scientific*; *historic*.

Ish. Belonging to; like or characteristic of; tending to; somewhat or rather; about. 9

Spanish—belonging to Spain; *Danish*—belonging to Denmark; *devilish*—like or characteristic of a devil; *boyish*—like or characteristic of a boy; *bookish*—

inclined to books or involved with books; *tallish*—rather tall; *bluish*—rather blue; *thirtyish*—about thirty.

Ism. Act of, practice of, or result of; condition of being; action or quality of. 8

terrorism—practice of terror or the use of fear to frighten or intimidate; *barbarism*—the condition of being primitive or brutal; *pauperism*—the condition of being very poor; *patriotism*—the quality of being a patriot; *Americanism*—practice of values characteristic of Americans. Others: *socialism*; *nationalism.*

Ite. A native or inhabitant of; a person associated with; a mineral or a rock substance. 13

New Jerseyite—a native of New Jersey; *laborite*—a person associated with labor; *graphite*—carbon used in lead pencils.

Ity. Quality of being; state of; condition of; degree. 10

nobility—the state or quality of being noble; *complexity*—the state of being complex. Others: *sovereignty*; *activity*; *reality*; *sincerity*; *alkalinity*; *brutality*; *absurdity*; *hostility*; *frugality*; *artificiality*; *cordiality*; *fraternity*; *civility*; *jollity*; *unity*; *safety*; *liberty.*

Ive. Of; relating to; belonging to; having the nature or quality of; tending to. 8

legislative—relating to the body of lawmakers; *affirmative*—having the quality of a positive statement; *derogative*—tending to belittle; *native*—belonging to a country by birth; *creative*—tending to be able to create; *destructive*—tending to cause destruction or the tearing down of things; *massive*—having the quality of being very large.

Ly. Like; characteristic of; every; in the manner of. 17

hourly—every hour; *quarterly*—every quarter; *monthly*—every month; *manly*—like a man; *fatherly*—like a father; *friendly*—in the manner of being a friend; *nicely*—characteristic of being nice. Others: *womanly*; *saintly*; *queenly*; *gladly*; *happily*; *merrily*; *cheerfully*; *justly*; *sadly*; *literally.*

Ment. The act of; the result of; the state of. 11

amazement—the state of being amazed; *development*—the act or result of developing. Others: *enjoyment*; *advancement*; *improvement*; *pavement*; *measurement*; *entanglement.*

Ob. Against; toward; to; over. 18

obstacle—something that stands in the way of; *obscure*—to darken; *obscene*—against decency; *oblige*—to bind to.

Per. Throughout; through. 15

percolate—to filter through; *persuade*—to win over; *perplex*—to bewilder; *permit*—to allow through; *peruse*—to read thoroughly; *perfume*—to fill with sweet odor.

Semi. Half; not fully; partly; occurring twice in a period. 14

semicircle—a half circle; *semimonthly*—occurring twice a month; *semiweekly*—occurring twice a week; *semirigid*—not fully rigid; *semiprivate*—not fully private. Others: *semiyearly*; *semiprecious*; *semiprofessional*; *semiskilled.*

Ship. State, condition, or quality of; office, rank, or dignity; art or skill. 5
kingship—dignity or rank of king; *governorship*—rank or office of governor; *citizenship*—state or quality of being a citizen; *penmanship*—art or skill of handwriting. Others: *lordship*; *dictatorship*; *friendship*; *leadership.*

Super. Above in position; over; above or beyond; greater than or superior to; extra; in the highest degree; in excessive degree. 6
superior—of higher degree; *superb*—of the highest quality; *superlative*—of the highest degree; *supercritical*—highly critical. Others: *supersafe*; *supersweet*; *superabundance*; *superacid.*

Ty. (Same as *ity*). At the end of numerals such as *twenty, thirty,* and *forty, ty* means "tens; times ten." Example: twenty is two times ten.

Ure. Act; result of an action; agent of action; state of. 7
legislature—body of lawmakers; *exposure*—state of being exposed or laid bare; *posture*—state of carriage (how one carries oneself); *rupture*—the act of something breaking apart; *torture*—act of causing severe pain; *temperature*—degree of hotness or coldness of something.

Y. Having; full of; tending to; like; somewhat. 2
dirty—full of dirt; *sticky*—tending to stick; *wavy*—like a wave. Others: *healthy*; *horsy*; *salty.*